Ian Thomson was born in London in 1961, and educated at Dulwich College and Cambridge University, where he read English literature. He then lived in Rome for two years, where he worked as a journalist and taught. It was during this time that he first travelled extensively in the South of Italy, a region he got to know well.

As a journalist in London, publications he has written for include the *Independent*, *Financial Times*, *Sunday Times* and *Spectator*. He has also written on Italian literature for more specialist publications, such as *Encounter* and *London Magazine*, and has translated the Sicilian writer, Leonardo Sciascia, into English. He was recently commissioned to write a biography of Primo Levi. He now divides his time between Italy, Switzerland and London.

Other Collins Independent Travellers Guides include:

South-west France
Soviet Union
Greek Islands
Mainland Greece
Turkey
Spain
Portugal

SOUTHERN ITALY

IAN THOMSON

Series Editor Robin Dewhurst

Collins
8 Grafton Street, London
1989

Note

Whilst every effort is made to ensure that prices, hotel and restaurant recommendations, opening hours and similar factual information in this book are accurate at the time of going to press, the Publishers cannot be held responsible for any changes found by readers using this guide.

To my parents

William Collins Sons & Co. Ltd
London · Glasgow · Sydney
Auckland · Toronto · Johannesburg

First published in 1989
© Ian Thomson 1989

Series Commissioning Editor: Louise Haines
Maps by Maltings Partnership

Cover photographs: front *Bay of Naples and Mount Vesuvius (Zefa);* back *Rivello, Basilicata (Tony Stone Worldwide).*

BRITISH LIBRARY CATALOGUING IN PUBLICATION DATA
Thomson, Ian
Southern Italy.—(Collins independent travellers guide).
1. Southern Italy—Visitors' guides
I. Title
914.5'704928

ISBN 0 00 410977 5

Typeset by Ace Filmsetting Ltd, Frome, Somerset.
Printed and bound in Great Britain by Mackays of Chatham plc.

Contents

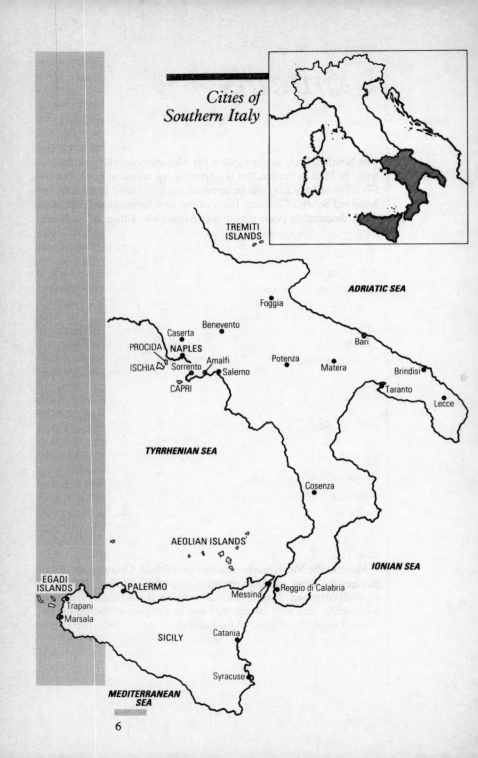

*Cities of
Southern Italy*

TREMITI
ISLANDS

ADRIATIC SEA

Foggia

Caserta
Benevento

PROCIDA
ISCHIA
NAPLES
Sorrento
Amalfi
Salerno
CAPRI

Bari

Potenza
Matera

Brindisi
Taranto
Lecce

TYRRHENIAN SEA

Cosenza

AEOLIAN ISLANDS

IONIAN SEA

EGADI
ISLANDS
PALERMO
Trapani
Marsala

Messina
Reggio di Calabria

SICILY
Catania

Syracuse

MEDITERRANEAN
SEA

Introduction

The South of Italy is often called the Mezzogiorno, the 'midday'; as with the Midi in France, this is where the sun stands at noon. But the Noonday of Italy has little in common with its Gallic namesake, the moneyed South of France. Parts of the Mezzogiorno are still backward, desperately poor; if you visit Aliano, the village in Basilicata where Carlo Levi set *Christ Stopped at Eboli*, you may think little has changed since 1945, when the book was published. Parts of the village are reserved only for men; you see them of an evening, their backs to a wall, smoking and playing at cards. Barnacled limpet-like to the stone, they never seem to move. There is a darkness in their eyes of earth and death. The women are subservient – no better, it seems, than the donkeys burdened with great bushels of firewood. They balance on their heads heavy amphora-type jars, like the gipsy women of Rajasthan.

That is the unchanging face of the Mezzogiorno; you will not find such villages in the North of Italy. Despite the pouring of thousands of millions of pounds of taxpayers' money into the South during the last forty years to implant new industries, the image of the two Italies – the go-ahead North and the sluggish South – seems more, not less, real.

Changes in living standards are superficial. The inhabitants of Milan and Naples may be able to watch the same television programmes, but they live in different worlds. Naples is the Belfast, Milan the Geneva of the Mediterranean; the one smells of rotten fish, the other of cigar smoke. And when you see how people live in the more remote pockets of the Southern interior –isolated from their fellow-countrymen by impassable mountains and inadequate communications – you begin to see why an 1873 handbook to the Mezzogiorno was able to pontificate: 'Patience and flea-powder are the two essential requisites for the traveller in Southern Italy.' And you may need them still.

Much of the Mezzogiorno remains untouched. Calabria, for example, has the most striking scenery of any part of Italy – 700 km of unspoilt coastland, forests, lakes, mountains. But attempts to exploit, touristically, the very nature that was in the past so damaging, the cause of so much suffering to the Calabrians, have failed. This failure to capitalise, commercially, on the Mezzogiorno is not without advantage to you as an independent traveller; it is perhaps what makes the region such a delight to explore.

Nowhere is this more true than of Naples, a magnificent city which is still, in this dreary age of confectioned travel, a stranger to sight-seers. Many of her major attractions are left unattended, without sign-posting. Take the eighteenth-century Sessa Palace, ambassadorial seat of Sir William Hamilton, British Envoy-Extraordinary and Plenipotentiary at the Court of Naples during Admiral Nelson's day. The dilapidated walls of this once fabulous *palazzo*, concealed in an alley off the ritzy Via Chiaia shopping area, are spray-gunned with graffiti of the 'Diego Maradona – Rambo di Napoli!' variety. One would hardly think that this was where Hamilton's wife, the divine Emma, once flirted with Horatio Nelson behind the unsuspecting ambassador's back. There is not even a plaque to mark the spot.

Much, of course, could be done to turn the Mezzogiorno into a des-tination for tourists; Naples itself has enormous untapped potential. Beneath its streets are an estimated 1,000,000 square metres of aque-ducts, tunnels, cisterns and funerary chambers built by the Ancient Greeks and Romans. To date only 600,000 square metres of this sub-terranean city have been placed on an archaeological map. An area roughly equivalent to half the size of Hyde Park in London, it has not been exploited in any way for the purposes of tourism.

This is a shame; the possibilities are infinite. Dim and cathedral-like, the echoing, subterranean vaults of ancient Neapolis could be converted into theatres, libraries, tennis-courts, museums, prome-nades and, most important, a new underground railway network, sorely needed in ramshackle Naples. In April 1988, the Agip pet-roleum company helped set up an international laboratory of archi-tects and archaeologists to investigate underground Neapolis. As you read, though, I doubt whether anything has been done to fathom the depths of this Greco-Roman underbelly; notoriously, such plans die a quick death in Naples, strangled by red tape.

If tourists tend these days to avoid the great cities of the Mezzogiorno – Palermo, Bari, Cosenza, Naples – it is partly because their finest monuments are to be found in the most bustling and dusty of places. People are put off by the dirt. And, it must be said, by the crime. Between 1982 and 1983 there was a massive 80 per cent reduc-tion of British visitors to Palermo, owing to a series of almost simul-taneous articles on the Mafia in the *Sunday Times* and the *Sunday Express*. The overall decline for all nationalities was only 10 per cent. Although an understanding of the Mafia is vital for an appreciation of the Mezzogiorno, tourists are in absolutely no danger from the Cosa Nostra; big-time hoodlums, those Edward G. Robinson lookalikes with violin cases, are not interested in small-fry sightseers. The dan-ger, rather, is in petty crime. In the section on Naples (see pp. 73–4) you will find a list of suggestions on how to avoid losing your wallet or handbag to *scippatori*, young boys who have turned to crime through dependency on drugs. Be cautious.

Change for Southern Italy is slow – if anything, along the lines of that riddling aphorism from Giuseppe di Lampedusa's Sicilian novel *The Leopard*: 'If you want things to stay as they are, things will have to change.' New museums have opened, but are often 'under restoration'; motorway networks have branched out, but require extensive repair work. Nevertheless, the Mezzogiorno is now in a stage of transition; for the independent traveller, this can only add to its fascination. A really comprehensive exploration of the region – the Norman castles, Roman theatres, Arab pleasure palaces, the ruined temples of Ancient Greece, the beaches, pine forests and the sea of a deep, dark blue – is an unforgettable experience.

History

The following is intended primarily as a guide to Southern Italy's more recent history. The ancient is covered in more detail in the Gazetteer, and especially in the introductory sections to Naples and Palermo.

Briefly, the historical influence in the South is Greek, Arab and Spanish; in the North it is German and Celtic. The Greeks colonised between the eighth and sixth centuries BC, and their occupation lasted sporadically until medieval times with the prolongation of the Byzantine Empire in the South. Even today, there are mountain villages in Calabria where a Greco–Byzantine dialect is spoken. Saracen invaders from North Africa conquered Sicily in the ninth century, to be evicted two hundred years later by the Normans. But Barbary pirates, descendants of the invading Arabs, were to harass the southern coasts for centuries to come. The Norman line merged in the Hohenstaufen; and was succeeded in turn by Angevin and Aragonese, French and Spanish, rules. The Bourbons, last of the rulers in the Italian South, were in outlook thoroughly Italianate, but bore with them traces of the earlier Spanish influence.

All of which meant that the Mezzogiorno had a Mediterranean rather than a continental European history. The flowering of interest in the arts and literature symbolised by the Renaissance up in the North had comparatively little influence down in the South – it bypassed Sicily altogether. One of the joys of Dante (a Northerner, of course, from Florence) was that he could find verses that described with matchless exactitude the views and landscapes of Northern Italy. From Lake Maggiore to Carrara and from Venice to Florence – the reader could travel, across the written word, to all these places. But there was rarely a word about the Mezzogiorno; outside time and place, the region had been forgotten by history.

During the Renaissance, feudal conditions still prevailed in the South. Barons were interested more in solving petty disputes among themselves than in exercising proper patronage. Neither did the Mezzogiorno share in the evolution of a merchant and banking class of bourgeoisie, which was so formative a development in the peninsula's more northerly parts, where for centuries there was rule under the Austrians. Economic efficiency was the hallmark of this rule; the Austrian domination is now regarded as having paved the way for the commercial success of Lombardy, a province that contains all the major industrial towns of Northern Italy. There is a popular dialect poem about Maria Theresa, Empress of Austria and ruler of a large part of Northern Italy from 1740 to 1780, which speaks of her as *'una bona mama'*, a good mother, who ruled for the progress of the people. *'E tuti i citadini la stimava'*, and all the citizens esteemed her.

There was, briefly, Spanish rule in the North. The effects were disastrous. They were written about by the great Alessandro Manzoni, Northern Italy's enlightened answer to Voltaire. In his classic 1827 novel *I Promessi Sposi* (studied and groaned at by all Italian schoolchildren), Manzoni presents a Spanish-dominated Lombardy of the early seventeenth century where 'honour' is vital, government corrupt and inefficient, and the people, collectively, irrational. From this it probably follows that the entire Lombardy region would today be suffering from the same problems as the Mezzogiorno if in Manzoni's day it had still been under Spanish rule. History moves in strange and mysterious ways . . .

Unification

In 1861, Victor Emanuel was proclaimed King of a unified Italy. In the same year, his Prime Minister Cavour, a Northerner, died. These are his last words: 'North Italy has been established. There are no more Lombards, Piedmontese, Tuscans, Romagnuols, we are all Italians, but there are still the Neapolitans. Oh! There is a lot of corruption in their country. It is not their fault, poor people. They have always been so badly governed . . . We must bring morality to their country, educate the children and the youth, create nurseries and military schools. We must not dream of changing the Neapolitans by insulting them. They ask me for government posts, decorations, promotions. They must work, they must be honest, and then I will give them knighthoods, promotions, decorations.'

Famous last words: the providing of economic patronage and special aid for the Mezzogiorno has been a policy of post-unification governments ever since. Cavour himself had done much to accelerate the unification of Italy, to bridge the divide between South and North, with his *'cura di ferro'*, roughly translated as 'cure of iron'. This involved the creation, at enormous expense, of a railway system stretching from the North right down to the toe of the Italian boot. But railways were hardly to improve the miserable lot of the Southern peasant: Alexandre Dumas *père* described what he found in Naples in 1862: 'While the gentleman feeds his dogs on white bread, the people live on roots and grass, eked out with an insufficient quantity of coarse bread.'

There was industrialisation in the North, but virtually none in the agricultural South. It was the North that had capital, contact with the rest of Europe, a more enlightened ruling class, a better climate and more raw materials. By the turn of the century, peasants were rebelling at the heavy taxations imposed on them by the government in Rome, and at a sharp decline in agricultural prices, caused by the steamships and railways – the famous railways! – which brought competition from American grain. A depression was further intensified by the trade war that Francesco Crispi, Prime Minister of Italy from 1893 to 1896, had conducted with France, by the arrival of a vine disease and by a reduction in mining wages. In 1891, the revolutionary *Fasci* movement was born, with its headquarters in the Sicilian city of Catania. Embryonic trade union movements were founded, cooperative shops established. Members advocated socialisation of the land and the mines. But Crispi, fearing that the *Fasci* were battling for Sicilian independence, sent a fleet and 30,000 soldiers to wipe them out. And wiped out they were – brutally.

In response, a group of ardent protagonists of the South, the so-called *Meridionalisti*, began lobbying Rome for parliamentary action. Most famous among them was Francesco Nitti, born in Basilicata, whose monumental 1901 book *Nord e Sud* was a landmark in social commentary on the problems of the Mezzogiorno. The book prompted the eighty-year-old Prime Minister Zanardelli to make a tour of Basilicata on muleback. Consequently, a parliamentary enquiry of 1906–11 produced an immense report, running to eleven volumes, on the condition of the Southern peasant. It was not without success: from one lira a day, wages rose for the Southern peasant to three and even five lire.

Fascism

With the advent of Fascism, the Mezzogiorno was plunged into a dark age. Its net total of agricultural produce declined by more than 40 per cent – hardly surprising, as Mussolini's chief interest was to make Italy into a strong military nation, which meant industrialisation and investment in the North, but not in the South. After 1926, when it was taboo even to talk about the *questione meridionale*, the South became the Cinderella of the State – useful only as a region to which anti-Fascists from the North, such as Carlo Levi, could be exiled.

Under Fascism, the South entered into the economic affairs of the nation only once – 1926, when Mussolini opened up his national Battle for Grain. Thenceforth, Southern farmers were encouraged to extract the maximum amount of wheat from their soil, often on quite unsuitable hillside land. The battle was highly successful: since 1870 the annual production of wheat in the South had been little more than forty million quintals, but by 1939 it had risen to eighty million. The price, however, was high: marginal land was changed over from cattle pasture, fruit and olives to the cultivation of wheat alone; and the economy of the Mezzogiorno, if indeed it ever had one, was knocked for six. At the end of the day, despite all the medals awarded to Southerners who had contributed the most towards the Battle, the cost of Italian grain was 50 per cent higher than of American.

After the war

Just how far the Mezzogiorno stagnated during the years of Fascism was revealed in the results of political and administrative elections and referenda for 1946. Of Northerners, 66.5 per cent voted for the establishment of a republic; of Southerners, 67.4 per cent for the return of a monarchy; 51 per cent of Northerners wanted a liberal government, 39 per cent of Southerners wanted a right-wing one. Extraordinary results, when one considers that Mussolini had claimed to have actually solved the Southern problem (a magazine entitled *The Problems of Sicily* had had to change its name). The reality, of course, was different: splendid roads had been constructed in the former African colonies whilst numerous Southern villages were linked only by the dried bed of a river. Agriculture was still in great part nomadic; and most country roads could not be used by even a rough cart.

According to a 1950 census, the South accounted for one-third of the total population of Italy, but for little more than a fifth of its gross national product. Over half the population of the South depended on agriculture for its livelihood, and the cultivable land available in the Mezzogiorno was then reckoned to be the lowest of any southern European country except Greece.

But then the problem of the South – '*la problema del Mezzogiorno*' – has always been one of land. Quite simply, the land below Rome is infinitely poorer than that of the North: parched, arid, hostile to the cultivation even of wheat. Instead of a river Po, Arno or Tiber, there are in the Mezzogiorno only torrents – stony beds during the arid summer months that rise to destructive fury during the winter. For a region almost entirely devoted to agriculture, it would be hard to think of a more difficult terrain. In Basilicata, which is 90 per cent mountain, lemon trees are grown on the face of sheer cliffs on tiny terraces (they seem accessible only to goats), where the soil has often to be carried up in baskets. Northerners coming to the South often wonder how a land of enchanting vistas like Naples, Sorrento and Palermo, where the coastal regions are thick with orange and olive groves, could be so poor. They forget that behind the heavenly coast the desert reigns.

Something had to be done. And, after a fashion, it was. In 1950, thanks in no small part to Carlo Levi's *Christ Stopped at Eboli*, a memoir that dramatically awoke the North to the plight of the Southern peasant, a co-ordinated campaign was launched to unite the two Italies with the founding of the Cassa per il Mezzogiorno. Until given another name in 1984, this was Europe's largest development fund. Since 1950 it has spent the staggering sum of $17,400 million – much of which should be valued in pre-inflationary prices – on the 40 per cent of Italians who live in the South.

Today

The question is: what, if anything, has the Cassa achieved? Many would say next to nothing. True, malaria has been eliminated (perhaps flea-powder is no longer an essential requisite of the traveller in the South), illiteracy lowered, and hospitals, schools and services have been established where there were none before. And there has been industrialisation, the most dramatic results of which you can see along the stretch of coast between Syracuse and Augusta, in Eastern Sicily – until recently there were only flocks of sheep grazing amid the olive groves; now the whole area resembles Newark, New Jersey, crowded with chemical factories, smokestacks, intricate metal structures rising in the sky. It is not a pretty sight.

A major criticism of the Cassa, however, is that numerous of its grandiose initiatives are white elephants – or, as the Italians would say, cathedrals in the desert. They cost vast sums of money, but employ relatively few people, and are of limited advantage to the local economy. Worse still, the builders and suppliers of materials for factories in the South are often Northerners who benefit from an appreciable proportion of the funds earmarked for the Mezzogiorno. The Taranto steel works, constructed in 1960, are a sorry case in point: the overalls used are imported from the North and paid for by subsidies which were destined for the South. And the factories themselves, rising like so many pyramids in the desert, are in a district too backward to make use of the advantages their presence might provide. They have resulted only in a sharp rise in the cost of living as well as in serious pollution. As Luigi Barzini, author of a marvellous book, *The Italians*, has written: 'The South is known by many as the cemetery of public works. But it may now be the cemetery of industrial plants as well.'

The failure of the Cassa to bridge the economic divide between the Two Italies is illustrated, depressingly, by the investment figures released for the period 1966–69: they showed an increase in the North of 45 per cent; and in the South, despite plans to build new industrial plants, of only 13 per cent. So the North–South gap remains stubbornly there, and seems destined to grow. In June 1988 the *Corriere della Sera* newspaper carried a gloomy story about the failure of the South to catch up with the North. It was headlined '*Il Sud muore coperto di milliardi* [The South dies, covered in thousands of lire]'.

Organised Crime

Organised crime is a fact of life in both North and South. The roots of the Mafia are of course in Sicily; but the so-called *Piovra*, Octopus, has spread its tentacles far and wide. It has become a multi-national criminal network with operations not only in Sicily and the rest of Italy but in Europe and America too.

Traditionally, the Mafia have nicknamed the Italian judicial system *la sonnambola*, the sleep-walker. In recent years, though, the sleeper seems to have stirred; some would say, awoken. On 10 January 1986 – a historic date – the Mafia 'maxi-trial' opened in Palermo. It was the first time ever that the Honoured Society had been trapped under the legislative net of the Italian State. The indictment ran to 8,007 pages; some 475 suspected Mafiosi were put behind bars.

The proceedings came to an end on 12 November 1987, and were held in Palermo's Ucciardine prison, a grim legacy of the Bourbon era down by the docks. Connected to this prison via an underground tunnel is a maximum security bunker specially designed to hold the trial. From the outside, it resembles a high-tech fortress: spring-loaded doors that close behind you with a heavy clunk, security guards to scan you with an electronic bleeper at just about every corner, closed-circuit televisions suspended from the ceilings on lengths of flex. On the last day of the trial, the entrance was guarded by an enormous space-age tank – like Cerberus at the gates of hell, I fancied.

Inside, the bunker is a space-age zoo. Peering over the rails of the public gallery, one could see, way down below, some thirty cages in which the imprisoned Mafiosi were pacing restlessly up and down, several of them hurling abuse at an Italian television crew. Many of them, relieved that the trial had finally come to an end, were thanking their lawyers (*avvocati-mafiosi* as the press had contemptuously termed the 180 Cosa Nostra defence counsels); seemingly hundreds of hands were being shaken through the prison bars. 'Ah well, Uncle Pippo, this torment is finally coming to an end, eh?' And even: 'May the Virgin be with you, Don Ciccio.' On hearing this last, I remembered how it is usually only after a Mafiosi has murdered that he is awarded the honorific title of 'Don'.

Before the *Gran Giudizio*, explained the President, the accused had the right to protest their innocence for the last time. At first, no such protestations were forthcoming. Then a mobster began in near-hysterical tones to defame those penitent Men of Honour who had squealed to the magistracy and so made possible the trial: 'The calumny of the *pentiti* will be the harbinger of the most atrocious consequences . . .'

The super-grass and arch-penitent, not referred to by name, was Tommaso Buscetta, one-time patron of several New York pizzerias who in 1984 was extradited from Brazil on request of the authorities in both Italy and America. Single-handedly, Buscetta had managed to put Sicily's most powerful mobsters in the dock, though at the same time committing what is for all Mafia men the ultimate crime – *infamità*, or talking to the authorities. Due to Buscetta's 'confessions', one of the most vital tentacles of the Octopus had been as good as lopped off: the Italo–American 'Pizza Connection', until recently the world's largest heroin network, trafficking in some $1.65 billion worth of drugs.

. And so, after 1,638 days of court hearings, judge and jury retired to prepare what was billed in Palermo as the 'longest sentence in the history of the world'. As they did so, applause went up; even the Mafiosi clapped and cheered, rattling the bars of their cages. The results were made public just before Christmas 1987: 338 Mafiosi were convicted. A stake had been driven through the heart of the vampire.

Or had it? Nine months later, 226 of the original defendants had been released. Typically in such cases, the Men of Honour had been acquitted through lack of evidence. Any Italians – particularly Northerners – who hoped that the Mafia had been reduced to a shell of its former power soon changed their minds. Added to this, people began to suspect Tommaso Buscetta's motives. As an old-style Man of Honour, Buscetta had originally claimed that he wanted to bring to book all those hoodlums making a fortune out of heroin – in his eyes, a dishonourable practice. But it is most unlikely that a long-standing Mafioso (and Buscetta first came to the attention of the Cosa Nostra at the age of fifteen, when he killed a group of German soldiers) would deliberately set out to violate the hallowed code of secrecy, *omertà*. And second, it is entirely possible that Buscetta was wreaking revenge on his old enemies – especially as his two sons, brother, nephew and son-in-law have all vanished without trace. Just after the brutal murder in 1982 of General Dalla Chiesa, prefect in charge of Mafia investigations in Palermo for precisely 100 days, Buscetta had returned to Sicily from America with the express intention of 'rubbing out' fifteen members of the Riccobono clan, who had been among the most successful survivors in Palermo's constant family feuds. Buscetta invited the mobsters to a dinner party where the food, need one say, was poisoned. Revenge is sweet indeed. Or rather savoury, as it was the seafood pasta, I believe, that floored the mobsters.

From Buscetta's lethal banquet it would seem that the men who most effectively destroy the Mafia are the Mafiosi themselves – chopping one another up into little pieces or submerging one another in barrels of wet concrete (only thus can one eliminate the possibility of a decent Catholic burial). The Italian judiciary, on the other hand, is not so adept at balancing Mafia accounts. Long ago, honest Sicilians suspected that the 'maxi-trial' would achieve next to nothing; people I spoke to in Palermo dismissed the trial as *una bolla di sapone*, a soap bubble. The new financial power of the Mafia, acquired through laundering drug profits into the legitimate economy, and the alleged links between gangsters and politicians, were never touched upon.

Nor are they likely to be touched upon. On 30 July 1988, Palermo Investigating Magistrate Giovanni Falcone, the most prominent of lawyers entrusted with Mafia prosecutions, handed in his resignation. As it was Falcone who had so patiently transcribed Buscetta's revelations (a staggering 3,000 pages of type), his resignation came as bad news indeed. It symbolised a complete loss of faith among the Sicilian judiciary in the capacity, or the inclination, of elected politicians to sustain a battle against criminals whose traditional influence in the network of patronage and favouritism, *clientelismo*, is now matched by enormous sums of money.

In the wake of Falcone's resignation, the Honoured Society can only expand its empire ever further into business, banking and drugs, infiltrating 'clean' economies until it expels them altogether. Dismantling the Mafia at this stage would mean dismantling huge tracts of Southern Italy's economic base; the social chaos, even in terms of unemployment, would be unimaginable.

There was serious unemployment even at the time of the 'maxi-trial', as I found out from a taxi-driver who drove me to the top of Palermo's Monte Pellegrino. The lower reaches of this great headland are disfigured by ugly tenement blocks which from the late 1950s right up to the present day have almost all been constructed with Cosa Nostra money. But because so many Mafiosi building speculators had been slammed in jail awaiting trial, construction had simply come to a standstill. 'See those villas,' said the driver. 'Well, I used to mix concrete there. Thanks to Buscetta – that dirty *infame*! – I was out of a job for eight months. And with my family to support too . . .' The driver had recently taken part in a *Viva la Mafia* march. The Mafia, it seems, has won at last.

The origins of the Mafia

To write a conventional history of the Mafia is almost impossible. Words normally associated with the phenomenon – *vendetta, rispetto, omertà* – are ways of behaviour handed down from generation to generation, aspects of what a socio-anthropologist might call an 'oral' culture. And so there is a consequent paucity of information. Anyone wishing to gather information on the Cosa Nostra would do best to scrutinise the few records of criminal proceedings that exist in penal and tribunal archives, in the Assize Court of Palermo in particular. But the task is as good as insuperable: the Mafia have always been careful to destroy all traces of their activity, erasing footprints in front of their lairs like animals. For they have a terror of the written word, of ink on paper. As a Mafia proverb has it: 'White soil, black seed. Beware of the man who sows it. He never forgets.'

The Mafia was first brought to the knowledge of the Anglo-Saxon world by the eighteenth-century travel writer Patrick Brydone, whose jaunts about Sicily included a description of a mysterious 'Honoured Confraternity'. In Italy, the word 'Mafia' first appeared in the title of a Sicilian dialect play, *I Mafiusi di Vicaria*. First performed in Palermo in 1863, the rough translation at that time would have been 'The handsome and daring men of La Vicaria'. The word 'Mafia' has stuck ever since. This play, amounting to an apology for the Mafia (as though it were an association for mutual aid, a sort of benevolent free-masonry), helped reinforce the idea that Sicily is really a nation unto itself, that the Mafia is its true constitution, an invisible state behind the visible but apparently useless screen of the Italian State; some-thing, in other words, of which the Sicilian should feel truly proud.

From the beginning, the Mafia has indeed always set itself up as a state within a State. Prior to the unification of Italy in 1861, Western Sicily was in fact made up of a plurality of states within the State, rep-resented by a multitude of feudal farmlands. There is no doubt that the Mafia grew up as a kind of intermediary force between the absen-tee landlord and his peasants: landlords set up private little armies, *campagnie d'armi*, to defend their families and estates from marauding bandits. In the absence of the law, these armies founded their own law, primitive and bloody though it was.

By the turn of the century, however, Sicilian landlords had become so decadent ('immersed in sated ease and tinged with disgust', as we read in *The Leopard*) that they were obliged to sell their feudal rights to the highest bidder. These invariably went to the *gabelloto*, a resident tax-collector on the estate. Usually, he was also a prototype Capo Mafia, the representative of a class which was on its way up, and which, in the guise of a pseudo-aristocracy, is the Cosa Nostra of today. Soon enough, the *gabelloto* involved himself in extortion and racketeering.

For the first quarter of the twentieth century, the Mafia was essen-tially an agrarian phenomenon, a semi-feudal confederation; it was deeply rooted in the old *cultura dell'appartenza* – roughly speaking, the mentality that sought strength in a feeling of belonging. Family and group loyalties took precedence over civic pride or the State. It was the criminal face of a peasant society. Accordingly, the village Capo Mafia controlled the local wholesale fruit, vegetable, flower and fish markets. He affected the airs of a gentleman – aloof, withdrawn and silent. At that time, the Mafia's code of silence had points in common with customs prevailing among gentlemen elsewhere – Southern US plantation owners, members of the Paris Jockey Club, Prussian cavalry officers, Monte Carlo gamblers. As a 'gentleman', the Mafioso would only resort to crime if absolutely necessary, and he would never sully his hands through work. He was the great overseer, a man to whom the peasants turned in times of need – the *amico degli amici*, friend of friends.

He was a supremely political animal, obtaining pre-eminence through a dense capillary network of clientelistic contacts. The most powerful Men of Respect therefore owned haulage companies, small banks and rural co-operatives – anything, in other words, that would advantage their relations with the outside world, and through which they could spread their tentacles into what Machiavelli would have called the *alti luoghi*, the high places of local power élites. For favours returned, politicians would often ask the Mafia for help at election time. Orlando, the Sicilian-born Prime Minister of Italy in 1918, always welcomed a little help from The Friends. In 1946, a large canvas sign was put up in Partinicio, a small Mafia stronghold near Palermo, with the words, 'Vote for Vittorio Emanuele Orlando, *l'amico degli amici*'. There was no doubt as to the identity of these friends – they were not the sort you would want to take home to show your mother.

Politically, the Mafia have usually veered towards the Right. You can bet your bottom lira that the Christian Democrat headquarters in any provincial town of Southern Italy is a front for something rather more sinister than politics. But corruption is no respecter of ideology; the Cosa Nostra have aided every successful revolution and landing of foreigners in Sicily, whether of the Left or Right – including that of Garibaldi in 1860. They cannot afford to be on the side of the losers – in the past, they have collaborated with the Bourbons, with the *Liberali* and, for a while, with the Fascists. But under Mussolini they were dealt a severe blow.

The methods used by the Duce, however, to obliterate the Mob were more reminiscent of the Spanish Inquisition than anything else. Mussolini's Chief of Police, Cesare Mori, was quite probably a madman. Armed with a *carte blanche*, he put into operation what he jokingly called his 'Plan Attila'. This involved the setting up of kangaroo courts, and the torture of Mafioso suspects by forcing huge quantities of salt water into their stomachs, removing their fingernails, twisting and crushing their genitals and other such delights. Mori's descent on a Sicilian village sometimes meant the arrest and removal of its entire male population; the only way of mollifying him when a visit was expected was to erect a triumphal arch bearing the words 'Ave Cesare'.

The Mafia was only temporarily anaesthetised under Fascism: it soon came back with a terrible vengeance. The big break was 10 July 1943, when the Allied armies landed on the south coast of Sicily. In return for furnishing US emissaries with intelligence information, high-ranking Mafiosi were made offers they simply couldn't refuse. One such mobster, Lucky Luciano, had his prison sentence for peddling drugs and running prostitutes reduced from fifty years to precisely two.

When Luciano was released, the New Mafioso was born. He single-handedly turned the Mafia from parasitical intermediary between employer and employee, producer and consumer, citizen and State, into a confederation of organisations dealing in large-scale entrepreneurial activities for the first time. Instead of loan-sharking, labour and protection racketeering the Mafia was now producing heroin. The old self-styled arbiter of justice became the modern urban gangster.

Proceeds from heroin, a commodity for which there is an ideal structure of supply and demand, were soon pumped into building speculation. Fortunes were made out of rebuilding Palermo and Naples in the wake of their war-time destruction. In Naples, the initial abusive building boom took place between 1952 and 1958, while the pro-monarchist ship-owner Achille Lauro was mayor. Before 1952, the coastline immediately west of Naples was known for its beauty as the 'miglio d'oro [the golden mile]'; now it is called the 'miglio del cemento d'oro'. The great Neapolitan film director Francesco Rosi condemned this illegal speculation in his 1963 film, Hands Over the City, which starred Rod Steiger as a pro-Lauro Mafioso, hell-bent on making a fast lira out of the construction business. You will not fail to notice how human greed has disfigured this most beautiful part of the Mezzogiorno.

Clientelismo

In his 1961 novel, The Day of the Owl, the excellent Sicilian writer Leonardo Sciascia used the chilling image of the 'palm-tree line' to illustrate what he saw as a Mafia takeover of all Italy, both North and South. These words are spoken by a carabinieri officer from the North: 'Maybe the whole of Italy is becoming a sort of Sicily . . . scientists say that the palm-tree line, that is the climate suitable to the growth of the palm, is moving north, five hundred metres, I think it was, every year . . . The palm-tree line . . . I call it the coffee line, the strong black scandal line . . . It's rising like mercury in the thermometer, this palm-tree line, this strong coffee line, this scandal line, rising up throughout Italy and it has already passed Rome.'

It passed Rome long ago: Mafia money is behind casinos as far north as the Ligurian coast. On St Valentine's Day 1983 arrests were made in Milan of numerous 'white-collar workers': financiers and businessmen who had channelled profits from heroin into property development. On 6 November 1988, a Turin court sentenced twenty-six Mafia gangsters to life imprisonment and convicted a hundred and four others in connection with a clan war for control of a drug trafficking network between Sicily and Northern Italy. The roots and the recruiting ground of Mafia leadership remain in Sicily, but the real corruption is in Rome, with the Christian Democrat parliamentarians. As long ago as 1915 Norman Douglas had written, in *Old Calabria*, of 'the unseen hand in Rome – a hand which is held out for blackmail, and not vainly, from the highest ministerial benches'.

Of course, systems of patronage exist everywhere in the world. There is corruption in London and New York. There is a very intricate network of favouritism in careers such as journalism and publishing – indeed, Sicilians always express surprise when you tell them that it is actually possible to get into journalism without any *raccomandazione*, recommendations from friends in the right places. All over the world, people know that they must aid each other, side with their friends, and with the friends of those friends, to fight the common enemy. John F. Kennedy was said to have filled the White House with an Irish Mafia, called the Murphia. And, in equally facetious usage, there is the Kosher Nostra for an alleged Jewish conspiracy, and the Taffia for a Welsh one.

In Southern Italy, there are no fewer than three types of Mafia: in Sicily, there is the Mafia proper; in Calabria there is the *'Ndrangheta*, a name stemming from an ancient Greek-dialect word meaning prowess; and in Campania, particularly Naples, there is the *Camorra*, derived from the Spanish *gamurra*, meaning extortion money. All of them operate through systems of *clientelismo*, political favouritism and nepotism – all too human vices. Organised crime in Southern Italy is indeed human nature writ large and bloody; it is all about the pursuit of power and money, which steadily works ever greater degradation.

Southern Italy Today

The differences between North and South. And racialism

For those in the industrial North, Southerners are *terroni* – literally, 'earth people'. As peasants, they till the soil, and that's about all they're good for. In Visconti's 1960 film *Rocco and his Brothers* a Southern family, in dire poverty, migrate to Milan; on arrival there, the brothers find work shovelling snow from the roads at dead of night. They have never seen snow before; but at least they can earn their keep, suffering work the Milanese would never undertake. Visconti was trying to say something about the Two Italies, the divide between North and South.

There is racialism on both sides, but it is more pronounced in the North. The Milanese talk about Sicily as though the island were a colonial land where European standards no longer exist, the inhabitants dirty and barbarous. Just how many Milanese have ever been to Sicily is another matter; Milan is closer to London than to Palermo. Nevertheless, there is a host of racist, and very unfunny, jokes. For example, why do the Americans have the blacks and the Italians the Sicilians? Answer: because the Americans had first choice. And so on, I regret to say.

As far as the North is concerned, the racial stereotype of the Mezzogiorno male is something like this: short and dark, he will have slicked-back hair, flashing black eyes and a low, neanderthal forehead. He will wear some sort of an amulet round his neck, exposed by a manfully open shirt front – a medallion of St Christopher, probably. He will be mad about spaghetti and mandolins. And he will be dishonest; a famous handbook on how to play *scopa*, a common Italian card game, written in Naples, begins: 'Rule Number One: always try to see your opponent's cards.'

If he is a Calabrian (a people reputed, like the Syrians in relation to other Arabs, to be more conspiratorial than any other type of Italian), he will also be sly and underhand, involved in subterfuges and shenan-

Regions of Southern Italy

Naples

Campania

Apulia

Basilicata

Calabria

Palermo

Sicily

igans so shady they would bring a blush to the cheeks even of Machiavelli. And if he is Sicilian, he will be a member of numerous masonic cliques, camarillas, mafias, cabalas or, as Northern Italians call them, *consorterie*. His every action will be borne out by the lyrics of a 1950 popular song, which goes:

> *Io ti do una cosa a ti,*
> *Tu mi da una cosa a mi.*

Or, 'I give you something for you, You give me something for me', a simple variation on the 'You scratch my back . . .' theme. The Mafia more or less functions according to this principle of favours reciprocated.

The Southerner is generally considered more calorific, much more live-wire, than his Northern counterpart. Suffering periodically from earthquakes and the isolated outbreak of cholera, sweltering under a summer heat that would fairly sandbag a Bedouin, the Neapolitan in particular is possessed of a happy-go-lucky exuberance, a near-oriental fatalism in the face of desperation. It is a frame of mind called *dolce far niente*, living from day to day in a devil-may-care sort of way. The Sicilian, though, is different: suspicious, silent, withdrawn. His taciturnity is perhaps a result of the Mafia's code of silence, *omertà* (which derives from the Sardinian dialect word *omu*, meaning man). The workings of this code are illustrated by a legend about a young man from Agrigento who is accused of murder. His mother, rightly convinced of a miscarriage of justice, drags the local padre to the victim's tomb, to see whether he can use his apparently magical powers to summon up the identity of the killer from beyond the grave. The priest reluctantly enjoins the dead man to confess the name of the assassin. There followed a long silence and then 'No', came a voice from the earth, 'I will not tell you his name. This mother's son is innocent, but do not ask further of me, for I know nothing.' Sicily is a land where crimes pass unnoticed, where no questions are asked under any circumstances.

The Southern man will certainly be a prey to *mammismo*, a mental disorder involving an infantile dependence on his mother. And he will probably know the joke – funny, for once – that Christ must have been Southern Italian as he lived at home until he was thirty, presumed his mother was a virgin, and she certainly believed he was God. The mother, by the way, will be perpetually dressed in black and conspicuously overweight. She will have just the faint soupçon of a moustache.

He will also suffer, as a Southern Italian, from *gallismo* – that is, from lady-killing, the word derived from *gallo*, meaning cock. And because he is such a prideful cock, no woman submits him to her will – apart from Mamma, that is. Which means he will tear out her hair by the roots if she proves unfaithful. 'A woman', runs a Sicilian proverb, 'is like an egg. The more she is beaten, the better she becomes.' As for the chap with whom the woman conducts her amorous dalliance, he will have his head blown off. The Southern male must be feared and respected. And he must be powerful, well-known. Hence the prestige attached in the South to such terms of respect as *Eccellenza*, *Professore*, *Ingegnere* and even *Geometra*, or Surveyor. In Naples, everyone is a *Dottore*, no matter what rank or profession. If you keep an ear open to the language, you will notice how these honorific titles are used all over the Mezzogiorno.

This is, of course, an absurdly generalised picture of the Southern Italian. The truth is, all Italians have a family resemblance. Not all the South is purely southern, nor is the North only northern. And it is not enough to say that all Southerners are dark and all Northerners fair; since Sicily was for many years colonised by the Normans, you will find that numerous of the islanders have blue eyes. But differences remain; and the reason the North is productive and the South not, that the biggest Fiat car plant is in Turin rather than Naples, is that Southerners are interested in ideals that are not economic. Unlike their cousins up North, they prefer to sacrifice wealth to positions of command, authority and prestige. For the Northerner, the acquisition of wealth is all-important. As Luigi Barzini writes in *The Italians*, 'Southerners tend to make money in order to rule, Northerners to rule in order to make money.'

The family

There is something in the theory that the Mafia is a debased form, a grotesque parody, of Mediterranean family life. For the first nucleus of the Mafia is the family. A group of Cosa Nostra clans are often referred to as a *cosca*, derived from the dialect term for an artichoke – the idea being that the clans all fit snugly inside each other, tightly bound like an overlapping of leaves. For rival Mafia *cosche*, there is strength in numbers. So families must be large; the women must be strong; and the children had better be male. Otherwise the father of the family is dead meat; or as the Sicilians, who have a nice sense of humour, would say, '*morto nel cuore degli amici* [dead to his friends]'. So the family is everything. As Leonardo Sciascia has said: 'The family is the State for the Sicilian . . . Perhaps he will become excited by the idea of the State and will go out to lead the government. But the exact definition of his rights and duties will be that of the family.'

Not surprisingly, then, the largest family in Italy – and, for all I know, in Europe – is to be found in the Sicilian town of Giarra. It consists of ten males and ten females and there is a nice symmetry to those numbers. I met the twenty members, plus progenitors, in March 1988. They were all of them doing just fine, from the oldest, who was thirty-one years old, down to the youngest, who was four. 'God has sent me so many children,' sighed the rather large Signora Mercurio, aged fifty, as 5 kg of spaghetti boiled in two cauldrons on top of the cooker. 'And I have fed, loved and nurtured every single one of the little ones.' Signora Mercurio, a biological wonder, explained that she had been pregnant for a total of 180 months, which is no mean portion of the human life. 'It's always growing, this blessed family,' she said, not without affection. The problem is one of space; and, of course, the cost of feeding so many mouths. To save money, the Mercurio family will only eat meat on alternate Sundays. Unfortunately for me, I had to make do with the mushy pasta.

Between the years 1951 and 1976 the population of the Mezzogiorno increased by 12 per cent. But this figure is diminishing with every year. More people are divorcing; there is education about birth control; fewer people are marrying. And families – excepting, of course, the amazing Mercurio tribe – are dwindling in size. Significantly, this is much more the case in those areas of the Mezzogiorno that have recently been industrialised, such as around the enormous Alfasud car plant near Naples.

Nevertheless, the demographic picture varies radically between the Two Italies. Southerners have an average of two or three children, while the typical family in the North has one child. And abortion, now legal in Italy, is practised much more in the North than in the Catholic South, where there have always been stronger patriarchal and matriarchal bonds.

Emigration and depopulation

There is still vast emigration from the South. During the quarter-century following the end of the last war, it is estimated that six million left their homes in the Mezzogiorno, two million of them in the early 1960s. At least half of them moved northwards; Turin almost doubled in size when half a million workers were imported from the South to work for Fiat.

Many of these emigrants do not mix easily in Northern Italy, where they are often mocked as spaghetti-crazed cave people, and where they have helped create, it must be said, a serious problem of violence in Northern cities. Whilst as a result of this emigration there was a significant reduction of unemployment in the South, there was nevertheless the simultaneous problem of depopulation. Some villages in Sicily were entirely bereft of their male inhabitants. In 1984, 244,000 people in Sicily – 15 per cent of the workforce – were officially registered as unemployed. Of these almost half were travelling north in search of their first job: a frightening statistic.

Emigration has been a problem particularly in Calabria, where flight is the theme, one might say, of everyday life. In the summer of 1988, whilst travelling down the Ionian Coast, I visited a medieval mountain town in Calabria called Badolate. Walking around, I had the impression that it had been visited by some terrible plague: the wooden doors to peasants' huts were padlocked; windows were shuttered; the streets deserted. Emigration from Badolate began in the early 1960s; the population has now been reduced from 4,300 to 700. The dead have already superseded the living; in 1983, three babies were born, whilst twenty-five adults died.

It is hard to believe, therefore, that between 1500 and 1700 Badolate was one of the wealthiest villages in Calabria, made rich from its production of wine and olive oil, fruit and grain. The village has a grand total of fourteen churches, proof if ever of its former eminence. Today, it gets not so much as even a mention in any guide book. Depopulated almost entirely, Badolate is an extreme example of what is happening in the rest of the Mezzogiorno.

These days, though, fewer Southerners pack their bags for that great El Dorado of opportunity and new-found wealth, the United States of America. It was not always the case. In *Christ Stopped at Eboli* Carlo Levi wrote: 'New York, rather than Rome or Naples, would be the real capital for the peasants of Basilicata, if these men and women without a country could have a capital at all.' Between 1901 and 1913 some 4,711,000 Southerners left for America. Not a few of them joined criminal organisations in the States; it was the only way to earn a living – better, at any rate, than tilling the fields back home. The Godfather, certainly, did rather well for himself.

Emigration to the States was not without its benefits for the Mezzogiorno. Each Southerner who became an American citizen was not only one mouth less to feed on fish or fruit; he also helped the economy of the Mezzogiorno by sending remittances to relatives back home. But the *Americani* are now a dying breed; as time moves on, they are forgetting the land of their ancestors. Remittances have dwindled. Nevertheless, you will still find in Sicily the old man who once trafficked with the Americans in contraband cigarettes ('Lucky Strike', of course), nylon stockings and penicillin. He will talk about the 'aischoola', a 'washtubba', the 'shoppa', 'jobba' or 'storo'. And he will say 'Shurrup' quite a lot, too. A friend of mine was once reading a copy of *The Times* in a Palermo café; an old man in a battered felt fedora and corduroy pants with a length of string for a belt leant over from a nearby table and, in conspiratorial tones, whispered, 'Psssst – you speaka English?' (The newspaper must have given him away.) 'Me, I lived in Nuova Yorka – 1948, that was. Olive oil exportation.'

Religious superstitions

The Mezzogiorno is uniformly a land of backward-looking beliefs and superstitions. In Naples, much hoo-ha is made about the bi-annual liquefaction of the blood of San Gennaro, patron of the city; in Bari, capital of Apulia, the bones of St Nicholas exude a mysterious manna believed to possess miraculous or curative properties; in Palermo, there is the extraordinary cult of Santa Rosalia, a superstition that came into being when the plague of 1625 devastated half of the city's population when it was under the 'protection' of Santa Cristina. Because of the terrible loss of life, the Palermans decided to get rid of Santa Cristina and replace her with Santa Rosalia. The Palermans had regarded Santa Cristina as a sort of old and powerless Capo Mafia that had to be supplanted by a younger and more dynamic Mafia Boss. As in heaven as it is on earth – superstitious.

In Carlo Levi's village of Aliano, for example, the peasants believe that it is ill-advised to urinate in the direction of a rainbow, as the curved jet of urine resembles and reflects the curved bow in the sky, and the whole man may be turned into an image of the rainbow. That is a magic, not a religious, belief. Tilling the fields from morning to evening, pressing the olives for their oil, the grapes for wine, the peasants of Southern Italy have little time for religion. Everything for them participates in the divinity. The sun, the moon and the stars, the slow changing of the seasons – all are bound up in a natural magic. As Carlo Levi wrote, 'The seasons pass today over the toil of these peasants just as they did three thousand years before Christ.'

Naples is the superstitious capital of Europe; the city is full of amulets to ward off the Evil Eye. If you are in Naples during the Easter period, you will not want to miss the procession in remembrance of the Madonna dell'Arco – a sanctuary founded on the spot where, in 1500, two youths kicked a sort of football against an image of the Virgin, causing it apparently to spout blood. The celebration shows Southern Italy at its most superstitious and, one is tempted to say, voodooistic. As the solemn cortège snakes its way through the heart of Naples (causing many a traffic jam en route), countless fireworks are exploded. Tasselled standards, embroidered with an image of the Virgin, sway precariously in procession, often snagging on overhanging washing-lines. A massive monstrance bearing a plaster-cast effigy of the Madonna, swathed in wreaths of pink tulle and bedded in a nest of palm-tree fronds, is bravely shouldered by six or seven young men, huffing and puffing under the holy weight of it. As the procession approaches the Madonna dell'Arco, girls and boys prostrate themselves in humble supplication. Old women, tearful with emotion, hobble shrinewards on their knees, seemingly oblivious of any pain.

Certainly, you will not find such processions in the enlightened North of Italy; perhaps they are a legacy of the Spanish domination – the grandiloquent buffooneries, the sacramental ceremonials, of the Bourbons. Whatever the verdict, religion is considered a more 'serious' affair in the North. For a start, there is a better training of priests up there, originating in the reform of seminaries by St Charles Borromeo, back in the sixteenth century.

A word on gestures

All Italians use gestures to emphasise a point, to insult a rival, to put people generally in their rightful place. Southerners are past masters at the art of gesture – and particularly at expressing emotions that are not always polite enough to put into words. An early nineteenth-century book entitled *La mimica degli antichi investigata nel gestire napoletana* [The Mimicry of Ancient People Interpreted Through the Gestures of the Neapolitans] lists ten possible gestures for expressing an emotion of rage. They range from 'biting one's hands and single fingers' to – weirdest of all – 'pretending to bite one's elbows'. But then Neapolitans are the most demonstrative of all Southerners, inflammable as a piece of tinder.

The foulest, the most heinous and unforgivable gesture a Neapolitan male can make in the direction of another male is to raise two fingers, the little and index, in the shape of imaginary horns. This means *cornuto*, or cuckold. Another insult is to fondle the lobe of one's ear between thumb and finger, indicating of someone that he is *frocio*, or homosexual. The tip of the index finger placed beneath an eye (right or left) means that the absent subject of a conversation is *furbo*, or cunning. The slowly raised chin means 'I don't know', or 'Perhaps I know but I will not tell you' – particularly useful when a Mafioso is being interrogated by the police.

There are other, less deprecatory gestures. The knuckle of the index finger ground vigorously into one's cheek means that food tastes exceptionally good (a favourite with Southern Italian waiters); twisting the end of one's moustache (if you have one) is a way of asking, 'Is it good to eat?' Placing the two hands together as though in prayer, accompanied by a world-weary raising to heaven of one's eyebrows, means 'Give us a break', or 'Leave it out'. Making a scissor-like movement with index and middle fingers means 'Get off the telephone.' And so on.

Customs and courtesies

Southern Italians are a supremely tactile people. Shaking hands is an essential part of leave-taking; and everybody kisses everybody else, even – and perhaps especially – when they hate each other. Usually, the kiss amounts to a couple of perfunctory pecks on each cheek, à la de Gaulle. You will notice how it is vital that the *noise* of kissing (two short, sharp sounds as of suction) be made, even if lips do not touch. The kiss is, of course, a mere formality, as when actors greet each other with an obligatory, 'Oh, daaarling!', but you would do best, as a foreigner in Southern Italy, to observe the custom. You will otherwise be considered rude.

In general, Southern Italians are polite – obsessed, indeed, with the codes of etiquette. It is customary to say *'Piacere* [It's my pleasure]' after shaking hands with a stranger, even if you dislike the look of him. Usually, you will be wished *'Buon appetito'* before beginning a meal, a pleasant custom that is extended just about everywhere – in a train compartment, on a beach, on a park bench. I was even wished a good appetite as I was about to open a packed lunch on top of Stromboli volcano.

Not so civilised is the Southern Italian's seeming inability to queue. In Milan, people file up in an orderly fashion outside cinemas and football matches; in Naples, wherever you are, it is a scrummage. And there is always the queue-jumper; he is usually short, and very dexterous at weaving his way to the front. You find him everywhere, but particularly in banks – institutions that function, in Southern Italy, like broken grandfather clocks. The best thing to do with a queue-jumper is accidentally to tread on his or her (usually his) toes. It is no good telling the jumper that you live in a country 'where people *always* queue' – he'll take you for a nincompoop.

The passeggiata

A civilised custom that harks back to Bourbon times, the Friday evening stroll is when the entire population (or so it seems) of a town or village will promenade up and down the same stretch of pavement until it is time to dine. It is when Southern Italians put on their finest suits and hand-me-downs, dressed competitively to the nines. Young couples stroll arm-in-arm, the boy casting a condescending glance or two at rival males from the corner of his lowered eyes, the girl assessing the cut of a best friend's dress. The old men walk arm-in-arm, dressed in suits of sombre grey, war-time medals pinned to lapels, the shoes a shiny black. The old women cradle in their arms a grandchild (or two), spoiling the creature with ice-creams or party balloons.

The *passeggiata* is a solely Southern custom. The best places in the Mezzogiorno to take part in the evening stroll are: Salerno in Campania, Bari in Apulia, Matera in Basilicata, Tropea in Calabria and Monreale in Sicily.

The balcony

In Southern Italy, the balcony has a cultural and social significance. It is not just there for the pretty views. In Palermo, where one's appearance counts for everything, washing is often hung out on a balcony to display the quality of one's underwear to neighbours. The larger or more frilly the bloomers, the higher the social standing of the woman that wears them. It is the same with flowers; that is, the more flower pots that are hung in the curve of the metalwork, the wealthier the occupants of the flat. (Washing in the North of Italy is hung under grey plastic coverings, to protect it from dirt; in the South, where the inhabitants are apparently less fastidious about matters of cleanliness, linen is left to drip from balconies no matter how dusty the street below.)

In Naples, where the streets are sometimes so narrow that pedestrians have difficulty in passing one another, the balconies of opposite houses often seem to be *touching*. As a result, neighbours can communicate from their respective balconies in near whispers. In the poorer parts of the city, seemingly hundreds of *balcone* are connected to each other by an intricate cat's-cradle of criss-crossing washing-lines (in some upper-class areas, on the other hand, outside washing-lines are banned); these lines connecting every house to every other house are an important part of Neapolitan life. In the words of the Neapolitan writer Luciano de Crescenzo: 'Just imagine, if God decided to transport one's house from Naples to Heaven, He would soon notice, to His utter amazement, that as He lifted it up all the houses in Naples were rising after it, one after the other like a vast line of bunting, houses and washing-lines and washing and all the singing . . .'

In the Mezzogiorno, balconies are often equipped with a plastic bucket and a length of cord. With these, provisions can be winched up to a third- or fourth-floor flat from street level. The men rarely do the winching; since the Mamma is the divine mistress of creation, it is her job to feed and nurture. In the Mezzogiorno, balconies are without doubt the province of women. In Sicily, the wonderful iron balconies billow outwards in a breast-shaped curve because they were built at a time when ladies wore crinolines; the balconies had to accommodate the stiff material, the hoop-shaped petticoats.

For the woman of the Mezzogiorno, the balcony provides a vantage point from which to observe, without being observed. Up on the balcony, she can eavesdrop on the latest gossip as it reaches her from the pavement below; transactions can be witnessed, passers-by recognised, and she can keep an eye on her husband's desirable – or undesirable – friends. When the woman has surveyed the street, taken in the scene, she can retire into the cool darkness of her flat, closing the green-painted wooden blinds behind her (which are anyway made up of slats through which she can peep if there is a definite danger of being seen). Occasionally, she will step out on to the balcony wearing only a nightdress; this is because the balcony often looks out from the bedroom. There is no shame in this; remember that the woman can see without being seen, or so she thinks. In this respect, the Southern Italian balcony is like a private theatre or opera box: standing (or sitting) on it, the woman feels herself a privileged spectator at the music, the complicated sub-plots, of life as it is acted out on the stage way down below.

Women travelling alone

Southern Italians are generally polite to tourists, but more so in small towns and villages, where an antique respect survives. Unfurl a map, and they automatically assail you with a *'Posso aiutarle?* [Can I help you?]' If you are a woman, however (and particularly if you have blonde hair, about which Italian males are bonkers), you should be on your guard against offers of help, no matter how politely phrased. Unfortunately, Italian males consider themselves irresistible to women. If you are seriously pestered, it's best to throw a *'Va fa'n culo!'* in their general direction – a phrase which is best left untranslated. But it usually does the trick, I'm told. Italian girls just don't swear like that.

If a Southern Italian considers a woman attractive, he will inform her that she is very *bella* and *molto elegante* (even if she has a wooden leg). They will assail her with such mouth-watering blandishments as *'Vieni qua, piccola!* [Come here, little one!]', or, more simply, *'Vieni con mi* [Come with me].' They may open a conversation with a *'Dove vai?* [Where are you going?]', though the more goatish may come straight to the point: *'Dove facciamo amore?* [Where shall we make love?]'

If you fancy Italian men, fair enough; but you may consider their attitudes towards women grievously behind the courtesies of this our feminist age. But at least a woman will not be refused service in a restaurant, bar or nightclub simply because she is unaccompanied. She will certainly be thought odd, though; Southern Italy is still the province of men.

Homosexuality and unmarried couples

Southern Italians are commendably liberal in their attitude towards homosexuals. Possibly this has something to do with the fact that males – straight or gay – will often walk arm-in-arm, a perfectly acceptable custom in the Mezzogiorno. Male transvestites are tolerated too; at night, in the railway stations at Palermo and Naples, you will see them skulking in the shadows. From afar, they look quite pretty, until you notice the unshaven legs and the 4 a.m. stubble beneath the rouge. The boys are accepted by just about everybody except the true prostitutes, who see them as a threat to trade. In Naples, call girls sometimes advertise themselves as 'Vere puttane [Real prostitutes]', to eliminate the possibility of any confusion. However, there are few gay bars in the major cities of the Mezzogiorno.

And with the advent of AIDS, Italians are becoming more frightened by the day. The Neapolitans in particular are suspicious about bad blood; should there be an epidemic, they fear that the blood – good blood – of their patron San Gennaro will not liquefy. In which case, it is the end of the world.

If you are travelling as an unmarried couple, you should not encounter any difficulties, especially as divorce is now legal. Nevertheless, there are the oddball owners of small pensioni who will not, if you are unmarried, provide you with a bed for the night. I once stayed in a small hotel in Naples where the landlady (large and intensely religious) would grudgingly allow unmarried couples to sleep in separate beds in the same room, but would throw them out if she found, the next day, that the sheets of one of the beds had remained unruffled. Extraordinary behaviour, when one thinks how she could have saved on laundry bills.

Drugs

The South has not been so badly hit by drug addiction as the North. Nevertheless, Sicily is the island through which heroin travels up to the North of Italy. No heroin refineries have been found in Palermo since 1980, but addiction is nevertheless a serious problem in that city; the estimated 7,000 addicts need the equivalent of $20 each a day to feed their habits. So petty crime is almost always drug-related.

In Naples, too, drug abuse is a serious problem, particularly in the ramshackle quarter of the city known as La Sanità. A disused hospital there, its courtyard piled high with rusty filing cabinets, has been converted into one of the most important heroin rehabilitation centres in Southern Italy, closely supervised by the Archbishopric of Naples. I talked to the priest in charge of the San Camillo centre, Antonio Vitiello. 'The Camorra', he said, 'buy the heroin from Marseilles or Sicily. It's sold on the streets for about 24,000 lire a shot – usually by the so-called *muschili*, young boys of nine or ten, many of them addicts too.' Monsignor Vitiello said there was very little he could do about the heroin problem in an area of Naples like La Sanità: one family in every three now has an addict in its midst. 'Religion only matters in Naples today in so far as it's absent.'

Penalties for any tourists coming into Southern Italy with drugs are more severe than in former years. Instead of the old maximum thirty-year prison sentence for pushers, there is now the penalty of a life-sentence. Also, there is fear of AIDS (which the Mafia indirectly help to spread). Cracking down on drugs is the most effective way Italy has of dealing with organised crime. The poppy fields of Thailand and Afghanistan are in the false-bottomed suitcases of small-time hoodlums; the airport sniffer-dogs tell you as much. The Mafia now also control cocaine distribution in Italy for the Colombian Medellín cartel: investigators say the Cosa Nostra are trading heroin for cocaine with the Colombians, at a rate of 4 kg of cocaine for 2 kg of heroin.

The Weather and When to Go

The further south you go in Italy, the warmer it is. But the weather in the South is less uniformly reliable than northern visitors might expect. In Naples, temperatures fluctuate wildly: between October and December it rains an average of ninety days. The lowest recorded temperature for January is 7°C, and the highest for July 30°C. In general, the lowest temperatures in Southern Italy can drop to zero, and the maximum heat for the period July–August can soar to 35°C. In Sicily, the African *sirocco*, which blows for four or five days at a time, raises the temperature to 40°C. But you are advised, even in summer, to take a raincoat and pullover; if you climb Mount Etna in Sicily, whatever the season, expect some blustery gales.

The heat between July and August is unpleasant in the large cities (Palermo becomes a giant black hole of Calcutta). The best time to visit the South is in spring – from the end of March to the end of May; or in autumn – from the middle of September to the end of November. Accommodation is more easily found in the autumn. But whatever, it is better to book in advance.

Travelling Around

By air

There are flights between Italy and every country in the world through the intercontinental airports at Rome and Milan. As far as the South is concerned, Naples, Catania and Palermo all operate direct international flights; and Bari, Brindisi, Reggio Calabria, Trapani and Lamezia Terme in Calabria domestic ones. Flights between Northern and Southern cities will save you an enormous amount of time over any other means of transport. Domestic routes are serviced by the **Alitalia** group, which includes **ATI**, and by the **Alisarda** and **Aligulia** companies. A 50 per cent discount is available on all domestic Alitalia day-return flights on Sundays; and there is a 30 per cent Alitalia reduction (the *Tariffe Nastro Verde*) for anyone travelling under the age of twenty-two.

Generally, you should make reservations in advance, since flights are often fully booked one or two days ahead. The Rome reservations office is open 24 hours a day for Alitalia and ATI flights; for domestic flights, telephone 06-5454, and for international, 06-5455. Lines are open from 6.45 a.m. to 11 p.m. At other times, telephone 601 03746/7. Domestic bookings can be made, changed or cancelled up to two hours before take-off time.

By boat

All Southern Italian islands from Sicily to the small and remote Lampedusa are linked to mainland Italy and other islands by efficient ferry and hydrofoil services. Services vary in frequency according to the season. A 24-hour two-way ferry service across the Straits of Messina links Sicily to the mainland (see p. 193), with daytime departures approximately every 15 minutes. The island of Capri may be reached from Naples in under one hour (see p. 121).

There are ferry services to the main international destinations around the Mediterranean – to Yugoslavia from Bari; to Greece from Brindisi and Otranto; to Malta from Naples, Reggio Calabria, Catania and Syracuse, and to Tunisia from Naples, Palermo and Trapani.

Though it takes twice the time, travelling by ferry is a more civilised business than travelling by hydrofoil. With a ferry, you can take the sun on deck, stretch out and read a book, eat a meal or drink a bottle of wine. Best of all, you can watch your destination as it looms into view; approaching the volcanic island of Stromboli by ferry is an unforgettable experience. By hydrofoil, seating is often cramped, and the plastic windows so scratched that you can barely see out of them. Hydrofoil is in general three times as expensive as ferry.

By train

Trains in Southern Italy are of an often biblical slowness; in Calabria, they may as well be powered by a rubber band. But on the whole, travelling by train in the South is fun; you will often share a carriage with an entire family, the mother large and dressed in black, the father a touch embarrassed by the wailing of his offspring. Eating lunch is a ritual – *panini*, ham rolls and lumps of cheese are removed from their wrappings of greaseproof paper with infinite care, and bottles of wine opened with relish. In Sicily, the compartment will fill with the pungent whiff of sardine sandwiches. If you strike up a conversation with fellow-passengers, expect to discourse at length on the United States of America – still, for so many Southerners, a land of hope. Often, empty carriages are strewn with bits of orange peel – unpleasant if you are allergic to citrus fruit. Southern Italian trains are not always clean or comfortable.

But no matter. Italy has over 16,000 km of railway, linking all the major cities in the South along the coastal routes. In addition, Italian railway fares are among the lowest in Europe. Numerous special rates and rail passes are available, all of them available at CIT and authorised agencies abroad, or at the main railway stations in Southern Italy. Among them are:

● The **Biglietto turistico di libera circolazione** or, more simply, the **BTCL**. This is an individual pass for unlimited distances, valid for periods of 8, 15, 21 or 30 days, for first or second class.

● The **Biglietto Chilometrico (BC)** is a rail pass valid for two months which gives you a maximum of twenty journeys totalling 3,000 km. It may be issued in the names of up to five people. If you are planning to travel long distances, the BC is recommended.

● If travelling as a family, the **Carta Famiglia** (Family Card) will prove indispensable: one adult pays the ordinary fare, whilst the other members of the family get a 50 per cent reduction.

Trains in Italy, both North and South, are classified as follows:

● **Super Rapido Inter City**, luxury first-class trains running between the main Italian cities, for which a special supplement is charged – well worth the money on long hauls.

- **Rapido**, fast trains running between main towns, many of which carry only first-class coaches. A special supplement (about 30 per cent on top of the ordinary fare) is charged. Children pay the full supplement.
- **Espresso**, long-distance express trains with both first- and second-class compartments. They stop only at main stations.
- **Diretto**, trains stopping at most – usually too many – stations; first- and second-class.
- **Locale**, local trains stopping at all stations. Excruciatingly slow, and very much a question of grinning and bearing it. To kill time, a good book is essential: *War and Peace* weighs in at 2,000 pages.

Restaurant cars are attached to all long-distance trains. A luncheon tray is available on most trains; snacks, soft drinks and coffee are also served. A proper dinner – about 35,000 lire for a three-course meal with a bottle of wine – is recommended.

By bus

If you do not have a car, bus is the swiftest form of travel, the best way to get around. Buses are often horribly air-conditioned, though, so that you come out feeling as though cold air had been blown on you by an unrelenting hair-drier (the answer, perhaps, is to wear a hat). Local buses abound between the main towns, and many of the principal Italian coach companies operate regular long-distance services. Buses are particularly recommended in Sicily, where a superb *autostrada* cleaves the island in two.

As a rule, buses are less comfortable than trains; they can often get very crowded. There are about seventeen different bus companies in Italy, so one is rather spoilt for choice.

By car

Italians drive like maniacs. In Naples, just crossing the road is an exercise in the logistics of survival. Men, it seems, like to model themselves on Steve McQueen, or on Yves Montand in the film *Grand Prix*: their funeral, in every sense of the word. Still, the ideal way to get around the South is in fact by car; in Sicily, where there is often no public transportation to the interior, you may think it is the *only* way.

Italy has the finest motorways in Europe. If driving your own car, you must carry a 'Green Card', which is an international insurance guarantee. You must also have an Italian translation of your driving licence, available at AA and RAC offices.

For what they are worth, here are some points of the Italian Highway Code:

● Speed limits vary according to the size and power of the vehicle, but the average maximum speed on motorways is 130 kph, and 50 kph in built-up areas.

● Vehicles must keep to the right-hand side of the road or street and close to the kerb, even when the road is clear.

● On three-lane roads, the middle lane is reserved for overtaking, which must always be signalled in advance.

● Seat belts are not compulsory (but I would certainly wear one).

● Vehicles in motion must keep at a distance which will enable them 'to stop without collision'. This article of the Highway Code comes in for a lot of abuse.

● All vehicles must be equipped with a portable danger signal, obtainable on hire from all Italian Automobile Club offices by paying a refundable deposit of 1,500 lire.

These translations of common Italian road-signs may be useful: *Vietato Ingresso Veicoli*, No entry for vehicles; *Rallentare*, Slow down; *Incrocio*, Crossroads; *Uscita*, Exit; *Lavori in Corso*, Road works ahead.

In Southern Italy, some of the motorways are free, but most are toll-roads. The toll depends on the length of the vehicle, and charges are higher on mountain motorways than in the plains. An average car will cost 60 lire per kilometre, and tolls are usually paid at the exit stations on presentation of the computerised ticket issued on entry.

As a tourist, you are entitled to a reduction on the normal price of petrol (supergrade only) and on the tolls, too. The concessions apply only to cars and motorcycles with foreign registration numbers, not to Italian hired cars. You can buy both petrol coupons and motorway vouchers at most garages along the main *autostrade* or, in advance, at UK motoring organisations. For motorists in Southern Italy, there is a special UK package, costing about £160, comprising twelve petrol coupons worth 15,000 lire each, ten motorway coupons worth 2,000 lire each and one petrol voucher worth 240,000 lire.

Most service stations close for lunch between approximately 12.30 and 3 p.m., except on the motorways where they are open 24 hours a day.

Hire cars

Compared to the UK or the USA, hire cars are expensive. You should avoid local companies in small towns – their rates may be cheaper, but the cars are probably falling to pieces. Rates generally include breakdown service, maintenance, oil and seat belts, but not petrol. Basic insurance is always included. Remember that VAT at 18 per cent will be added to the total cost. In general, the smallest car available for hire (Fiat Panda) should cost the equivalent of around £100 for three days, and the largest (Alfa Romeo 90) about £250 for three days.

By taxi

In Naples, taxi is a dodgy way to travel. Meters are often fixed, but usually there is no meter. Whatever the city, agree a price before you get into the taxi, and ask the driver to write it down for you on a piece of paper. Fares vary from city to city, but are generally cheaper than in London or New York. No tip is expected, but you will probably want to give one. In the event of the fare being 'modified', a taxi-driver is obliged by law to show a supplementary table in which the updated fares and the relative extras (for luggage, night-time journey, etc.) are written.

Hitch-hiking

Women are advised to refrain from hitch-hiking, even in pairs. They will get a lift much more quickly than men (Italian women drivers never give lifts), but there may be a price to pay. At all costs, always refuse rides in the back of two-door cars and do not let anyone put your luggage in the boot. Remember that hitching on a motorway is illegal in Italy (and you will also get dusty, sticking your thumb out like that).

Where to Stay

Hotels and pensions

Hotels are cheap in Italy, and the more so the further south you go. There are, of course, dives that you would do well to avoid, such as the 'hotels' around the Naples railway station that double up as brothels. But otherwise, follow these recommendations.

Hotels are classified into five categories: de luxe, first, second, third and fourth. Since 1986, the category of *pensione* has been abolished; instead of having their own overlapping system, *pensioni* now correspond to the third and fourth categories. All hotels, no matter how they are categorised, are subjected to regular inspections to ensure that minimum standards are maintained.

Usually, standards range from adequate to excellent. The days when one had to sprinkle camphor on one's bed-sheets to deter what an early nineteenth-century guidebook to Southern Italy called 'the enemies of repose' are over. *Pensioni*, particularly in small towns, are usually clean, and recommended to travellers staying more than a few days in one place. In the lowest-grade hotel there are often such inconveniences as having to ask for a special spanner from reception in order to loosen the shower tap for hot water, and lavatories are often communal. But these are a small price to pay, if you want – or can only afford – to slum it. In general, it is best to aim for the second category mark – clean, simple, moderately priced.

For convenience, hotels are classified in this book as top range, mid range and bottom range, with the accent on the mid range. Some hotels charge the same prices all year round, but prices will usually vary according to the season – cheaper in winter, becoming more expensive by the month as you move towards the peak tourist season of August.

Farm holidays

In 1988, half a million tourists to Italy spent their holidays on farms. Farm accommodation in Southern Italy varies from elegant country houses to spartan cottages; they offer home-grown vegetables and locally produced sausages, wine, milk, oil and cheese. You can horse-ride and fish, or you can pick and thresh grapes. In short, you can get back to nature. If you are interested in such a holiday, write for a copy of the **Rural Hospitality Guide** to Agriturist, 101 Corso Vittorio Emanuele, 00186 Rome (tel. 06-651 2342). The guide will wax lyrical about all things bucolic: 'Gathering mushrooms . . . enjoying the scent of pistachio or the view of a stretch of tangerine groves'. Farmhouse prices range from 4,000 to 10,000 lire per night per person.

Camping

Camping is popular in Italy. The Local Tourist Board of the nearest town will give information and particulars of the most suitable sites, of which there are over 16,000, most of them in Southern Italy. Calabria is the best region in the South for camping, particularly in the pine-forests of the Sila.

Prices depend on the category and popularity of the site, and on the number of people in a party. For further information, write to **Centro Internazionale Prenotazioni Campeggio**, Casella Postale 23, Florence (tel. 055-882391). The Touring Club Italiano publishes an annual directory of all the campsites in Italy, *Campeggi e Villaggi Turistici in Italia*.

Spas

There are all categories of thermal waters in Southern Italy, from low mineral content to high, from sulphurous to muddy, cold to tepid. The Germans, in particular, are keen on the regenerative effects thermal water is supposed to have on the liver, and they flock to spas on the island of Ischia, near Naples.

Campania is *the* region in Southern Italy for spas. Around Vesuvius the land is sulphurous and the air you breathe is highly beneficial to the health (though it is probably an old wives' tale). For a list of Southern Italian spas, write to **Assoterme**, 19 Via Margutta, 00187 Rome (tel. 06-361 4044). They will send you a brochure claiming that the spas have 'an elegant setting of colourful and flower-scented parks and gardens which raise their voices in an anthem to life'.

Eating and Drinking

Some years ago, in Sicily, I once asked a chef in a restaurant why he had named one of his house specialities *macaroni alla lupara*. Patiently, he explained that the *lupara* was a sawn-off shotgun once used by Sicilian shepherds to kill *lupi*, wolves. I did not immediately see the connection, though there was, I suppose, a just-detectable echo of squat gun-barrels hovering over the shapes of the macaroni on my plate.

Dishes vary from region to region, but Southern Italian cooking, as you can see from the shotgun anecdote, is not renowned for its subtlety. Pasta (first brought to Italy in the form of noodles from China by Marco Polo), olive oil, peppers, fish and beans – such are the Southerner's staple fare. It is a healthy, peasant food, unspoilt by cloying sauces – *cucina rustica*, they call it. In the North, on the other hand, the food is more continental-European – rice, dairy products, red meat.

Neapolitan cookery is in many ways typical of Southern cuisine. Here is the sort of menu that you are as likely to find in Naples as in Palermo or Bari (and remember that Italians buy their food fresh from markets, and would die at the thought of tinned spaghetti):

Antipasti, Hors d'oeuvre

Sarde	fresh sardines with olive oil and oregano
Salsicce	dried sausage
Alici al limone	fresh anchovies baked with lemon juice
Caponata	a dish of olives, anchovies and aubergines
Prosciutto crudo o cotto	ham, raw or cooked
Antipasto di mare	seafood hors d'oeuvre
Fagiole e cipolle	beans with onions

Minestre e Pasta, Soups and pasta

Zuppa di cozze	mussel soup with white wine and tomatoes
Zuppa alla verdura	green vegetable soup
Minestrone alla Toscana	Tuscan vegetable soup
Spaghetti alla Caprese	spaghetti with tunny fish, tomatoes and olives
Spaghetti al sugo	spaghetti with meat sauce
Spaghetti alle vongole	spaghetti with clams
Pasta con le sarde	pasta with fresh sardines

Pietanze, Entrées (meat and fish)

Bistecca alla pizzaiola	steak with a sauce of fresh tomatoes, garlic and oregano
Coniglio ai caperi	rabbit cooked with capers
Saltimbocca	rolled veal with ham
Ossobuco	stewed shin of veal
Pollo alla cacciatore	chicken with herbs, tomato and pimento
Pescespada	swordfish
Triglie alla Siciliana	grilled red mullet with orange peel and white wine
Sogliola	sole

Dolci, Sweets

Cassata	ice-cream with candied fruits
Sfogliatelle	sweet ricotta turnovers
Gelato	ice-cream
Torta	tart
Monte Bianco	chestnut-flavoured pudding

Vegetarians, who will not like all of the above, are advised to obtain assistance from the **Associazione Vegetariana Italiana**, Viale Gran Sasso 38, Milan. For Kosher restaurants, contact the **Unione Comunita Israelitiche Italiana**, Lungotevere Cenci 9, Rome.

Restaurants

In general, you cannot go wrong with Southern Italian food, but avoid restaurants that have a *menu turistico* (greasy, plastic-covered menus with such gastronomic delights as egg and chips, Würstel, hamburgers and French fries), and go to where the locals eat. Often, the cheaper the restaurant, the better the food. *Trattorie* are less posh than restaurants, but the fare is sometimes just as good; after you have eaten, your tablecloth will be scrunched up into a ball of paper and thrown in a bin – with such places, the emphasis is on eating, not on interior decoration. Usually, prices on the menu do not include a cover charge, *coperto*. Since a service charge is now always added to the bill, tipping is not a necessity, but Italian waiters are a proud, serious and very professional breed and do not take kindly to the snapping of fingers.

Prices

Prices tend to be much higher in the major cities – and at their highest on the islands off Sicily and Naples, where the food has to be specially ferried in. Wherever you are, fish is more expensive than meat. Average prices (per person) for a Naples or Palermo restaurant would be approximately the following:

● **Expensive.** A meal in one of the best restaurants will cost you about 80,000 lire. That would include wine, pudding and cheese.

● **Moderate.** In the average restaurants such as you find listed in this book, the price of a meal (simple, unadorned, excellent) will be about 30,000 lire.

● **Economical.** A restaurant where you can eat satisfactorily (in a *trattoria*, say) will charge about 15,000 lire or less.

Opening hours

Southern Italian restaurants keep simple, not very sophisticated hours – open from 12 noon to 2.30 p.m. for lunch; 7.30 till about 10.30 p.m. for dinner, rarely later than 11 p.m. If starving, you can always get a meal in a railway station, or from one of the hamburger joints that are now springing up all over Italy. (In Rome they have recently opened a McDonalds next to the lodging house where the poet Keats died; the next thing we'll have is a Wimpy next to Dante Alighieri's house in Florence!)

Snacks

In Naples, you might want to eat in a **pizzeria** – the pizza is the culinary pride of Campania. Otherwise, pretty well anywhere in Southern Italy you can eat an inexpensive, light lunch at a **tavola calda** (literally, 'hot table') or at a **rosticceria**, grill. For picnic food, it is a good idea to find a grocery store (**alimentari** or **salumeria**) and ask them to make a cheese or ham sandwich – the cold cuts are sliced right off the block. For a light snack, you can buy a roll or a small pizza from a **bar**.

In Sicily, the selection of sweets available from behind a bar-counter is particularly impressive: *Torrone gelato*, chocolate-covered nougat; *Cannoli*, fried pastries stuffed with ricotta, candied fruits and bitter chocolate; *Frutti di marturana*, miniature marzipan fruits.

In all bars, you should pay at the cash desk ('*alla cassa*') first, and then take your receipt – with a couple of hundred-lire coins by way of tip – to the counter. In the dog days of summer, bars are an excellent place to repair for a thirst-quenching *spremuta di limone*, fresh lemon and iced water – remember to add lots of sugar as it will be very, very sour.

Wine

Italy is the largest wine-producing country in the world. In 1982, she produced more than seventy million hectolitres – about one fifth of the world's total. With so much wine floating about, it may seem surprising that one rarely sees a drunken Italian, but inebriation is a loss of face, and there is never any low boasting, on the part of Italian men, about their drinking.

The South is more prodigious a producer of wine than the North of Italy; Apulia is the biggest producer, followed by Sicily. Although wines from the Mezzogiorno are unable to compete with the top French *crus*, many of them are excellent. Some are, of course, paint-strippers (so strong they would etch the bottom out of a copper cauldron), but others deserve more attention than they have so far received in the English-speaking world. At the very least they should be taken seriously – an American television commercial for Italian wine is typical, being heavy on Old Masters, with a breathless hint of sex, but notably light on the drink itself.

From the five regions of Southern Italy covered in this book, here are some recommendations:

Campania. Ischia, near Naples, was one of the first wines to claim a DOC, *Denominazione di Origine Controllata*, a system of governmental control similar to the French Appellation Controlée. The island produces the wine for which Campania is the most well known – *Lacrima Christi*, also grown on the slopes of Vesuvius. It is a wonderful, gunpowdery wine, with a barely perceptible tang of sulphur, which takes its name from a legend: God, looking down on His new-born world on the seventh day of creation, was so moved by the sight of the Bay of Naples that He shed a tear, which became the vine from which the Lacrima Christi grape is now grown.

Among the other excellent wines of Campania are *Falerno*, a full-blooded wine praised by Pliny and Horace, and *Taurasi*, which is broad, dark and deep, like the Sybil's cave in the ancient fields outside Naples.

Apulia. Many of the wines here – strong, potent whites – are used as a base for vermouth; the best of this kind are *Locorotondo* and *Martinafranca*. The rosés of *Castel del Monte* are also worth tasting; they are perhaps the most attractive product of the region at present.

Basilicata. There is only one DOC from this region, the *Asprinio*. Pale and crisp, it is not a particularly potent white, but refreshing. It makes an ideal accompaniment to salads.

Calabria. The best wine of this region is *Ciro*, an almost treacly red (but not in the slightest cloying), so highly esteemed by the ancients that it was offered to winners of the Olympic Games. Calabria's most unusual wine is the *Greco di Gerace*, made from a sweetly perfumed grape that grows on the south coast.

Sicily. This area produces some of the best wines in Italy. Recommended are *Regaliali*, a refreshing and slightly astringent white; *Corvo*, an extremely successful wine, imported to both the UK and the USA (the red is far superior to the white), and *Marsala*, a sweet fortified wine which is a distant cousin of sherry, used in the making of the dessert *Zabaglione*, and in Italian cooking generally.

Entertainment

Religious festivities, village fêtes, tournaments and jousting matches –
all are to be found in Southern Italy (see pp. 58–61, Public Holidays
and Festas). But the principal entertainment is the **opera**. The season begins in December and continues through to May or June. The
principal opera house in the South is the San Carlo in Naples, Via
Vittorio Emanuele; tel. 081-79 72 370.

Music and drama festivals take place all the year round; performances of Greek tragedies in the Greek Theatre at Syracuse (May
and June), and the classical drama festival in the Roman Theatre at
Pompeii (July and August) are among the best. As far as folklore is
concerned, Sicily is famous for its puppet shows, depicting scenes
from the Norman and Arab invasions of that island. The shows last all
the year round (see p. 216 for details).

Film festivals are held at both Messina and Taormina, in Sicily,
during the month of July. In Taormina, films are projected at night in
the Greek Theatre.

Nightlife

There are shows and activities for all tastes in the big towns and cities
of the Mezzogiorno. In both Palermo and Naples, the biggest cities,
there are nightclubs and piano bars, gay hot-spots and discothèques.
In August, however, when there is a mass exodus of Italians away
from the towns to holiday resorts, even restaurants and cinemas will
shut.

There are only four **casinos** in Italy – San Remo, Campione, Venice, St Vincent. Curious that they should all be in the North, when the
Mafia have such a financial stranglehold on the South.

Sport

For the sportive, Southern Italy is a haven. **Underwater fishing** is the ticket – and **scuba-diving**, too. The most suitable coasts for these activities are those of Sicily, particularly off the Aeolian Islands. Underwater fishing with aqualungs in all the waters off Sicily is not always permitted, although you can use them for other purposes. Only those over sixteen are allowed to use underwater guns, harpoons and other such implements of destruction. When submerged, you are required by law to indicate your underwater whereabouts with a float bearing a red flag with a yellow diagonal stripe; otherwise, there is a danger that a speedboat may not see you and the consequences will be messy, to put it mildly. When fishing underwater, you must operate within a radius of 50 metres of the float bearing this flag. Compressed-air service stations (for oxygen cylinders, canisters and aqualungs) are available at all main seaside resorts.

The South of Italy is not so good as the North for **golf**, presumably because so much of the area is mountainous. However, the main course in Campania is the *Naples–Afsouth* Golf Club (9 holes), 80078 Pozzuoli; in Apulia, the *Riva dei Tessali* (18 holes), 74025 Riva di Ginosa; and in Calabria, the *Porto d'Orra* (9 holes), 88063 Catanzaro Lido.

Hunting: as far as birds are concerned, Italians shoot pretty well any species that moves, whether the birds be up in the trees, in the air, or on the ground. Sicily is renowned for hunting, particularly on the Egadi Islands, where the land is strewn with spent cartridges. To conserve the bird population, there are now restrictions on the importation and use of firearms. Further information may be obtained from *Federazione Italiana Caccia*, Viale Tiziano 70, Rome; tel. 06-394871.

Shopping

These days, Italy is no better than any other Mediterranean country for shopping. However, Campania is good for coral and pottery; and Sicily is renowned for wooden puppets (ideal gifts for children), majolica tiles, and interesting-looking shells and natural sponges, which are best purchased on the Sicilian island of Lampedusa.

Otherwise, there is always olive oil, nectar of the Mediterranean. It is consumed by Southerners in enormous quantities – the Sicilians not only eat (or drink) it, they are also in the habit of rubbing it into chapped or grazed skin, rather like the oil with which those classical Greek athletes massaged themselves. Then again, I know of an elderly Neapolitan lady who lubricates the wheels of her Hoover with the stuff. You may not want to do quite *that* with the oil, but if you are thinking about stocking up on a couple of extra bottles, make sure the label says *Extra Vergine*: it is the best quality.

From the healthy to the unhealthy. A couple of bottles of Marsala may go down very nicely with grandma; and a box of *Toscani*, perhaps, for grandfather, a cheap type of hand-rolled cigar so irregular in shape that Northern Italians joke they are rolled on the sweaty bellies of Southern peasants. They may well be right. If you smoke cigarettes, you might like to buy a carton of the extremely cheap (though eminently puffable) MS brand. The initials stand for 'State Monopoly', though are more commonly understood to mean '*Morte Sicuro*', certain death. Probably, that's not such a bad joke.

General Basics

Naples
- **British Consulate**, Via Crispi 122; tel. 041-664647.
- **United States Consulate**, Piazza della Repubblica; tel. 041-660966.
- **South African Consulate**, Corso Umberto Primo 7; tel. 041-206931.

Palermo
- **United States Consulate**, Via Vaccarini 1; tel. 091-291532.
- The British Consulate was closed in 1980.

Documents needed to enter Southern Italy

EEC citizens do not need a passport if they have valid national identification papers, such as a Visitor's Card; however, citizens of the UK and Eire need passports, since they do not have such papers. So long as the period of stay in Italy does not exceed three months, holders of passports for the following countries do not need a visa: Australia, Canada, New Zealand, the USA. Also exempt from visas (for the same period of stay) are holders of a British passport whose national status is defined as 'British Subject and Citizen of the United Kingdom and Colonies' or of a British passport issued in Hong Kong. Tourists are not authorised to work in Southern Italy; for that you need work and residence permits.

Electrical current

Throughout Southern Italy, the current is 220 volts, 50 cycles. Hotel sockets usually indicate this voltage. In cheaper hotels, there are often no sockets. British and American plugs do not fit standard Italian sockets; you will need an adapter. Do not attempt to interfere with the wiring yourself; the further south you go, the less safe the electrics – there is a danger of electrocution.

Finding your way around

This can be a problem. It is not that Southern Italians are unwilling to help when giving street directions; on the contrary, they fall over backwards in trying to help. The problem, rather, is that the directions they give are invariably wrong, or confused. On a bad day, one's conversation with a Southerner may begin to sound like something out of a Marx Brothers script, such as this colloquy conducted by Edward Lear with a peasant outside Naples:

'How far is it to Spiaggia?'
'Who knows?'
'Is it a town or a village?'
'How can anybody tell?'
'Are there any inns?'
'I don't live there.'

That was in 1838, but little has changed. As a rule of thumb, double check all the directions you get. In smaller towns, even the information given at a Tourist Office should not be trusted – particularly when it comes to the opening hours (so called) of churches, castles and museums, which often vary according to the whim of a custodian or sacristan. Remember, too, that travelling anywhere in Southern Italy on a Sunday is a bad idea; buses are slow, trains snail-like.

Health

Malaria is a thing of the past: today, you need no pills or vaccinations. Temporary upsets, though, may be caused by over-exposure to the sun, and by troubled stomachs. For the first, take a bottle of high-protection sun tan oil, for the second, stock up on a packet or two of the aptly-named 'Arret' if you can get it – an excellent pill. You should also take a hat or a parasol. Drinking the water is generally okay, but avoid drinking the stuff when a sign says *Non Potabile*, not drinkable – often indicated by a crossed-out P.

Do not consume too much cheap wine (the white will give you a hangover like seven Swedes). Avoid eating mussels in Naples; it is through these crustaceans that viral hepatitis is often transmitted. Avoid all dishes and cakes made from mayonnaise or cream which are displayed in fly-blown bars. Do not consume too many ice-cold drinks in a broiling heat. And do not leave your hotel bedroom with the lights on and the windows open; you might come back from your candle-lit dinner to find the place aswarm with mosquitoes – creatures that may be slain with a rolled-up newspaper, or with a single flip-flop.

Since Italy and the UK are both members of the EEC, British visitors now have the right to claim health services available to Italians. Before leaving for Southern Italy, it is a good idea to obtain Form E111 from the Department of Health, which entitles you to free medical service. At every chemist's shop (*farmacia*) there is a list of chemists open at night and on Sundays. First aid service (*pronto soccorso*) may be found at all airports, railway stations and in all hospitals. For an emergency – ambulance, fire or police – dial 113.

But you should at all costs avoid being hospitalised in the Mezzogiorno; hospitals south of and including Rome are no joke. After being operated on in Rome for a fractured skull, I woke up with a shaved head outside a lavatory in a hospital corridor, strapped to some sort of iron trolley. That was not so unusual, as I later found out; owing to a grave shortage of space in Italian hospitals, old women, men and children are often to be seen sleeping out in the corridors, suffering their post-operative slumbers on iron trolleys.

The lavatories were bad news, too: so squalid, one could best liken them to those on board the Naples–Palermo express. And the food was certainly remarkable – always *pasta con carne*. Nobody dared ask from what sort of animal the meat came, but resignedly referred to it as *grasso di rinoceronte*, 'rhino-fat'. An elderly chap in the bed next to me was more fortunate; every second day, he was visited by a brigade of black-clad Calabrian relatives who would bring with them lengths of salami, pungent wedges of goat's cheese, loaves of unleavened bread. Most extraordinary was the way these terrifying women would prostrate themselves in the presence of the chief surgeon, at times even offering him some of their unusual food; less an entreaty, perhaps, than some obscure remnant of feudalism.

So it was bedlam generally. And that was Rome; things are much worse in Naples, where the old Policlinico hospital is always in the local news for its *degradazione inumana*. One day, a priest there showed me a subterranean 'recuperation ward'. It was nothing but a grotto – windowless, without air. 'I don't call this a centre for recuperation,' he said, touching the red cross emblazoned on the front of his cassock, 'but for suffocation. It's a shameful room where even rabbits and hens would not survive.' If you can at all help it, please do not get yourself run over in Naples – or anywhere else in the Mezzogiorno, for that matter.

If you are unable to produce your Form E111, it is advisable all the same to go to the Local Health Centre (USL) to solve the problem there.

Insurance

The EEC insurance card E111 does not cover all medical expenses (such as the cost of an operation); and it is advisable to take out separate medical insurance for full cover. Only holiday insurance schemes and private patient schemes such as BUPA cover the cost of an emergency return to the UK or USA in the event of an illness while abroad.

The standard 'green card', used throughout the European Community, will provide sufficient insurance for your car. Remember that claims must always be accompanied by a police report of the incident. For disputes or legal or police problems, the American or British Consulate will find you lawyers. Finally, do not carry all of your documents and all of your money in the same wallet or purse.

Laundry, dry-cleaning and shoeshine

In general, laundries should be avoided; they are terribly slow. So take with you a large bag of detergent, and a travel iron. Most hotels allow you to wash and dry clothes in your room. But in case there is no balcony, take with you a washing line and clothes pegs and you can rig the thing up in your room. Obviously, no dry-cleaner will have anything to do with your *biancheria intima*, 'intimate white things' – underpants, knickers, bras etc. The best hotels have cleaning and laundry facilities. But having one's shirts pressed and ironed is an expensive business – about 10,000 lire per shirt.

I have always found shoeshining an embarrassing business, too much a master–slave set-up. In Palermo, the ambulatory bootblacks look so bedraggled, and the men whose shoes they are shining so imperious, well-fed and generally pleased with themselves, that one wonders whether man is moving forward at all through the centuries. Most bootblacks are so hard up, they will even persuade you that your suede shoes could do with a polish. But there is, no doubt, a luxury in sitting down and having your shoes shined while you wait. You may feel as contented and as comfortable as a bug in a rose. Bootblacks are to be found in all the major towns and cities of the Mezzogiorno. Women are never to be seen having their shoes shined. Perhaps they have less leather to shine?

Money matters

The unit of currency is the lira – plural lire. There are coins in circulation of 10, 20, 50, 100, 200 and 500 lire. Often, these useless coins are in short supply, and change will be given in the form of hard-boiled sweets or *gettoni*, special tokens used for making telephone calls. When an article is priced at, say, 995 lire, you will never get change. Banknotes are issued for 500, 1,000, 2,000, 5,000, 10,000, 20,000, 50,000 and 100,000 lire. You should get an awful lot of boiled sweets for the 100,000 lire note.

The amount of Italian money allowed in and out of Italy is 400,000 lire, but check with your bank before departure. There are no restrictions on any other currency. But if you intend to re-export out of Italy at the end of your stay more than 1,000,000 lire valued in other currencies, then you have to fill in Form V2 at the customs on entry.

Major credit cards – American Express, Visa, Access, Diner – are accepted in most big shops, restaurants and hotels, but *not* at petrol stations. However, many rural places are still pretty backward in this respect.

Banks are open in the mornings from 8.30 a.m. to 12.30 p.m., and for one hour in the afternoon – generally from 3 to 4 p.m.

Newspapers

The South has an excellent selection of local newspapers. But whereas the bigger papers of the North are sold all over Italy and abroad, those of the Mezzogiorno lack the structure which makes this possible. As a result, Northern points of view predominate. And because so many cultural luminaries of the South, such as the excellent Sicilian writer Leonardo Sciascia, publish articles condemning the Mafia in the Milanese quality paper *Corriere della Sera*, there is a danger that the Northerner might be fooled into thinking that the Mezzogiorno is uniformly a land of hoods and delinquents. It is quite a problem.

The only Southern paper that can compete on the national scene with the *Corriere della Sera* is the Neapolitan *Mattino*, an excellent publication with a more than competent coverage of international affairs. As with most of the papers of the South, though, the *Mattino* is biased towards the political right; both Gianni Agnelli, chairman of Fiat, and Ciriaco De Mita, secretary of the conservative Christian Democratic Party, have a share in its ownership. Since 1985, the paper has been under the control of the Banco di Napoli. Founded in 1891, the *Mattino* has an impressive circulation of over 180,000 copies. If you speak Italian, it is the best paper for you, in whatever part of the South you happen to be.

Otherwise, the major paper of the Italian South is the *Gazzeta del Sud*. Based in the Sicilian town of Messina, this too is under the thumb of the Christian Democrats. Its late owner, the Cavaliere Uberto Bonino, even received the last rites from the Pope when he died in June 1988 – over the telephone. The paper is sold principally in Calabria, and tends to the sensationalist.

The major paper in Sicily – and the longest established in all the Mezzogiorno – is the *Giornale della Sicilia*. This is a quality publication with a circulation of 80,000. It specialises in the coverage of what Italians call *cronache nere* – literally, 'black chronicles': Mafia killings, kidnappings, political assassinations, corruption in high places.

The fiercest critic of the Mafia remains Palermo's afternoon daily, *L'Ora*. A supporter since 1900 of the Italian Communist Party, its most illustrious journalist was Mauro De Mauro. An expert on the Mafia's interest in drug-trafficking, De Mauro was kidnapped outside his house in September 1970, while he was investigating the last days of the oil magnate Enrico Mattei on behalf of the film director Francesco Rosi. De Mauro has never been heard of since; he was the first journalist murdered by the Cosa Nostra. *L'Ora* is an excellent paper, with a particularly good listings page for theatre and cinema.

The principal English-language newspaper in Italy is the *Daily American*, based in Rome; if you can get hold of a copy further down south, the paper has first-class coverage of the arts. Otherwise, your best bet in Campania is *Qui Napoli*, a monthly 'What's On' translated into English rather oddly as *Here Naples*! and, in the capital city of Sicily, a similar sort of publication entitled *A Month in Palermo*. Both are available from the Tourist Office. Foreign newspapers are obtainable at main railway stations and airports; usually they are on sale two days after the date of publication.

Photography

There are few restrictions on photography in Southern Italy, but you will need to obtain permission from priest, custodian or sacristan if you want to photograph the interior of a church. Often, permission to do so will not be granted; obviously, churches make a reasonable amount of money out of the sale of postcards. You are forbidden to take pictures of military installations, and you should be careful about photographing people in uniform – *carabinieri*, policemen, soldiers.

Places of worship

Here is a typical church notice: *'Agli signori e vietato l'ingresso in calzoncini, in abiti corti, scollati o comunque vestite indecentemente. A TUTTI e severemente vietato fotografare o andare in giro durante le sacre celebrazioni.'* Translated, this reads: 'Entrance is forbidden to those dressed in shorts, mini-skirts, low-cut dresses or indecently dressed in any way. FOR EVERYBODY it is severely forbidden to take photographs or to walk about during the services.' One need not add to this, except to say that talking loudly is taboo (church acoustics are such that they usually amplify your voice threefold), church custodians will often badger you for money, and women do not have to cover their heads. In general, move about noiselessly, and keep away from the altar when the clergy are officiating. You may otherwise get some nasty looks.

Pornography (and cinema)

In every Southern Italian town you visit, most cinemas will be showing *lucce rosse*, red light films. These are the equivalent of our blue movies. That pornography should be so popular a form of entertainment in the Catholic South is a mystery. Whatever the verdict, most films carry the warning *'Vietato ai Minori di 18 Anni* [forbidden to those under 18]'.

Things have got worse – or improved, depending on how you look at it – since the general election campaigns of 1987 when Ilona Staller, Italian MP and sex enthusiast, toured the Mezzogiorno with a series of markedly lewd porno-shows. These featured a leather-clad Neapolitan nymphette wielding a whip or machine-gun, steel-studded gloves and sundry bottle-sized gadgets of an irrefutably sexual nature. When I met Signorina Staller, otherwise known as Cicciolina (Italian for 'Sweetiepie'), outside Parliament in Rome one day, the last thing she said was, 'But I just don't agree with lover boy John Paul II. When he says, "Make love to procreate", I say, "Do it for pleasure." '

Well, the Hon. Sweetiepie seems finally to have won her naughty way; one is hard pushed these days to find a film – *lucce rosse*, of course – which does not feature this eminent parliamentarian in the lead sex role. Pornography is an enormous, money-spinning business in the South (and in the North, too). Take, for example, the Calabrian town of Cosenza: the cinematic life of the place seems entirely to have been commandeered by some lewd entrepreneur of the flesh.

That said, films by the great directors of the Italian cinema – Pasolini, Fellini, Francesco Rosi – are still to be seen. To find out what's showing, check one of the English-language publications. Italian daily newspapers also carry a list of cinemas and films. All foreign films in Italy are dubbed (and often atrociously so); and all films are interrupted by an often interminably long *intervallo*. But no matter; the cinema is still an enjoyable way to spend an evening.

Post offices

You need not to go a post office (open from 9 a.m. till 7 p.m. on weekdays) to buy stamps; you can get them from tobacconists, where there is usually less of a queue. Parcels, registered and express letters are of course a different matter; for these, you will need to go to a post office. Correspondence can be addressed c/o the Post Office by adding *Fermo Posta* to the name of the locality. Delivery will be made at the local central post office, and you can collect after providing identification by a passport, and on payment of a small fee. Telex and fax services are available only at the central post office in each city.

My favourite post offices in Southern Italy are both in Sicily: the elephantine building in Palermo on Via Roma, built under Mussolini in 1933, which has a certain brutal appeal, built as it is entirely of ferro-concrete; and the striking circular building, constructed in Art Deco black and silver in modern Agrigento. Both stand as ruined symbols of Fascism.

Public holidays and festas

Traditional festivals are celebrated in most Southern Italian towns and villages to commemorate local historical or religious events. There are an awful lot of such celebrations; here are the dates for a few of them.

Public holidays
- **1 January**, New Year's Day.
- **Good Friday**, a movable feast.
- **25 April**, Liberation Day.
- **1 May**, Labour Day.
- **15 August**, the Assumption.
- **1 November**, All Saints' Day.
- **8 December**, the Immaculate Conception.
- **Christmas Day**, needs no explanation.
- **26 December**, St Stephen.

And here are some of the most popular *festas*. Whether or not you will be able to attend depends on whichever part of Southern Italy you happen to be in at the time.

January
6 Epiphany. Solemn celebrations in the Byzantine rite feature a procession of womenfolk in Albanian costume, accompanied by a benediction and distribution of oranges; takes place in Piana degli Albanesi, near Palermo.

Procession of the Magi; a movable festival recalling the journey of the Magi to where Christ was born. Held in most major towns and cities of Southern Italy.

February
3 Feast of St Agata. A procession bearing gilt wooden candlesticks 6 metres high marks the Saint's feast day, and the following day a huge silver cart heads a procession of white-robed faithful through the city; held in Catania, Sicily.

9 Pomigliano d'Arco. Five characters representing the family of Pulcinella (the model for the puppet Punch) perform the farce known as *la zesa*; held in Naples.

16 Palio del Viccio. The *viccio* is a turkey, the prize awarded to the best of ten horsemen who tilt at and attempt to break a suspended water bag; an unusual *festa* held in Bari.

April
1 Procession of the Vattienti. Like the flagellants of the Middle Ages, the *vattienti* accompany a statue of Christ to a symbolic Calvary, scouring their legs with discs of cork bristling with shards of glass; a foolish and harmful *festa* held in the Calabrian town of Catanzaro.

Procession of the Mysteries. The Congregation of the Turchini organises a procession of adolescents and children. The youngest children, who wear black costumes and are called 'the little black angels', are carried by the adults. Painted panels representing scenes from Christ's Passion are executed by the children and bring the procession to a close. Takes place on the Island of Procida, near Naples.

Procession of the Mysteries. Sculpted groups representing scenes from the Passion of Christ are carried in procession; takes place in the Sicilian town of Ragusa.

3 La Diavolata. At the end of a fierce verbal battle in the town's main square between five devils headed by Lucifer and a child who impersonates an angel, good wins over evil; takes place in the Sicilian town of Catania.

Easter Monday In the chapel of San Vito, men and women of various sizes and statures attempt to pass through the aperture in a large stone, to the amusement of all. Tradition holds that those who pass through the hole will be healthy and fecund. Takes place in the Apulian city of Lecce.

May

7 Feast of St Nicholas. Recalling the arrival in the Apulian city of Bari of the bones of the Saint, brought from the Near East by sailors in the eleventh century, a caravelle on wheels bears an antique icon of the Saint to the Basilica of San Nicola. The following day the Saint's statue is mounted on a boat which leads a waterborne procession. Held in Bari and great fun.

28 Procession of the Caparisoned Horse. This is a theatrical reconstruction of the legend of the knight returned from the Crusades who consigns the consecrated Host to the bishop, who carries it in procession on a large white horse. Held in the Apulian city of Brindisi.

31 Cavalcade of the Turks. In this traditional parade, figures in period costume ride through the city on floats resembling galleons. The Turks get beaten up. Held in the capital city of Basilicata, Potenza.

June

24 *U pisci a'mmare*. A comic pantomime of fishermen catching a swordfish and a contest for the most beautifully painted boat; held in the Sicilian city of Catania.

26 Feast of the Lilies. Gigantic constructions in wood, as much as 30 metres tall, the 'lilies' are carried by bearers to the beach, where they are jigged about in a dance called the *ballata*; takes place in Naples.

July

3 Feast of the Bruna. After a procession, the statue of the Madonna Bruna (Black Madonna) is solemnly returned to its church while, outside, an excited crowd destroys the cart that carried it. Weird and violent; takes place in the town of Matera, in the region of Basilicata.

11 *U fistinu*. A procession is led by a huge cart, about 12 metres high, which bears the urn containing the relics of Santa Rosalia. The festivities end on the evening of the 15th with a spectacular fireworks display; held in Palermo, capital of Sicily.

August

15 Procession of the Giants. A small Black Madonna covered with silver is carried in procession and followed by a bagpipe player. The following day, figures of the Giants, the Black King and the White Queen – marionettes moved by puppeteers – act out the story of their unhappy love affair. Held in Reggio di Calabria.

Feast of the Assumption. After the religious procession, a papier-mâché donkey is pulled through the streets; the animal, stuffed with firecrackers, is subsequently set on fire. No way to treat a beast of burden, but there you are. Takes place in the Campanian town of Salerno.

16 Feast of San Rocco. A procession involving the *spinati*, penitents who have pierced their flesh with thorns; votive offerings of wax are sold at street stalls. Takes place in Reggio di Calabria.

21 Wedding March. In a re-enactment of an ancient wedding ritual, a cortège follows the bride from her father's house to her new home. A group of dancers perform the 'dance of the cord', intertwining coloured cards hanging from a pole to form a canopy-like net. Takes place in the Sicilian village of Pettralia Sottana, near Palermo.

September
1 Feast of Piedigrotta. A festival celebrating the pilgrimage to the Sanctuary of Piedigrotta with music, parades and fireworks; one of the most famous of all *festas* held in Naples.
11 Madonna della Consolazione. The festivities, lasting several days, include folk and religious celebrations, and parades of floats and fireworks; held in Reggio di Calabria.

December
25 Christmas and New Year festivities. Throughout Southern Italy, every town, village and city celebrates. Not all observances are of ancient origin, but for the most part they reflect the traditions of the Roman Catholic church.

Restoration

Since the 1980 earthquake that killed over 5,000 people in the Campania area of which Naples is capital, numerous buildings have been *sotto restauro*. Many are simply *chiuso*, closed. The wings of museums are cordoned off, church treasuries bolted shut, castles covered in scaffolding. Despite the 750 million dollars shelled out in earthquake relief, the progress of restoration is slow. It can make for a very frustrating day's travel. Nevertheless, the Mezzogiorno is so wonderfully rich in things to see that for one church closed there are always two or three open. So despair not.

Telephoning

A public telephone is nearly always at hand in Southern Italy; that there is usually a long queue outside it is another matter. To make calls inside Italy, you need special *gettoni* (tokens), available from post offices, tobacconists and bars, worth 200 lire each. Otherwise, you can use 100 and 200 lire coins. For local directory enquiries, dial 12; for the operator, 13; for emergencies, 113.

International and long-distance calls can be made in every major town from the offices of SIP (Società Italiana Posta/Telefoni), pronounced 'seep'. Here are some of the country codes:

- **United Kingdom:** 0044.
- **Eire:** 00353.
- **United States and Canada:** 001.
- **Australia:** 0061.
- **New Zealand:** 0064.
- **South Africa:** 0027.
- **Hong Kong:** 00852.

Codes for capital cities are as follows:

- **London:** 1.
- **Dublin:** 1.
- **Washington DC:** 202.
- **Ottawa:** 613.
- **Canberra:** 62.
- **Auckland:** 9.
- **Pretoria:** 12.
- **New Territories (Hong Kong):** 0.

Time differences

Italian summer time is in force from the last weekend of March to the last weekend of September. Clocks in Southern Italy are one hour later than in the UK and Eire, except for the brief period when clocks are changed over from winter to summer time, when for a few days Italy and Britain have the same hour.

It is six hours later in Italy than on the east coast of the United States in winter, and five hours in summer.

Tipping

In restaurants, a service charge is usually included. Like anywhere else in the world, though, it is customary to give a 10 per cent tip in addition – if you are pleased with the service, that is. The absolute minimum would be 500 lire. You should tip the usherette in cinemas. It is also polite to tip the garageman who cleans your windscreen. Hotel porters will expect some sort of *douceur*.

Toilets

On his first day in Italy, Goethe asked an innkeeper for the lavatory. The publican gestured vaguely to the courtyard. But where in the courtyard, insisted the German poet. *'Ma da per tutto,'* came the answer, *'dove vuole'* – 'Wherever you wish, anywhere.'

Things are not quite like that any more, of course. But standards of cleanliness in the few public facilities that exist in railway stations etc. leave much to be desired. Privately owned loos in bars and cheap restaurants are worse, though; often the owners are so ashamed of their closets that they will tell tourists that they are out of order – 'under restoration', even. Such loos as are open for your delectation are usually without a waste bin for soiled sanitary towels, babies' nappies and the like. So carry a plastic bag with you.

As far as I can make out, there are no decent public lavatories in the major cities of the Mezzogiorno. Instead, I recommend the Art Nouveau loos in the Grand Hotel des Palmes in Palermo, and the no less elegant WCs in the Excelsior Hotel, Naples. You can also take the soap.

Vocabulary and learning the language

Italian is perhaps the most musical, the most mellifluous, language in the Western world. German, which by comparison sounds like a throat disease, is an excellent language in which to be raucous, to bark out orders; Italian, with its lilting words that trill so softly, like the arpeggios in a musical scale, from the tip of one's tongue, is a language in which to become amorous, joyful, reckless, and – once you have dimmed the bedroom lights – aphrodisiac. Indeed, one is surprised that Casanova chose to write his salacious memoirs in French, for he was born in Venice.

But it can be no accident that so many librettos, so many operas, have been written in this most melodious language. Basso profundo, and dozens of other musical terms, have over the years been smuggled from the Italian into the English language. But not just musical: think of la dolce vita (Fellini's film has no doubt helped here), inamorata, magnifico and prima donna. And so on – the list could fill a small book. In fact, we could add a few more loan-words to our collection: concerto, impresario, oratorio, solo, soprano, violoncello.

It is almost, some might say, worth travelling to Italy simply to learn the language. With its grounding in Latin, it is the lingua franca (and there we have another expression which has been absorbed into English), the mother tongue, of the European community. The great Dr Johnson, who certainly knew his Latin, would have agreed: 'A man who has not been to Italy', came his Olympian judgement, 'is always conscious of an inferiority.'

Learning Italian is not difficult (though it helps to have that Latin).

Unlike English, which is a lovely, though irregular and thoroughly vexing language, Italian is a purely phonetic tongue: that is, you pronounce the words as they are written. There are no, or very few, exceptions to this rule. Moreover, Italian is 100 per cent euphonic – a naturally beautiful language; if you string an Italian sentence together, and it sounds ugly, you have got the grammar wrong. It is as simple as that – *armoniosa*, they call this indeed most harmonious language. Accordingly, there is little discord in the way its verbs decline, or words pronounced. Remember, too, that the letters j, k, x, y and w do not belong to the Italian alphabet, so you have less letters to worry about. Most Italians, though, are by now familiar with the letter j, which wormed its way into their language during the early 1960s, when everyone began to wear jeans. (Though you will notice how Italians will still say 'yeans': the j, as Anglo-Saxons pronounce it, is too hard, not sufficiently harmonious, for the dulcet-toned *lingua italiana*.)

At the risk of sounding fogeyish, anyone wishing to learn Italian must start with the grammar: that, of course, is the same with any language, but particularly so with Italian, which is by and large constructed on the regularities of a chalk-and-blackboard logic. When Dante wrote the *Divine Comedy*, he did so whilst paying minute attention to the building bricks of his mother-tongue, the component parts of the Italian grammar. Alessandro Manzoni, author of that great nineteenth-century classic *I Promessi Sposi*, was an obsessive observer of philology, of grammatical moods, voices, genders, tenses and, above all, verbs. Indeed, the Italian in which Manzoni chose to write his novel is now the common language, the Standard Italian, of united Italy. Manzoni, a northerner, gave it the name 'Tuscan-Milanese'. And this is the language, perfected by Manzoni with so diligent a scrupulosity, with so fine an attention to the niceties of grammar, that you yourself will learn – or, more likely, already have learned. For the Italian as spoken today originated in Tuscany. 'Tuscans polish the air around them' is an Italian saying. And the very best Italian (according, that is, to Northerners) is spoken in the Tuscan city of Siena.

But even in matters of language, see how there is in Italy a great divide between the North and South: after all, Manzoni never wrote in anything called a 'Sicilian-Campanian'. Why should the Italian spoken in the North be the Standard, textbook Italian? Why should it not have been a language that evolved in the South? Such questions are bedevilled with political complexities, perplexing enough for even the most accomplished of grammarians. Suffice it to say, there is an enormous, a quite mind-boggling, diversity of dialects in Italy: after learning your pure, Manzoni-based Italian, you may feel disappointed that some peasant in the deep South will have difficulty in understanding you.

And misunderstandings there will certainly be: it is estimated that only 2 per cent of Italians are unable to speak a dialect; during the First World War, and to a certain extent during the Second, operations were hampered because so many in the army could speak dialect only, and so could not understand one another. Go to Florence, and you will find that the people there speak an Italian with a difference noticeable even to foreigners: they pronounce 'c' and 'h' as in the Scottish word 'loch'. Years ago, when I once asked for a Coca Cola in a Florentine bar (a simple enough request), the chap behind the counter appeared very confused indeed: it turned out that he pronounced the name of this drink 'Hocha Hola'. Which, if you ask me, sounds more Arab than European.

Italy, then, is a Babel of warring tongues; no single person agrees on how an individual word should be pronounced. In Calabria, the inhabitants of certain mountain villages speak a dialect that is derived from a Byzantine Greek language. In Naples, people speak with such rapidity, spitting out ten words to your one, that they can talk you down by sheer breathing power. In Rome, the people speak a terrible slang, as though they were eating their words: hence *andiamo*, let's go, becomes *'nammo*; and *eh bene?*, well then?, becomes, more condensed still, *mbeh?* Such mispronunciations are sprinkled into Roman conversation like paprika. It can be a little galling.

When written, though, the dialects of Italy can probably be understood by anyone who knows the language. Take a look at the following Sicilianism, concerning the name of a dance much beloved of the inhabitants of Catania.

In Sicilian dialect: *'Ti fazzu abballari la Gran Surdana'*.

In Italian: *'Ti faccio ballare la Gran Sardana'*.

In English: 'I'll make you dance the Great Sardana'.

Not surprisingly for a land infested by the Mafia, this Sicilian phrase has menacing overtones: quite literally it means: 'I'll whip you so hard, you'll dance with pain'. But that is another story.

With every year that passes, the Italian language is becoming more standardised. Unquestionably, this has been as a result – a pernicious result, some would say – of television. With the advent, in the early 1950s, of the magic box (television came late to Italy), dialects have increasingly been whittled down to a kind of consumeristic 'Esperanto' consisting of half-garbled Americanisms gleaned from cop films and pop songs. So much so, wrote the film director Pier Paolo Pasolini in 1974, that if he wanted to make his 1961 Roman dialect film *Accatone* again he would not be able to, as both the language and the way it was pronounced in the original version have now vanished. Pasolini gave the name *'aphasia'* – loss of the faculty of speech – to the phenomenon. But this gradual destruction of the diverse dialects of Italy is not without advantage to anyone who has only recently learnt a Manzoni textbook Italian; certainly, it makes for less confusion on the linguistic front.

Anyway, here are a few useful words:

one	*uno*
two	*due*
three	*tre*
four	*quattro*
five	*cinque*
six	*sei*
seven	*sette*
eight	*otto*
nine	*nove*
ten	*dieci*
eleven	*undici*
twelve	*dodici*
twenty	*venti*
thirty	*trenta*
forty	*quaranta*
fifty	*cinquanta*
sixty	*sessanta*
seventy	*settanta*
eighty	*ottanta*
ninety	*novanta*
one hundred	*cento*
one thousand	*mille*
one room	*una camera*
two rooms	*due camere*
three rooms	*tre camere*
shower	*doccia*
terrace	*terrazza*
with	*con*
front room	*camera sul davanti*
bath	*bagno*
lavatory	*gabinetto*
back room	*camera sul dietro*
sea-view	*vista sul mare*
deposit	*deposito*
spring	*primavera*
summer	*estate*
autumn	*autonno*
winter	*inverno*
months	*mesi*
days	*giorni*
aeroplane	*aeroplano*
airport	*aeroporto*

bank	*banca*
beach	*spiagga*
beer	*birra*
bus	*autobus*
bus station	*stazione d'autobus*
butcher's shop	*macelleria*
church	*chiesa*
coffee	*caffè*
doctor (medical)	*medico*
drink (noun)	*bibita*
electrician	*elettricista*
ferry	*traghetto*
fishmonger's	*pescheria*
food	*cibo*
gas (bottled)	*butano*
greengrocer's	*fruttaiolo*
help!	*aiuto! aiutami!*
hospital	*ospedale*
how much is it?	*quanto?*
I need	*ho bisogno*
information office	*ufficio d'informazione*
mechanic	*meccanico*
medicine	*medicino*
milk	*latte*
mineral water	*acqua minerale*
motor car	*machina*
museum	*museo*
petrol	*gasolio*
please	*per favore*
police	*polizia*
post office	*ufficio di posta*
river	*fiume*
road	*strada*
speak slowly	*parla lentamente*
swimming pool	*piscina*
thank you	*grazie*
tobacconist's	*tabaccaio*
tourist office	*ufficio di turismo*
train	*treno*
waiter	*cameriere*
water	*acqua*
what?	*cosa?*
what is it?	*che cosa e?*
when?	*quando?*
where is?	*dov'e?*
who?	*chi?*

Gazetteer

Introduction

Italy is boot-shaped, as everybody knows. It is a very long boot, with the toe poised to kick Sicily, a break-away part of the boot. This guide deals with the toe, the stiletto heel, the spur and the instep: together, they form Southern Italy, part of the Italian boot which many tourists are still unwilling, in this age of packaged tourism, to try for size. For Northern Italians, at any rate, the South is the unacceptable, the dirty, part of the boot: Europe ends at Naples, and everywhere else is an African darkness.

Attitudes, of course, are changing; stretches of the Southern boot are a world away from the decorous suavities of Tuscany, but at least they have the fascination of the undiscovered. And tourism is tugging at the Southern boot as never before; hotels have flourished where previously there was malarial swampland; airports and railways connect, quicker though you may sometimes find it to walk.

This guide assumes that you have no qualms about venturing into the unknown, that the offbeat has quite as much allure for you as the common or garden, that you do not mind a night or two in a fly-blown hotel. Thus, the guide will take you to those barren parts of the Southern hinterland where the people appear outside time and history, the villages hedged in by centuries of custom and sorrow. It will take you to islands known only to fishermen, and to mountain towns where the language is an Albanian or Greco–Byzantine dialect. Above all, it will assume that people, differences between regions in terms of history, customs and even language, are quite as interesting for you as monuments and buildings, that the living holds an equal fascination with the dead. It will assume, too, that you like your drink and food.

The guide is comprehensive enough: every nook and corner, every crease, ruck and wrinkle of the (sometimes surprisingly leathery or primitive) boot is wherever possible explored. The guide follows the regional divisions of Southern Italy as they are found on the Italian map; sometimes, though, villages are so out of the way that you will have a hard time finding them on the map. Aliano, in the region of Basilicata, where Carlo Levi's book *Christ Stopped at Eboli* (subsequently a film) was set, is a case in point.

The guide is divided into the following regions:

Campania, an at times fairly rough part of the boot, of which Naples, ramshackle capital of the Italian South, is the roughest. Considerable space has been devoted to this magnificent city, as in recent years it has suffered a shameful neglect.

Apulia, the spur of the Italian *stivale*; and, in general, the most polished, the most opulent part of the boot. Much attention is paid to the region's capital of Bari, a fascinating city famous for its possession of the remains of St Nicholas, our Father Christmas.

Basilicata, a largely forgotten part of the boot, overshadowed by neighbouring Apulia. The smallest of Southern Italian regions, this is perhaps the *Mezzogiorno*, the 'Noonday', of Italy at its most primitive. Up in the limestone mountains, you feel miles from anywhere.

Calabria, the toe of the boot. A fierce and barren land, infamous once upon a time for the bandits who infested the mountainous regions. Travellers these days take to Calabria for the forests and mountains of the Sila, an area that resembles as much the Highlands of Scotland as the uplands of the Italian South.

Sicily, the island which appears, on the map, as though it is about to be kicked by the boot. This is by far the richest part of Southern Italy, both in terms of monuments and natural scenery. Parts of Sicily appear more Moroccan than Mediterranean; and the fascination is in the atmosphere of the place – a dangerous potion of exotic spices, pink-domed Arabic churches, and of violent puppet shows. There is no danger, to the ordinary traveller, from the Mafia – a point that cannot be stressed enough.

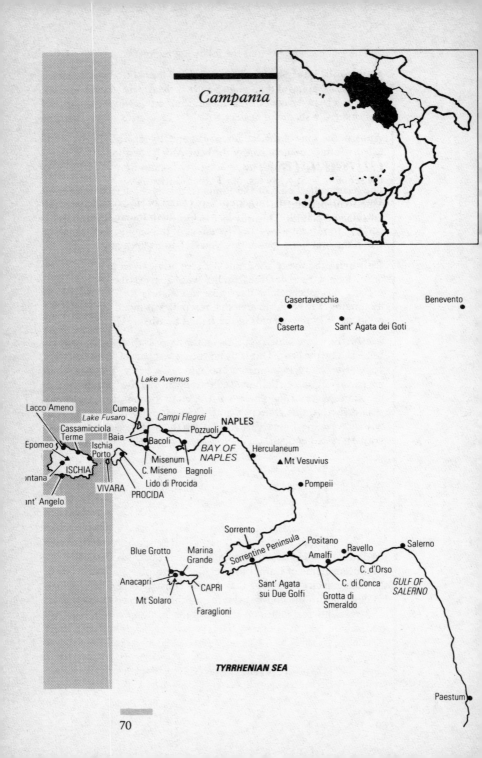

Campania

Casertavecchia

Benevento

Caserta

Sant' Agata dei Goti

Lake Avernus

Lacco Ameno

Cumae

Cassamicciola
Terme

Lake Fusaro

Campi Flegrei

NAPLES

Epomeo

Baia

Pozzuoli

Ischia
Porto

Bacoli

*BAY OF
NAPLES*

Herculaneum

ntana

ISCHIA

Misenum

▲ Mt Vesuvius

C. Miseno

Bagnoli

sant' Angelo

VIVARA

Lido di Procida

PROCIDA

● Pompeii

Sorrento

Blue Grotto

Marina
Grande

Sorrentine Peninsula

Positano

Ravello

Salerno

Amalfi

C. d'Orso

Anacapri

CAPRI

Sant' Agata
sui Due Golfi

C. di Conca

*GULF OF
SALERNO*

Mt Solaro

Grotta di
Smeraldo

Faraglioni

TYRRHENIAN SEA

Paestum

Campania

Introduction

The 'Campania Felix' of the Romans, this is the fertile and lovely region comprising the provinces of Avellino, Benevento, Salerno, Caserta and Naples. The area includes parts of the Apennine mountains, and a coastal strip along the Tyrrhenian Sea consisting of plains interrupted by hills, many of them volcanic. The world-famous sites and sights of Campania – the remains of castles, churches and palaces built by the invading Normans, Aragonese and Spanish, not to mention those illustrious victims of Mount Vesuvius, the dead cities of Pompeii and Herculaneum – make the region one of the most rewarding in Southern Italy to visit. The Amalfi coast itself, on the southern side of the Sorrento peninsula, is of an extraordinary picture-postcard picturesque: wild, precipitous, dramatic, sheer, this must be one of the most beautiful corners in all Europe. Without doubt, you could happily spend over a fortnight in Campania alone.

The region, some would say, is a paradise on earth: the Roman writer Pliny, himself an illustrious victim of Vesuvius, described the Campanian countryside as 'so blest with natural beauties and riches that it is clear that when Nature formed it she took delight in accumulating all her blessings in a single spot'. Little, it seems, has changed: on the coast are raised intensive crops of fruit, vegetables, vines, olives, tobacco and hemp. The interior produces wheat in abundance. Moreover, Campania has some 500 km of seashore, though the beaches are few, thin and usually rocky; if you want to flop on Southern Italian sand, I suggest you head for Calabria.

Classical associations lie thick on the ground in Campania: just west of Naples lies a volcanic peninsula which the ancients considered the entrance to Hades. Appropriately, the area smoulders under the sulphurous name of Campi Flegrei, or the Burning Fields. It was in the Flegrean city of Cumae that Aeneas consulted the Sibyl prior to his descent into the underworld; the soothsayer's cave (or presumed cave) is still there, tangled up in some of the lushest plant-life that you are likely to find in Southern Italy. As with all the most interesting parts of Campania, the Burning Fields are easily reached in a day from Naples. Naples is, in fact, the ideal place from which to explore Campania: capital of the region, a splendid city which is nevertheless unfairly neglected by sightseers, it is where the Italian South begins.

Campania is famed, too, for the beautiful islands of Capri, Ischia and Procida – semi-submerged leviathans laid out in the shape of a theatre across the Bay of Naples, keeping mysterious company with the twin, camel-like mounds of distant Vesuvius. For me, these islands present one of the most magical views in Italy: *'un pezzo di cielo caduto in terra'*, the Neapolitans call it. This is not to exaggerate: to look out across the Bay of Naples is a visual education in the grand style. And it must have been of this particular view that travellers (made delirious, perhaps, by the fumes of Vesuvius) were thinking when they used to sigh. 'See Naples and die!' But then to see the Gulf of Naples was once *de rigueur*, a gracious end to those Grand Tours of the seventeenth and eighteenth centuries.

Both ferries and hydrofoils ply a regular course to Capri, Ischia and Procida from the port of Naples. All three islands well repay a visit – particularly jet-set Capri, now notorious for the debauched excesses of the Emperor Tiberius, who held many a gory orgy, many a mass execution, in his palace there. Or so they say.

Industry   But Campania is not, uniformly, a heaven on earth. Parts of the region are heavily industrialised: the inland suburbs are dotted (disfigured, perhaps) with industrial plants, including iron works, food processing factories, an oil refinery, cement works and an aircraft assembly plant. Compared to their Northern Italian counterparts, most of these industries suffer drastically from low productivity through overmanning. At Bagnoli, west of Naples towards the Campi Flegrei, stands the enormous Italsider steel plant, a typical example of what Italians call a 'cathedral in the desert'. Technologically, it is one of the most advanced steel plants in Europe, and yet the Italian government would like to cut the workforce by some 25,000 men.

Due north of Vesuvius, in Pomigliano d'Arco, is a huge Alfasud car plant. This, too, is not without its problems: in June 1988, Red Brigade terrorists tried to incite industrial action on the shop floor, distributing propagandist leaflets and draping the factory gates with red flags. But low productivity notwithstanding, Campania does not compete unfavourably with Lombardy as far as the car industry is concerned: Turin may have the great Fiat factories, but Naples has the international centre for stolen cars and spare parts.

On a less frivolous note, the foothills of Vesuvius near Pomigliano d'Arco are thickly fertile with vineyards: Lacrima Christi, literally Tears of Christ, is the name of the wonderful wine the Vesuvian grapes produce. Blessed with a markedly sulphurous, not to say gunpowdery, tang, a bottle of this wine should be bought to celebrate your arrival in Naples: it will prepare you for the civic riot, the exuberant chaos, of this most tumbledown of Italian cities.

Naples – the city today

Naples has some 1,226,594 inhabitants: it is one of the most populous cities in Italy. It is, they say, halfway to Baghdad. The boisterous yelling in the corridor-like streets, the bustling markets, the barefoot immigrants from Ghana and Senegal who hawk their watermelons on every available stretch of pavement – it all owes something, you might think, to the *souks* of the Middle East, something to the Levant. At the end of the last century, Scarfoglio, the leading Italian journalist of his day, wrote of Naples: 'This is the only Eastern city where there is no European quarter.' You will probably still not think him far wrong.

On initial inspection, Naples may not be to your liking. The joke these days is to substitute for the expression 'See Naples and die' the rather less enthusiastic *'Vedi Napoli e scappa'* – see Naples and run away. I consider Naples the most beautiful of Italian cities, but here are some reasons why others may not.

Traffic In 1988 it was estimated that some 600,000 cars run through Naples every day. The historical centre is fouled with exhaust fumes, and you'll soon learn, when crossing its traffic-congested roads, to distinguish between the quick and the dead. This is not to put you off, but I may as well quote Mark Twain on the subject of congestion: visiting Naples a century ago, he afterwards complained, 'Why a thousand people are not run over every day is a mystery no man can solve.'

And Twain was only talking about horse-drawn carriages. Today, you'll also have to contend with the hundreds of air-conditioned coaches, shunting hordes of tourists to and from Pompeii. For every 7,000 cars in Naples, 1,000 are quite without a physical space to park – for many Neapolitans, there isn't even room to park their cars on the pavements.

Neapolitans, by the way, use their car horns constantly – and most of the time, it would seem, quite needlessly. And just what purpose the amber traffic light serves I have no idea: presumably it's only there to liven the place up.

Crime and the Camorra Prior to the terrible earthquake of 1980, which killed 2,570 people in the region of Campania alone, some 300,000 Neapolitans were estimated to live off sales of contraband cigarettes. Not surprisingly, the Camorra – the Neapolitan version of the Sicilian Mafia – were behind this contraband industry: it functioned as smoothly as a multinational, with a network of speedboats, couriers and corrupt *carabinieri*. But now that much of the government aid destined for the earthquake victims has, they say, been siphoned off into the coffers of a second generation of young and particularly ruthless Camorristi (members of the so-called Nuova Camorra Organizzata), organised crime in Naples has moved on from cigarettes to the infinitely more profitable heroin. On your walks around Naples, you will still see many a vendor of contraband cigarettes, though since 1980 their number has severely dwindled. Today, they mostly consist of impoverished old women (truly the very salt of the Italian South), selling from makeshift stalls their meagre supplies of Lucky Strike, Camel, Marlboro – the packets filched from cargo boats anchored in the Bay of Naples, traditional port of call after Morocco, Albania or Yugoslavia. If you yourself smoke, there's no real harm in buying them; they sell at considerably less than shop price. But the *contrabbandisti* of Naples are now a thing of the past; like the song 'O Sole Mio', maudlin with nostalgia for the mandolin and the knife, they have entered into Neapolitan folklore. You might even want to take a photograph of the old dears.

No, the big money these days is on drugs. And if your bag is snatched in Naples, or your wallet filched, it will almost certainly have been whipped by a young boy in need of money for a heroin fix. Because of the drug-related problem of crime in Naples, I suggest that you take the following precautions:

● Leave your passport, camera and any form of handbag behind in your hotel. Handbag-snatching is the most common form of crime in Naples: boys known as *scippatori* scoot about in pairs on souped-up Vespas, ever on the lookout for unsuspecting tourists . . .

● If you are driving a car around the isolated outskirts of Naples, do not on any account stop for a young man that you might suddenly see rolling in agony on the tarmac in front of you. The agony is only apparent: the moment you get out of your car to help, you may well be coshed and robbed of your possessions. In Naples, it's sometimes better to let the Good Samaritan ethic fall by the wayside. Recently there has been a reported increase in this highly imaginative form of crime.

● Do not wear a necklace: the infamous *scugnizzi* of Naples, ragamuffins who manage to survive only through resorting to crime, will have it off your neck in a second – a sudden yank and away they are with it. If it doesn't break, you may be hurt, even pulled to the ground, as the thief tugs at it.

● Make sure you have a record of the numbers of your credit cards and the numbers to ring if they are stolen (police 79 41 11; emergencies 112 or 113). By now, the *carabinieri* are expert in dealing with pickpockets; visiting Naples some 250 years ago, Casanova was in the space of a month robbed of twenty silk handkerchiefs.

Poverty   Poverty is actually respected in Naples. Often, even in the most expensive restaurants, you will find some toothless old troubadour serenading the clientele on a gourd-like mandolin; and always, his discordant twangings are financially rewarded. The Church undoubtedly helps here: Neapolitans give the odd coin to salve the conscience. However, 30 per cent of the entire population of Naples is now unemployed, so poverty is naturally a problem. The sorry squalor of certain Neapolitan streets, their violent shadows, their obscure exuberance of life, is a dramatic reminder of this unemployment.

The Spanish Quarter

Take, for instance, the ill-famed area of Naples known as the **Quartieri Spagnoli**, made up of dilapidated seventeenth-century houses built during the Spanish domination to house the occupying troops. Today, this quarter has a population density comparable only to that of Hong Kong; its streets are so cramped they barely admit the light of day, and 'where the sun does not enter,' runs a Neapolitan adage, 'the doctor does'.

With its rusty old balconies draggled with dripping linen, and the streets incongruously festooned with tiny flags (most of them bearing the image of the ubiquitous Diego Maradona, captain of the Naples football team), there is in the Quartieri Spagnoli something of what Henry James, when writing about Naples, called the 'picturesqueness of large poverty'. But only up to a point: numerous stone memorials here attest to the many thousands who have died in Naples from cholera over the centuries: unbelievably, the last epidemic broke out as recently as 1973.

The poverty in the Quartieri Spagnoli is such as you will find nowhere else in Italy, north or south: the streets are lined with typically Neapolitan *bassi*, one-room hovels opening directly on to the street with single doors, like coach-houses. With neither window nor chimney, the *basso* is both house and workshop, inhabited by a mechanic or carpenter, a cobbler or tinker. Many actually double up as sweatshops: down in the Victorian half-light, you see children hammering away at a piece of shoe-leather, or stitching together some counterfeit item of 'couture' clothing. (Avoid buying Louis Vuitton handbags in Naples.) Out of desperation, it seems, plastic altars to the Madonna are illuminated during the night at every street corner, garish with fluorescent hoops of neon.

Poverty notwithstanding, though, the Quartieri Spagnoli will well repay a visit, for it is here that some of the more bizarre Neapolitan customs and superstitions prevail: the habit, for example, of warding off the evil eye with an amulet shaped like a twisted red pepper – people hang them over their front doors, from car mirrors, and on chains around their necks. Another quaint little custom is that of wishing a woman *figli maschi*, male children, whenever she sneezes. Nobody seems to know whence such superstitions came – they are lost in the hoariest mists of antiquity.

Bella Napoli

After reading the above, you may well want to agree with John Ruskin, that sage old panjandrum of all things bright and beautifully Venetian, when he wrote, 'Naples is certainly the most disgusting place in Europe.' But read on – here are some reasons why you should spend at least a week there.

The people

There is something about the Neapolitan soul which has for centuries captivated even the most icy of Northern Europeans. It certainly got to Goethe: 'Naples is a paradise,' he enthused. 'Everyone lives in a state of intoxicated self-forgetfulness, myself included. I seem to be a completely different person whom I hardly recognise. Yesterday I thought to myself: "Either you were mad before, or you are mad now." '

What captivates me is the spirit of *dolce far niente*, living from day to day in a devil-may-care, not to say near-anarchic, sort of way. Deprived in this latter half of the twentieth century of their mandolins and guitars, street musicians and spontaneous refrains, the Neapolitans nevertheless continue to possess a physiognomy which is absolutely unique: they are a people of extraordinary vitality and theatricality, moved to laughter or tears at the drop of a hat. Often, you will see men and women engaged in the most explosive of arguments – when their language in general deteriorates medievally, and when things look as though they might degenerate into violent fisticuffs. (And perhaps it's no coincidence that one of the biggest firework factories is in Naples.) Usually, though, the argument will be resolved amicably, the snarls becoming smiles. Which is just to say that the stranger coming to Naples for the first time should avoid judging it over-hastily by his or her own standards, writing it off as uncivilised. If you are in Naples during the sultry months of summer, it is advisable to resign yourself to Goethe's condition of intoxicated self-forgetfulness. It is not a state of mind that one should choose to fight; surrender, rather, to the jolly carnival of it all.

Architecture

Now whilst Naples perhaps lacks the monumental grandeur of Rome, one can see why in the past visitors have been so smitten by this helter-skelter metropolis of the Italian South. The palaces, squares and streets of Naples all testify to an intense cultural tradition, to centuries of history stretching right back to the Greeks. The most significant medieval churches date from the time of the Angevins, and the traces of Palaeo-Christian art in Naples are among the most important in the Western world: you find them in numerous catacombs, and under the stone floor of Naples Cathedral itself. The city boasts some of the finest museums and art galleries in Europe.

The churches of Naples, including the oratories of numerous religious confraternities, are often exquisite examples of seventeenth-century Baroque – an architectural style magnificently reflected in the so-called *Spagnolesco*, a word the Neapolitans gave to the Spanish aristocracy, which formed a closed and proud society that despised work. And the palaces around the Piazza of San Domenico, or in the ancient Via dei Tribunali, are all possessed of immensely ornate doorways and staircases, which are indeed designed to dwarf the slums around them. The Baroque is found, too, in the famous *guglie* of Naples – obelisk-like pinnacles of stone round which cherubs, saints and flowers climb.

History

A popular Neapolitan saying runs: *'e meglio cumanna che fottere'*, domination is sweeter than fornication. Whereas Florence, Venice, Genoa, Milan, Turin and Rome can all boast their moments of conquering glory, Naples has never, throughout its long and sorry history, played an imperialistic role. She has always been the dominated, the vanquished city, rarely resisting, and sometimes even welcoming, the aggression of others.

It was the Greeks from neighbouring Cumae who first settled in what was to become modern-day Naples, calling their town Parthenope. Shortly after, they were joined by Athenian colonists, who set up the neighbouring Neapolis, meaning new town. Parthenope itself became Palaeopolis, or old town. At a very early period, both old and new towns joined to found a Greek Republic, and forgot their differences in nomenclature.

328 | The Republic was besieged by the Romans, and the Greeks must have surrendered, since their city walls had previously resisted attacks from such titans as Pyrrhus, Hannibal and Spartacus. The Romans chose to rehabilitate the name Neapolis for their new-found municipal town, preserving intact the Hellenistic customs and maintaining the use of Greek as an official language.

The vicinity of Neapolis to Rome meant that she was completely under the Romans' thumb. While the provinces further away from the Imperial City took advantage of distance to create a certain autonomy, Neapolis became a sort of holiday resort for the Roman aristocracy – 'otiosa Neapolis', Horace called it. Perhaps the most illustrious citizen of Neapolis was Virgil, who wrote his *Georgics* there. After the fall of the Western Empire, Neapolis came under the Goths for a while.

536 | Naples was subsumed into the Byzantine Empire.

1139 | The next to invade were the Normans: Roger II of Hauteville incorporated Naples into his Kingdom of Sicily – the city's fortunes were inextricably linked with those of Sicily for the next 700 years.

1268–1442 | The execution at Naples of the young Conradin, the last representative of the Norman dynasty, led to 176 years of rule by Angevin kings. The first to take over was Charles I, who seems to have been quite a reformer, removing the seat of government from Palermo in Sicily to Naples. But in 1282, when Sicily threw off the French yoke in the popular revolt known as the Sicilian Vespers, Charles was obliged to relinquish Naples.

His successors were Charles II (1285–1309) and then Robert the Wise (1309–43), a notable patron of the arts – both monarchs were members of the House of Anjou. During their rule, Naples became one of the most advanced cities in Europe, enjoying a political and administrative order of the highest quality. She even had a state university, and a legal system in no way inferior to the Roman.

1442 | Naples' dark period began when she was seized by Alfonso V of Aragon. For almost half a century the city was ruled by the distinctly unenlightened Aragonese, who were largely responsible for excluding Naples from the creative spirit of the Renaissance. Alfonso rarely lived up to his honorific title of 'Magnanimous': under his rule, the survivors of an Abruzzi earthquake were forced to go on paying the taxes of the dead.

Alfonso's successor, Ferdinand I, wasn't much better: it was his unusual habit to keep about him the bodies of his (usually murdered, often strangled) enemies, embalmed and fully dressed.

1503 The beginning of 200 years' rule of Naples by a string of Spanish viceroys. Few stood out as particularly worthy reformers, except Don Pedro de Toledo, who constructed drainage systems and sewers, some of which – suitably modernised – are still in use. Though the viceroys otherwise did little for Naples in the way of public works, it was under their governorship that the city flourished artistically. With the Spanish impetus of the Counter-Reformation, Neapolitan Baroque swirled dramatically into life. But burdensome taxations were otherwise the order of the dismal day.

1647 The Neapolitans were eventually roused to one of their rare flights of insurrection: on 7 July a fisherman named Masaniello armed two hundred rebels with long sticks, disguised them as Turks and paraded them in front of the Royal Palace. When the Viceroy and his attendant entourage of grandees appeared on the balcony, the rebels laid down their bamboo sticks and duly exposed their behinds. (I am indebted, here, to the Neapolitan writer Luciano de Crescenzo, who relates these events in his interesting book on Naples, *Thus Spoke Bellavista*.) The Spaniards were not amused. Miraculously, though, the tax on fruit which the Viceroy had imposed only a few months previously – with the consent, of course, of the Neapolitan nobility – was soon afterwards lifted.

After that, power rather went to Masaniello's head. He gave himself the modest title 'Generalissimo of the Most Serene Republic of Naples' and went on to found the singularly short-lived 'Parthenopean Republic'. Not surprisingly, his followers turned against him: they cut off his head and threw his body into a ditch.

Taking advantage of this most opportune execution, the Viceroy immediately put up the price of bread. A fatal error: Masaniello's former supporters soon resented having so cruelly disposed of their master. They recovered his body and stitched the head back in place, parading the whole through the streets of Naples in solemn procession.

Sadly, nobody today even knows what Masaniello looked like, since there is no surviving portrait. In contemporary Naples, he is something of a popular hero – the mythical symbol of a failed revolution.

1734 The Infante Charles of Bourbon (Charles VII, known to history books as Charles III) seized Sicily; thenceforth, Naples was the property of the Bourbons. Without more ado, Charles established himself as King of the Two Sicilies. It was during his rule that Naples truly flourished as a centre of tourism: a museum was opened to house the treasures recently unearthed at Pompeii and Herculaneum; English gentlemen flocked to the city as part of the Grand Tour, clutching copies of Virgil and Horace. Naples became irrefutably the artistic and cultural centre of Italy, the third largest city in Europe after Vienna and Paris. A Frenchman in 1739 found it 'the only city in Italy which really feels like a capital . . . a Court which is a proper court and a glittering one at that . . . the same busy and lively atmosphere that one finds in Paris or London and which does not even exist in Rome.' How the touristic tables have turned today!

1799–1815 | The Bourbon dynasty was interrupted when General Championnet, at the head of a Napoleonic army, invaded Naples and founded (taking a leaf, no doubt, out of the hapless Masaniello's book) the 'Second Parthenopean Republic'. This Republic was the natural daughter of the rather more famous French Revolution. Unlike that revolution, however, the people of Naples sided, unbelievably, with the King. Domination is sweeter than fornication; 'Hurrah for the King', they cried. Admiral Caracciolo and other Jacobin sympathisers involved in the French invasion were summarily executed on the orders of Admiral Nelson, who did not even grant Caracciolo the customary choice of death by rope or firing-squad. He was strung up instead on the frigate *Minerva* and thrown into the sea without funeral rites.

The Bourbons suffered a further setback when Joseph Bonaparte crowned himself King of Naples in 1806. In 1808, he was succeeded by the Frenchman Joachim Murat, also King of Naples. Murat, however, soon went the way of Caracciolo – executed by Bourbon supporters.

1815 | The Bourbons returned to Naples in the figure of Ferdinand I, King of the Two Sicilies. But with the accession of Ferdinand II – otherwise known as King Bomba for his bombardment of Messina in 1848 – Naples assumed a bad name. In 1851 Gladstone published a scathing attack on this monarch's regime, comparing it to 'the negation of God erected into a form of government'. The words which appeared the most frequently in the English Prime Minister's *j'accuse* were 'filth' and 'horror'.

1860 | Stubbornly, the Bourbons misgoverned Naples until 1860, when Garibaldi entered the city on 7 September, proclaiming Victor Emanuel of Savoy the new King of Italy. Sadly, Naples now took a turn for the worse: in 1884 a terrible cholera epidemic swept the streets. As a result, the government passed special laws to hasten the rebuilding of the city – *'Dobbiamo sventrare Napoli!'* was the government's legendary clarion-call, 'We must tear up Naples!' Sanitary conditions were certainly improved through rebuilding, but the aerial bombardments of the Second World War were to nullify these improvements more or less wholesale. The angry words of Matilde Serao, one of the greatest of Neapolitan journalists and writers, during the 1884 cholera outbreak now seem quite prophetic. '*Sventrare Napoli?*' she marvelled in an open letter to the government. 'Do you really think that will be enough? Do you delude yourselves that three or four new roads built through the slums will be enough to save our city? You'll see, you'll see just how tawdry the truth will appear when the plans for this holy work of redemption are put into action.' Furiously, she concluded, 'Tear up Naples? *Bisogna rifare*, we must make her anew!' One wonders what Signora Serao would think of the way the Camorra have remade Naples, with their thousands of illegally built, and very shoddy, tenement blocks, disfiguring a once-beautiful skyline.

Today, Naples is a city in decline, with a per capita income less than half that of Milan; the port itself is as dead a centre of commerce as the harbours of Alexandria, Tripoli or Tangier. And with the demise of the port came the demise of tourism: visitors will now use Naples only as a convenient point of departure for Pompeii or for Capri, or else they make lightning tours of the environs, ignoring the city itself, departing from nearby Rome in the early morning. Naples has become a city of transient tourism, a city through which people simply pass on their way from A to B.

That Naples today is so obviously a stranger to tourism is certainly not without its benefits. Without the crowds of camera-clicking globe-trotters, you are more or less able to visit the city as a traveller might have done during the Grand Tour. Whilst in the Uffizi at Florence you are unable to see the paintings for the crowds of people, in Naples you can wander about the often empty galleries of the splendid Capodimonte Museum in your own sweet time, taking in the Caravaggios and Titians, the Raphaels and Botticellis for all the world as if you owned them.

Getting there
By air

There are frequent air services between all the principal European centres and Naples' airport, Capodichino, 4 km north of the city. You can get direct flights from London, Frankfurt, Munich and Zurich – flying time from all these cities is, very roughly, one and a half hours. Domestic airlines – Alitalia, for example – connect with the main towns: Bologna, Pisa, Turin, Rome, Venice, Palermo, Catania, Genoa and others.

By train

The train journey from London to Naples takes about thirty hours – since a second-class return ticket is appreciably more expensive than a charter flight, the sensible way to get to Naples is by plane. Within Southern Italy, however, Naples is a principal railway station; to Rome alone, there are forty-three daily connections from Napoli Centrale (in Piazza Garibaldi). Main lines spread out from Naples like the spokes of a wheel.

By car

For those coming by road from somewhere north of Rome the approach to Naples is on the Autostrada del Sole, which comes down from Milan. It also links Naples and Salerno. Otherwise – assuming, again, that you will be coming from Rome – you have the choice of two delightful roads: the Via Casalina (which follows the route of the ancient Via Latina), and the Via Appia (another Roman road, built by the censor Appius Claudius Caecus in 312 BC). Both of these roads provide interesting stopovers en route.

However, I would strongly recommend that you do *not* come to Naples by car; certainly, when getting about the city itself, a car is no great advantage. For a start, you will be constantly badgered by those ragamuffins who, armed with buckets of soapy water, sponge for an often unreasonable price the windscreen of any car stuck in a traffic jam, whether the driver likes it or not. And the coastal road which skirts its way through Amalfi is so tortuous you will not be able to keep your eyes on the magnificent scenery for fear of crashing your car. Shameful to relate, I even crashed my *moped*.

By sea   Depending on where you are, Naples may be reached by sea from Catania, Syracuse, Palermo, Messina, and the Aeolian Islands – all in Sicily. There are ferries, too, from Cagliari in Sardinia, and from Malta and Tunis.

Getting about   Unlike Turin, the streets of Naples were never laid out on a logical grid-plan: the city is made up of many a blind alley, many a twisting and labyrinthine back street. It can all be a little confusing. To find your way around Naples, bear in mind that the city is bisected from north to south (from the Capodimonte and its splendid National Gallery to the Royal Palace at Piazza Trieste e Trento) by the Corso Amedeo di Savoia and the Via Toledo; and from east to west (from the main station to Via Toledo) by the Corso Umberto I, a broad boulevard ploughed through the city slums in the 1884 cholera outbreak.

The Old City proper is bisected by the Spaccanapoli, the street which, quite literally, splits Naples in two, running roughly parallel to the Corso Umberto. You will not find this street on any map as it links together several thoroughfares in a straight line – the longest being the Via dei Tribunali. Naples on the sea, the part of the city most celebrated for its views of Vesuvius, is marked by two parallel roads, the Riviera di Chiaia and the Via Partenope/Via Caracciolo. Sandwiched in between is the Villa Comunale, a delightful park with an aquarium. All the grand hotels and the best restaurants are in this part of the city, overlooking the Castel dell'Ovo (Egg Castle), a great sandstone fortress built by the Normans on a causeway linked to the mainland.

Beyond Egg Castle, following the Bay of Naples westwards, are the areas of Posillipo and Mergellina. Mergellina boasts the tomb of Virgil and, in the chaotic Piazza Sannazaro, some of the roughest (and best) pizzerias in town. From the heights of Posillipo you are afforded some superb views of Naples, best seen at night for the glittering necklace of lights around the bay. As for Naples on the hills, the most important area is the Vomero, a wonderfully tranquil, largely residential quarter (marred only by the Camorra-constructed tenements), which pro-

NAPLES STREET MAP

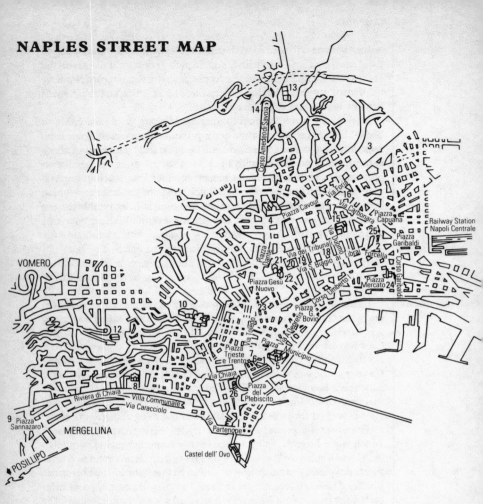

PLACES OF INTEREST		CHURCHES	
1	Tourist Office	15	Duomo
	Royal Palace	16	San Giovanni a Carbonara
2	Castel Capuana	17	Santa Maria Donnaregina
3	Botanic Garden	18	San Lorenzo Maggiore
4	Archaeological Museum	19	Cappella Sansevero
5	Castel Nuovo	20	San Domenico Maggiore
6	Teatro San Carlo	21	Gesù Nuovo
7	Galleria Umberto Primo	22	Santa Chiara
8	Villa Pignatelli	23	Sant' Anna dei Lombardi
9	Virgil's Tomb	24	Santa Maria del Carmine
10	Castel Sant' Elmo	25	Santissima Annunziata and
11	San Martino		Annunziata Orphanage
12	Villa Floridiana	26	San Francesco di Paola
13	Capodimonte Palace		
14	Catacombs of San Gennaro		

vides a welcome respite from the chaos of downtown Naples. It boasts the massive Castel Sant'Elmo, begun in 1349 during the Anjou dynasty, and the Carthusian monastery of San Martino, which houses a wonderful museum and art gallery. You might want to picnic in the nearby park of the Villa Floridiana.

The main Tourist Office is in the Royal Palace (telephone [081] 41 87 44). Whilst at the Palace, don't forget to pick up a copy of the monthly publication *Qui Napoli*: it is full of useful information about exhibitions, concerts and plays.

In Naples, getting about can be a bit of a problem. During the summer rush-hour, buses can be like Black Holes of Calcutta on wheels: bodies packed close to one another, tongues lolling out. When the buses are too crowded, people are regularly injured falling out. All I can say is: do not take any form of Neapolitan transport during the rush-hour – you may end up in a plaster-cast.

That said, Naples is well served as far as transport is concerned. Whilst it is certainly a good idea to investigate as much as possible of the city on foot, some of the most appealing parts of Naples are unfortunately far from the historical centre. Out of necessity, then, you will be obliged occasionally to rely on the buses, trams and trains – funicular, over- or underground.

By bus   Of the buses which leave Piazza Garibaldi, the square with the main train station, among the most useful are the numbers 150 and 106, which go via Piazza Municipio, and further on past the Riviera di Chiaia to Mergellina. A word of warning: always buy your ticket *before* you board the bus (most newsagents and tobacconists sell them), and don't forget to feed it through the clipping machine at the rear of the vehicle – otherwise, an inspector may fine you for fare-dodging.

By funicular   There are a total of four funiculars. The most important climbs up to the Vomero, connecting the lower city to the hills and San Martino. The funicular is a distinctly rickety affair, but fun to ride – it leaves from Piazzetta Duca d'Aosta, opposite the Galleria Umberto on Via Toledo.

By train   As for trains, the *Circumvesuviana* (caught from the main station at Piazza Garibaldi) is the swiftest way to get to Pompeii and Herculaneum – or to Sorrento, for that matter. It's cheap, and with the windows open in the summer, almost refreshing. The *Metropolitana*, or underground, will take you to Piazza Cavour (for the Museo Nazionale), Piazza Amedeo (for the Vomero funicular), Mergellina (for Virgil's tomb), and way out to the Campi Flegrei.

By taxi   You can of course take a taxi (all of them yellow), but Neapolitan cabbies are a breed apart – if you look like a newcomer to their city, and speak no Italian, they will almost certainly take you for a ride, fleece you something rotten. And it is certainly exasperating, watching the taxi meter tick over during a Naples traffic jam (assuming, of course, that there *is* a meter; often, there just isn't, or the thing has conveniently ceased to function). If taking a taxi from Naples airport, remember that you will have to pay a return fare too, and that there is a supplementary charge for each piece of luggage. Sometimes you will be charged for more pieces of luggage than you ever thought you were physically capable of carrying.

What to see

The following guide to Naples will assume that you have at least four days to spend in the city. During the summer, most of the sights should be visited in the morning, so as to avoid the afternoon heat. Remember that all museums are closed on Mondays, and that many are open only in the mornings. Churches close at midday; most of them open again at about 3.30 p.m., after the custodians have taken their siesta.

Since the earthquake of 1980, much of Naples has been under restoration – the words *'sotto restauro'* are often applied, with a world-weary shrug of the shoulders, to churches, to the cordoned-off wings of art galleries and museums, and even to such unlikely institutions as public lavatories and restaurants. Sometimes you may have the impression that the whole of Naples is *sotto restauro*. It's best to resign yourself to this fact – arguing with recalcitrant custodians is a waste of time and energy.

The Duomo

We begin our tour of Naples in the **Old City**, with the Cathedral, situated between the Via dei Tribunali (parallel to the Spaccanapoli) and the Via dell'Anticaglia. The present building was begun by Charles I of Anjou in 1272. It is now dedicated to the city's patron San Gennaro. As with so many Neapolitan churches, the Cathedral has over the centuries suffered serious damage: in 1877, the medieval façade, destroyed by an earthquake, was entirely reconstructed in a rather dreary grey stone of neo-Gothic aspect. It is not a wildly impressive façade: what impresses, rather, is the way in which it seems to be tucked away in a recess, so that you might easily miss its needle-like towers and pinnacles. In most Italian cities, the Duomo will occupy an absolutely central point, will loom large in the middle of a main square. Not so in Naples.

The interior is overwhelming. There's a great deal to see (and not all of it worth seeing), so I'll concentrate only on the most important works. Built to a Latin cross plan, the nave is supported on sixteen arches in which are incorporated over a hundred granite columns from the temples of Apollo and Neptune which once occupied the site of the church. (This quaint fusion of pagan and Catholic is most common in Southern Italy; you will meet with it several times.) On the walls above these arches are forty-six saints painted by Luca Giordano, one of the greatest representatives, along with Salvatore Rosa, of Neapolitan Baroque. Above the main portals – 'suspended like that of Mahomet between heaven and earth', according to Alexandre Dumas – is the tomb of Charles I of Anjou.

Protected by a beautiful seventeenth-century bronze grille is the **Cappella di San Gennaro**, the third chapel on the right side of the church. It was built in fulfilment of a vow made by the citizens to the saint during the terrible plague of 1527, and took twenty-nine years to complete. San Gennaro's skull, encased in a silver bust of French fourteenth-century workmanship, is preserved in a tabernacle behind the high altar. This treasure is studded with the most extraordinary variety of precious stones, including a mantle in emeralds and diamonds made at the behest of Joseph Bonaparte during his exceptionally short reign over Naples. Two ampoules of the saint's congealed blood are also kept behind the altar. The forty-five silver busts of other saintly patrons of Naples are taken out and paraded in the streets during the miraculous liquefaction of this blood.

'Miracle' of San Gennaro

As it is so important a part of Neapolitan life, a word or two about the 'miracle' of San Gennaro is, I think, in order. The liquefaction is celebrated by Neapolitans, here in the Duomo, on the Saturday preceding the first Sunday of May and on 19 September; if you are in Naples during those times, you should not miss the festivities, which are great fun. Although San Gennaro is not the only saint whose blood is held in a church reliquary (in Naples there are some 400 reliquaries containing holy blood), the melting of the patron's blood is nevertheless regarded by Neapolitans with superstitious dread. If San Gennaro's blood fails to liquefy, or if liquefaction is not exactly spontaneous, catastrophe is the order of the dismal day. After the failure of 1527, 40,000 people perished in a plague. Failures in 1550 and 1558 brought about the Turkish invasion, first of nearby Procida and then of Sorrento. In 1836, the stubborn blood caused 24,000 Neapolitans to die from a cholera outbreak; in 1973, when the blood, normally dark brown, assumed, without liquefaction, a sort of burnt sienna tint, the contagion broke out once more.

Prior to liquefaction, the bizarre activity beneath the rococo vault of the Duomo will bring to mind the delirious theatricality of a Fellini film. You must get to the Cathedral early in the morning, to secure a good seat. Down the nave a brass band oompah-oompahs to the martial strains of the Italian national anthem, while various Neapolitan notables mingle with nuns of every conceivable religious order. When I had to cover the liquefaction for an English newspaper in May 1988, I was on to an amusing story, as the blood failed to liquefy. The day after, Naples lost a home-game football match to the hated Milan – a sign, apparently, that the saint was far from pleased with his citizens. Had things gone according to plan, the two glass ampoules containing the liquefied blood of San Gennaro would have been fastened into a medieval monstrance of solid gold, and conveyed in joyous procession to the nearby convent of Santa Chiara, where the Archbishop of Naples would administer blessings to the assembled multitude, followed by a Te Deum. But the blood remained clotted in its ampoules, hard as a piece of pitch. Liquefy it did, but only after a week of solid prayer.

Incidentally, it was Montesquieu who first likened the glass ampoules of San Gennaro to a thermometer, and the solid substance inside to mercury. He suggested that the illuminated wax candles, the excited breathing and overwhelming presence of so many people in the Naples Duomo significantly raised the temperature, causing the blood to melt. Probably you will not want to question too strongly the good Frenchman's verdict.

Whilst in the Duomo, have a look at the tiny basilica of **Santa Restituta**, directly opposite the Cappella di San Gennaro; founded by the Emperor Constantine in around AD 324, it is the oldest building in Naples. The ancient Corinthian columns that surround the nave probably derive from a temple of Apollo, on the foundations of which the basilica was built. On the roof is a painting by Luca Giordano of Santa Restituta's body being carried by angels in a boat to Ischia. Note the **baptistry** and the remains of contemporary mosaics showing early Christian iconography. Underneath Santa Restituta is a fascinating network of Greek and Roman roads, complete with the remains of gutters, aqueducts and lead piping used to transport water; this sizeable part of ancient Neapolis was discovered in 1969. To see it – and a guided tour of the Duomo's underbelly is one of the most memorable things you can do in Naples – you should make enquiries at the Tourist Office in the Royal Palace.

Also worth seeing is the **Crypt of San Gennaro**, or the **Cappella Carafa**, beneath the main altar. Unquestionably, this is the masterpiece of Renaissance art in Naples: note the finely chiselled ceiling of white marble (no Baroque nightmares here!), the way in which the walls have been finely decorated with fruit, eagles, flaming torches, delicate curling leaves, flowers and ribbons, shields, lizards and lions, mermaids and strange mythical beasts. The tomb is that of Pope Innocent IV, the opponent of King Frederick II; a Latin inscription speaks of this Pope as the destroyer of the 'enemy of Christ, the snake Frederick'.

The Piazza Capuana

Between the Duomo and the Piazza Garibaldi is one of the most animated of Neapolitan squares, teeming with fish- and melon-sellers. Built across two mighty Aragonese towers is the noble Renaissance archway of **Porta Capuana**, one of the finest of its kind in Italy, with delicate marble-work, carved angels, and the martial paraphernalia of shields, breastplates and helmets. Nearby is the **Castel Capuana**, a royal palace built by the Norman King William I – otherwise known as 'Il Malo', the Wicked – and later converted into a court-house by the Spanish. Today, it is the seat of the Neapolitan Civil and Criminal Courts.

San Giovanni a Carbonara

From the Castle, walk eastwards down the busy Via Carbonara until you come to the neighbourhood church. An open double staircase leads up to the main portal, a fine specimen of Angevin Gothic. Inside, the wonderfully pretentious tomb of King Ladislaus (made in 1414) rises in three stages to the whole height of the church, decorated with colossal statues of Temperance, Fortitude, Prudence and Justice, Loyalty, Charity, Faith and Hope (I think this is enough to be getting on with). On the third storey, angels are drawing aside a curtain to reveal the sarcophagus containing the King's corpse. On the pinnacle stands an equestrian statue of the King, sword in hand. All in all, the tomb well conforms to the great Sir Thomas Browne's conviction that 'Man is a Noble Animal, splendid in ashes, and pompous in the Grave.' Note also the tomb of Gian Caracciolo, steward to and part-time lover of Queen Joan II. In 1432, he was murdered in the nearby Castel Capuana by the Duchess of Sessa, who afterwards stamped upon his body. The statue of Caracciolo holding a dagger in his hand is an allusion, presumably, to this sorry event.

Apparently, if you come to the **piazza** in front of San Giovanni a Carbonara at twilight, you'll see people crossing themselves when the street lights go on – a recent tradition which equates the lamps with the light of God.

The Botanic Garden

As a pleasant little detour out of Old Naples, you might want to walk from San Giovanni down the broad Via Foria until you come to the garden founded by Joseph Bonaparte in 1807. It has a superb collection of flora, including numerous aquatic plants; it houses, too, a nineteenth-century neo-Classical greenhouse – copied, I think, from the one in Kew Gardens, London. For some reason, there is a pen here full of wild billy goats. The garden is one of the very few places in Naples where you can actually escape the traffic and relax. I strongly recommend a visit. It is open Wednesdays and Thursdays only, 9.a.m.–2 p.m., and at other times by request (tel. 44 97 59).

Santa Maria Donnaregina

Returning to Old Naples along Via Foria, cut down the Via Duomo until you reach one of the most interesting medieval buildings in Naples. This church is situated behind the massy Baroque church of the same name, which is of little interest. Built in 1307–20 with the aid of Maria of Hungary, wife of Charles II of Anjou, the church is now used for lectures and exhibitions. Ring the bell, tip the custodian and, inside, you'll find Maria's splendid Gothic tomb: angels hold back curtains to show the figure of the dead queen, a motif literally done to death in this part of Naples. The sarcophagus is supported by figures of Fortitude, with a dead lion and cub; Justice, with a globe in her hand, and with a snake about her arm. Don't miss the old Nuns' Choir, with its extraordinary coffered ceiling of gold and dark mahogany, and the even more extraordinary fourteenth-century frescoes of the Last Judgement and Passion by the Roman painter Pietro Cavallino – comparable, stylistically, to the frescoes in Assisi by his more famous contemporary, Giotto.

Continuing down the Via Duomo, turn right into the Via dei Tribunali, passing the (uninteresting) Baroque church of **Girolomini**.

On your left soon after, there's the early fourteenth-century church of San Lorenzo: one of the finest examples of French Gothic architecture in Southern Italy. The beautiful apse – light, airy, lofty – is a refreshing change from the puffy cherubim and chiselled skulls of Neapolitan Baroque. It was here, in 1336, that Boccaccio (author of the *Decameron*) first set eyes on his beloved Fiammetta, daughter of King Robert of Anjou: 'Round her red garland and her golden hair,' wrote the excited poet, 'I saw a fire about my Little Flame's head.' In the numerous chapels are some interesting Angevin tombs, particularly that of Catherine of Austria.

At this point, you should take an immediate left down the Via Gregorio Armeno. This is one of the most typical of old Neapolitan streets; since time immemorial, families here have been making miniature Christmas cribs (*presepi*), and there are numerous stalls selling hand-made silk flowers. As in the bazaars and *souks* of Muslim countries, entire streets in Naples are given over to makers and vendors of particular kinds of merchandise – the nearby Via Duomo, for example, is *the* street for wedding dresses.

Retrace your steps and you will see opposite San Lorenzo Maggiore the curious early seventeenth-century **San Paolo Maggiore**. It occupies the site of a temple of Castor and Pollux, with two of the original Roman columns remaining on either side of the portico; in the corner is the mutilated antique torso of Castor or Pollux.

The Cappella
di Sansevero Continuing along the Via dei Tribunali, take a left down the Via De Sanctis and you will eventually come to what is for me the strangest church in all Italy – so strange, it deserves a longer than usual mention. Prince Raimondo di Sangro – a dubious character who christened himself 'Gran Maestro' of a Neapolitan Masonic Lodge and spent much of his life as an amateur alchemist trying to extract phosphorus from his urine – was the first to decorate this sixteenth-century family church with its bizarre profusion of Baroque frescoes and marble statuary. Above the door, Cecco di Sangro, bored with his tomb, is about to leave it, sword in hand. Another statue, 'Vice Undeceived', represents Raimondo's father struggling to free himself from a net with the gentle encouragement of a seated angel. Strangest of all is the 'Veiled Christ': laid out on a sort of operating-table, the figure is draped in a transparent marble shroud which, with an absolutely chilling realism, clings to the body with the very sweat of death. Incredibly, the 'Veiled Christ' has been carved out of one single piece of marble: it is one of the masterpieces of Italian Baroque. Legend has it that Raimondo afterwards blinded the sculptor, Giuseppe Sammartino, for having stumbled upon some alchemical or masonic secret.

Down in the crypt are examples of 'petrified humanity': the perfectly preserved cardio-vascular systems of two hapless mortals. Their veins, a network of interconnecting capillaries fine as filigree, have been conserved, they say, through some alchemical process formulated by the shady Prince. One thing is sure: whilst San Gennaro (the miracle of whose liquefying blood Raimondo boasted he could perform in the privacy of his own home) is irrefutably the symbol of all that's good in Naples, Prince Raimondo is representative of all that's bad. Shortly before he died from accidentally inhaling the fumes given off from one of his alchemical experiments, the Prince was excommunicated by the Pope.

The Cappella di Sansevero is now a sort of private museum; a small entrance fee is required. As you enter, the etherial strains of Mozart's 'Requiem' will mysteriously greet you. The custodian will tell you that the ceiling has in part been painted with the blood of animals, and that there is a real human being underneath the Veiled Christ. I don't know; an altogether freakish place.

San Domenico Maggiore

Walk down on to Via S. Biagio ai Librai (this is part of the Spaccanapoli, which incidentally follows the course of the old Roman Decamanus Maximus) and you soon come to the church which forms one side of the small square of the same name. The square is marked by a fancy Baroque obelisk raised to commemorate yet another Neapolitan plague, that of 1656.

This famous church is a motley assemblage of diverse architectural styles. But despite alterations in the fifteenth, seventeenth and eighteenth centuries (and note particularly the hideous nineteenth-century gilding and stuccoing in the interior), it still remains a noble building of Gothic origins. Charles II of Anjou founded it in 1289. Inside are some fascinating chapels: in the seventh (the Cappelone del Crocifisso) is the little painting of the Crucifixion that spoke to St Thomas Aquinas when he was living under the patronage of Charles II in the monastery next door. To the painting's question, 'Well hast thou written me, Thomas. What wouldst thou have as a reward?' St Thomas replied, 'None other than thee.' The church was richly patronised by the Aragonese nobility; in the sacristy are the tombs of no fewer than ten princes of Aragon, together with another thirty-five assorted notables. You may have difficulty in persuading the bad-tempered sacristan to show you these – '*sotto restauro*', I'm afraid. Still, there are always copies of Caravaggio's 'Flagellation' and Titian's 'Annunciation', the originals of which are in the Capodimonte.

By now you will probably need a short break from churches (there are upwards of 350 in Naples). If so, troop across the square from San Domenico to the famous Scaturchio patisserie. Here you will find the finest coffee in Naples (the water for which apparently comes from a spring in the Apennines), and the *cornetti* (croissant-like cakes) will very nicely accompany your *espresso*.

Thus repaired, we move on up the Spaccanapoli to the **Piazza Gesù Nuovo**, in the middle of which is the thoroughly Spanish **Guglia dell'Immacolata**, a grotesque obelisk sprouting saintly effigies and curlicued Baroqueries.

Gesù Nuovo

The church opposite has an extraordinary façade, the whole

embossed with diamond-shaped bricks of a forbidding grey-black. It doesn't look like a church façade, and it isn't one: it was originally part of a fifteenth-century Renaissance palace. In 1584, the Jesuits set about converting the *palazzo* into a church. The interior is a Baroque explosion of multi-coloured marble and crystal candelabra; the altar is a contorted specimen of decorative art. Note the shrine to the recently-dead Giuseppe Mosca, a Neapolitan doctor who in 1987 was canonised by the Pope for his good works.

Santa Chiara   On the other side of the square is one of the principal monuments of medieval Naples. In 1984, the body of the last King of Naples, Francis II, was brought here for burial, and the crowds shouted, 'Viva i Borbone!' – the church, founded by Robert the Wise in 1310, has always been patronised by the Neapolitan nobility. Unique to Naples, Santa Chiara is architecturally of the Provençal–Gothic style; from the outside it has almost the aspect of a fortress. The aisle-less interior, the largest in Naples, has been compared variously to a large banqueting hall, a ballroom and an indoor car-park. With its stall-like chapels, King Robert's son, Charles of Calabria, thought it resembled nothing so much as a stable. See what you make of it, bearing in mind that in 1943 the building was completely gutted by Allied incendiary bombs and the roof had to be replaced. Don't miss the Gothic tomb of Robert himself, to the right of the high altar, or the Santa Chiara **cloisters**, reached by a doorway outside and to the right of the church. Depending on the time of year, these cloisters are an arcadian haven of hyacinths and white daffodils, tiny vegetable allotments and fruit trees – you will not believe you are in Naples. Everywhere there are eighteenth-century majolica tiles depicting colourful scenes of country and town life – fishing, carnivals and mythological events. So proud are the monks of their little heaven on earth that they have put up the notice: 'If you think you are going to pass into history by writing your name on our walls, you're wrong: it will be removed shortly after.'

Sant'Anna dei   The last church on our visit of Old Naples is hidden halfway down
Lombardi   the road of the same name, which begins where the Spaccanapoli finally hits the busy Via Toledo. Erected in 1411 by Benedictine monks, this church is known to Neapolitans as a Renaissance museum because of the number and beauty of the Tuscan art treasures it contains. Among them is perhaps one of the most popular pieces of sculpture in Naples, the remarkably realistic **Pietà** by Mazzoni of Modena, found in the chapel of the Holy Sepulchre. The second chapel on the left is like a museum within a museum: there is the lovely Nativity by Antonio Rossellino in which, said the famous art historian and painter Vasari, 'the angels are singing with parted lips, and so exquisitely finished that they seem to breathe, and displaying in all their movements and expression such grace and refinement, that genius and the chisel can produce nothing in marble to surpass this work'. There is

also Rossellino's beautiful tomb of Mary of Aragon, daughter of King Ferdinand I; two angels hover at her side, and a gracious Madonna reposes in the arched compartment above. The bas-relief around the bottom of the tomb is delicately decorated with unicorns, flowers, fountains and two figures of Adonis bearing cornucopiae.

The Museo Archeologico Nazionale

Walking up the Via Toledo northwards towards Capodimonte, you will soon arrive at the Archaeological Museum (open Tuesday–Saturday 9 a.m.–2 p.m.; Sunday 9 a.m.–1 p.m.). It is an interesting walk: things have not changed very much since Alexandre Dumas wrote, 'Via Toledo is the road of all roads; it's the road of restaurants, of cafés, of shops; it's the artery which feeds and traverses all parts of the city; it's the river in which flow all the currents of the crowd.' You'll pass the busy **Piazza Dante** on your right (the monumental statue of the writer colourfully spray-gunned with Maradona graffiti), and the nearby **Port' Alba** (well worth walking up as this is *the* street in Naples for secondhand bookshops). The Museum – once a cavalry barracks and then, from 1616 to 1777, the seat of a university – is a huge red building. One of the finest archaeological museums in the world, it needs at least two hours to do it justice. There is so much to see (and most of it fascinating), that I'll limit myself to pointing out some of the more awe-inspiring treasures. Alexandre Dumas, by the way, was once chief custodian here.

Once your ticket is clipped, you'll find yourself in the enormous Great Masters Gallery, lined with tombs and equestrian statues from the Imperial Age of Rome. Dominant here are the colossal **Farnese Hercules**, a great muscular figure of a man bulging with weight-lift biceps, and the **Farnese Bull**, both found in the Baths of Caracalla at Rome. The latter is the largest known work of antique sculpture: it was carved from a single block of marble and was restored by Michelangelo himself. Don't miss the superb Greek and Roman copies of famous statues – the **Javelin Thrower** (surely one of the most famous statues of the ancient world) and the graceful **Venus Callipyge** (Venus of the Beautiful Bottom).

Climb the gargantuan marble staircase and, halfway up, turn into the mezzanine entrance for the **Mosaics of Pompeii**. Here you will find what are perhaps the finest examples of the mosaicist's art to have been preserved from the ancient world: they include death in the form of a skeleton holding a water-pitcher; a ferocious-looking guard-dog straining on its leash; wonderful fish, crustacea and marine creatures (all of them still available in Neapolitan restaurants) and doves pecking at a bowl of food. But most impressive is the huge mosaic of Alexander routing a confused army of Persians in retreat with King Darius: note the terrified expression of Alexander's horse (its flared nostrils) and the way in which a dying Persian catches a last glimpse of himself in the polished metal of his shield.

Some fascinating statues are to be found on the first floor: **Hermes**

at Rest, the fleet-footed messenger resting his winged sandals on a rock, taking a well-earned breather; and **The Drunken Silenus**, boozy companion of Dionysus, resting his heavy head on a swollen wineskin, hand raised tipsily like a wino asking for a cup of coffee.

Also not to be missed are rooms LXX–LXXIX containing gladiatorial gear found at Pompeii – breastplates, helmets with delicate reliefs and sinister visors of criss-crossed metal, trumpets and stabbing-swords. Fascinating, too, is room XCVI with the cork model of Pompeii: all around are cases containing carbonised items dug up from the city's lava-swamped houses – bars of soap, rope-soled shoes, dates, olives, onions, four cakes looking like burnt Bakewell tarts, a pan for poaching eggs, a sink plug, coils of hemp, divans and easy chairs. It all seems curiously modern, as though little has changed in 2,000 years.

From the Corso Umberto to the Royal Palace

It is perhaps off-putting, the scene that greets you at the top of Corso Umberto by the Napoli Centrale railway station: traffic, prostitutes and blackmarket racketeers. But fear not: the occasional detour off the Corso will take you to some interesting side-alleys, markets and churches.

First on the list of detours is Santa Maria del Carmine. Take the Corso Garibaldi, a broad thoroughfare that runs out to your immediate left from the station at the top of the Umberto. Pass on your right-hand side the massive **Porta Nolana**, an Aragonese gateway under whose arch is a madly animated fish-market – wooden pails full of black and blue-silver mussels, curious-looking slippery bivalves and the multi-tentacled squid. It's worth investigating.

From here it's a short step to the **Piazza del Mercato**, a square with a gruesome history. Here, a scaffold, gallows and gibbet once disposed of nobles, plebians and the socially unclassifiable. Poor Masaniello, whose revolution broke out on this very spot in 1647, was executed nearby; and it was here, too, that in 1799 the leaders of the 'Second Parthenopean Republic' were strung up.

Santa Maria del Carmine

Masaniello is buried in the nearby church, as is the young Conradin of Hohenstaufen, murdered by Charles I of Anjou: his body lies behind the high altar, under a stone marked 'R.C.C.' – Regis Corradini Corpus. The beautiful church, founded in the thirteenth century but not really completed until 1631, contains an enormous crucifix which is exposed only on the first and last days of the year. It is said to have bowed its head to avoid a cannonball which passed clean through the nave in 1439.

The great Swedish doctor and author Axel Munthe used every night to sleep in the pews of this church, after selflessly tending to the victims of the 1884 cholera outbreak. The church is to this day traditionally associated with the poor, particularly with impoverished families of fishermen or mariners. When living in Naples I would often talk to a young man sitting cross-legged outside the church on a flattened-out cardboard box. He had the saintly and tormented aspect, I thought, of an El Greco subject; it turned out that he had fallen on hard times after having been arrested for disembarking from an oil-tanker in the nearby harbour of Naples with two suitcases full of 'Lucky Strike' contraband cigarettes. For all I know, he is still there, out of his job as third petty officer in the engineering rooms. He spoke superb English, and had read both Joseph Conrad and Voltaire.

Santissima Annunziata

Return to the Corso Umberto via any street you choose – they are all equally colourful. Cross the Corso into the Via dell'Annunziata to what is, in point of classical architecture, one of the finest churches in Italy. With an interior stuccoed a cold white and grey, and a grand cornice supported by forty-four Corinthian columns of cool Carrara marble, its overall severity of design is a bracing tonic to the tortured ornamentation of Neapolitan Baroque. The trouble is that the church is in a dreadful state; with the earthquake of 1980 the sacristy windows were blown in and the aisles invaded by 4 metres of mud. Nothing very much has been done by way of repairs. A disgrace, some would say.

The Annunziata Orphanage

Until December 1988, this magnificent church was affiliated to the seventeenth-century building round the corner, an orphanage. It is perhaps no accident that the Via Annunziata is full of tumbledown maternity shops with names like 'Fantasy Baby'. It is worth taking a look at this orphanage: in a section of wall by the main gates is a very peculiar cavity, now blocked with concrete. Until 1875, it was through this hole that parents would secretly push their unwanted offspring, secure in the knowledge that their identities would remain a secret. On the other side of the wall was a rotating wooden drum – you can still see it – into which the child, via the infamous hole in the wall, was so cruelly deposited. Once gathered into the arms of an attendant nurse, the orphan was stamped with the sign of the Madonna and given a number.

Corso Umberto ends at the Piazza G. Bovio, in the middle of which stands the massive seventeenth-century **Fountain of Neptune**.

The Castel Nuovo

After that, it becomes the Via A. Depretis, which we now follow to the vast and gloomy fortress erected between the sea and some pleasant greenery; it is usually open to the public, but best apply to the custodian in the early morning. Built in the thirteenth century during the Angevin dynasty, the castle was later reconstructed under Alfonso of Aragon; the magnificent Triumphal Arch, which now serves as entrance, was begun by Alfonso in 1454 to commemorate his ousting of the French from Naples.

Don't miss the Barons' Hall (where the municipal council of Naples now sits): it was here, in 1486, that the Aragonese King Ferdinand I arrested and later put to death the ringleaders of an Angevin conspiracy to overthrow him. In the grimly named **Crypt of the Barons' Conspiracy** you can see the remains of four of his victims – one, a prelate, must have been strangled, to judge from his contorted face and bound hands. All the corpses have been lovingly mummified in the clothes they wore when living. He was certainly a man of unusual tastes, Ferdinand.

The Piazza del Plebiscito

We now come to the most monumental and harmonious square in Naples; it is also the biggest and most hectic car park that I have seen. The square is dominated by **San Francesco di Paola**, a monstrosity of a church built by Ferdinand I in slavish imitation of the Pantheon in Rome. Tourists coming to Naples for the first time often mistake this heap for the Duomo, as it hogs so central a part of town. In front of it stand two equestrian statues, the pair of them constantly rammed by cars in search of parking spaces: one is of Charles II, the other of Ferdinand I.

The Palazzo Reale

On the other side of the (incredibly) busy road stands the elegant façade of the palace built for the Spanish viceroys in the early seventeenth century. In a series of niches are fierce-looking statues (late nineteenth century) of the sundry kings who ruled Naples: the one of Murat on the extreme right is a study in regal pomposity – people joke that he has the expression of a *scugnizzo*. Inside, the handsome Staircase of Honour takes you up to the ritzy and really rather vulgar **Historical Apartments** (open Tuesday–Saturday 9 a.m.–2 p.m.; Sunday 9 a.m.–1 p.m.). As you climb the marble stairs, note the original bronze doors of the Castel Nuovo, on which six reliefs depict Ferdinand's struggle with the Angevin conspirators: amazingly, a cannonball is lodged in the lower relief of the left door. The apartments themselves are of little artistic interest, though it is quite fun to glide about under the chandeliers, as in a costume drama.

The **Court Theatre**, however, is a delight: a little masterpiece of eighteenth-century restraint and classical taste, decorated unobtrusively with marble figures of Apollo, Minerva and Mercury. The composer Scarlatti performed many of his works here.

The Teatro San Carlo

Next to the palace is the opera house. Work on this was begun on 4 March 1737 and finished, at breakneck speed, in time for the opening on 4 November, King Charles III of Bourbon's birthday. With its velvet curtains of thick red plush, its concentric rows of flickering candles (now artificially illuminated, of course), this fine theatre is even more stunning than the Scala in Milan. Rossini, Donizetti and Bellini all performed first works here. After Stendhal had seen San Carlo he wrote: 'Naples is the only capital of Italy.' All the rest he considered but 'aggrandised versions of Lyons'. The auditorium and foyer are usually open to the public daily, 9 a.m.–12 noon.

The Galleria Umberto Primo

The neighbouring shopping arcade is a wonderful late-Victorian construction made, like the old Crystal Palace in London, from glass and iron. It was the subject for one of the greatest books to have come out of the Second World War – *The Gallery*, by John Horne Burns: 'There's an arcade in Naples that they call the Galleria Umberto

Primo,' it begins. 'It's a cross between a railroad station and a church. You think you're in a museum till you see the bars and shops.' Nothing has changed, except that aerial bombardments during the last war collapsed the dome, 'and tinkling glass fell like snow to the pavement'. The Gallery is an excellent place to sip a cup of coffee, watching life go by; look out for (and by all means speak to) old Don Pasquale, who has for some forty years sold lottery tickets at the Via Toledo entrance to the arcade, togged out in a pork-pie hat and braces. Everyone knows Don Pasquale; in Naples, he's a contemporary myth.

Naples on the sea
Castel dell'Ovo

The Bay of Naples is dominated by the ponderous 'Egg Castle'. One of the most picturesque buildings in Naples, this is unfortunately closed to the public as it is a military establishment. Suffice it to know, however, that the castle was begun under the Norman King William I, and that in Roman times the outbuildings of the villa of the patrician Lucius Licinius Lucullus once stood here.

The Villa Comunale

Walk down the broad Via Caracciolo until you come to a green expanse dotted with sycamores and palms. A popular seaside promenade, beautifully shaded by sub-tropical trees and planted with acacias and azaleas, the Villa was laid out by the Bourbons in imitation of an English pleasure-ground. Sit under a fig tree and watch Naples go by: the *venditore di volante* (literally, 'sellers of flying things') with great clusters of bobbing balloons and multi-coloured kites for the children; couples ambling arm-in-arm for their *passeggiata* or evening stroll; and the ice-cream and coconut men, fast asleep beneath parasols striped the white and blue of the Naples football team.

But the chief attraction here is the **Aquarium** (open weekdays 9 a.m.–5 p.m.; Sundays 10 a.m.–7 p.m.). Founded in 1872 by a German follower of Darwin, it contains more than 200 species from the waters of the Bay, miniature sharks included. Look out for the giant turtle in tank number 10; it has been nosing around the Aquarium since 1928. And lucky for the creature that it survived the famines of the last war, when the Neapolitans boiled up all the tropical fish and served them in a variety of unusual pasta dishes.

The Villa Pignatelli

Across the Riviera di Chiaia (still one of the most elegant thoroughfares in Naples where, in bygone days, Alexandre Dumas, Nietzsche, Wagner and Shelley all stayed in hotels) stands a neo-Classical villa surrounded by a luscious park. It houses the **Museo Principe Diego Aragona Pignatelli Cortes** (open Tuesday–Saturday 9 a.m.–2 p.m.; Sunday 9 a.m.–1 p.m.), containing a collection of nineteenth-century furniture and china, as well as an eccentric coach-museum. At the end of the last century, this villa became the centre of Neapolitan intellectual and social life; today, its grounds are the ideal place to take a picnic.

Virgil's tomb

Continue down the Via Caracciolo and you eventually come to the colourful area known as **Mergellina**. Here, by the entrance to a dark tunnel called the Galleria Quattro Giornate, a gateway leads up a wooded hillside to the **Parco Virgiliano** (open daily 9 a.m.–1 p.m.). Close by a Roman columbarium, hung with festoons of hyacinth buzzing with giant-sized bumble-bees, is the spot where the poet Virgil is thought to be buried. It is marked by a monument, with an inscription in Latin: 'Ravaged the tomb, and broken the urn. Nothing remains. And yet the poet's name exalts the place.' The tomb was originally shaded by a gigantic bay tree which is said to have died on the decease of Dante. Nearby is the tomb of the poet Leopardi. Superb views of Naples are to be had from up here; and it was on this spot that Boccaccio renounced his career of merchant for that of poet.

Naples on the hills

Increasingly, the **Vomero** is becoming a built-up suburb of Naples; its hills crawl with illegally built tenements. But it is not simply a leafy hillside residential district; standing on a spur which dominates Naples, it boasts the massy fortress begun in 1349 during the reign of Robert of Anjou. Possession of the Castle was once essential to the defence of the city; from it there is a fine view of Old Naples, perfectly bisected by the Spaccanapoli. A military establishment, the Castle is sadly closed to the public. The Vomero also has a lovely park and museum. The area may be reached by funicular from the Stazione Funiculare Centrale, off the Via Toledo in Piazzetta Duca d'Aosta. You will probably want to spend the best part of two mornings in the Vomero; it is a very beautiful part of Naples.

Castel Sant'Elmo

San Martino

Near the Castel Sant'Elmo is the huge Carthusian monastery, founded in the fourteenth century but reconstructed in the seventeenth century in Baroque style. It houses the wonderful **Museo Nazionale di San Martino** (open Tuesday–Saturday 9 a.m.–2 p.m.; Sunday 9 a.m.–1 p.m.), chock-a-block with naval and folklore sections devoted to the history of the kingdom of Naples – costumes, coins, models of ships, prints, proclamations and theatre bills, together with extraordinary collections of glassware and Nativity cribs. Note the oil-portraits of Garibaldi and Alexandre Dumas. The beautifully kept **Cloisters** are one of the most striking achievements of Italian Baroque, the dazzling white of the surrounding arches a nice contrast to the tiny cemetery with its sixteen death's-head decorations (some of these marble skulls are in a pretty bad way: jaw-bones unhinged, craniums cracked).

The Villa Floridiana

Ten minutes' walk from San Martino (returning to the funicular station) will take you to this lovely park, famous for its camellias and views of faraway Capri. The villa itself, a graceful white mansion in early nineteenth-century neo-Classical style, houses the **Duca di Martina Museum** (open Tuesday–Saturday 9 a.m.–2 p.m.; Sunday 9 a.m.–1 p.m.). Its elegant rooms are crammed with valuable collections of European, Chinese and Japanese china, porcelain and majolica.

Capodimonte

Though not in the Vomero district, the **Museo e Gallerie di Capodimonte** (open Tuesday–Saturday 9 a.m.–1 p.m.; Sunday

9 a.m.–1 p.m.) lies in the hills to the north of Castel Sant'Elmo. You can take buses 160 and 161 from Piazza Dante, or 110 and 127 from the Central Station. It is best to visit the Capodimonte Palace as soon as it opens, so you will afterwards have time to descend the nearby Catacombs of San Gennaro, before the custodian shuts shop for lunch.

Set delightfully in a wooded park, this eighteenth-century gallery and museum – once a palace belonging to the Bourbons, built rather precariously over part of the catacombs – contains one of the most important collections of art in Europe. On the first floor are the Royal Apartments, containing a rather chocolate-boxy collection of Neapolitan kitsch, as well as some fine ceramics and ivories. The true masterpieces, however, are on the second floor, in the National Gallery proper. A word of warning: since the 1980 earthquake several rooms have been closed to the public. If you want to see them, you will need to obtain permission from 'La Direzione', a small building opposite the Palace itself – it is easily enough done, and worth it. Among the masterpieces are Masaccio's 1426 'Crucifixion' with a flaxen-haired Mary Magdalene in a luminous red cape (Room 6); an early *'Madonna col bambino e angeli'* by Botticelli, the Virgin's eyes cast downwards in mute admiration of her child (Room 7); Bellini's 'Transfiguration', one of his finest pictures, with the peasants ploughing the fields in the background, seemingly oblivious of the white-robed Christ in the foreground (room 8); Raphael's portrait of 'Pope Leo X and Two Cardinals' and his drawing of Moses (Room 12); two extraordinary Brueghels – 'The Allegory of the Blind' and the very peculiar 'Misanthrope' (Room 20); and Caravaggio's characteristically gruesome 'Flagellation' (Room 29).

Catacombs of San Gennaro

The catacombs (guided tours on Friday, Saturday and Sunday only, at 9.30, 10.15, 11 and 11.45 a.m.) are situated down the hill from the Capodimonte Palace, behind the Church of S. Gennaro Extra Moenia. Executed in AD 305 by the Emperor Diocletian, San Gennaro lies buried in one of the numerous honeycomb niches excavated out of the volcanic tufa with which the Greeks and Romans built the ancient city of Neapolis. Dim and cathedral-like, the funerary chambers of San Gennaro contain some of the most striking examples of Palaeo-Christian mosaics in the Western world. There is an episcopal throne cut into the tufa here, and an ithyphallic goat (curiously risqué for so Christian a place) which dances priapically on the wall above the entrance.

The Fontanella Cemetery

The ramshackle quarter which abuts the catacombs is known as La Sanità, a risky place to wander around with a handbag, but otherwise fine, and very interesting. Here, every Sunday at 11.30 a.m., a guide meets curious Italians (foreigners rarely come here) outside the Church of Maria Santissima del Carmine in the dusty Via Cavone Gerolomini and takes them on an extraordinary tour of the cemetery.

It consists of a network of underground tufa quarries piled sky-high (literally so!) with the skulls of those who perished in the plague of 1656; until quite recently, women would mutter prayers to a skull of their own choosing, so as to speed its owner to paradise. Many of the skulls, you will notice, have been lovingly polished, with a sheen to them like a pair of well-brushed shoes. As an independent traveller, you may want to take a look at this unknown part of Naples; you can always book an appointment with the *parroco* (parish priest) of the Santissima del Carmine, telephone 34 82 98. You will not be disappointed, though you may be a little . . . disturbed.

Nightclubs **Airone**, Via Petrarca 123; tel. 57 50 175. Ritzy piano bar; good for cocktails. Sometimes crowded as the club specialises in receptions and reunions of one kind or another.

Chez Moi, Parco Margherita 13; tel. 40 75 26. Piano bar with dancing at the weekends.

Kiss Kiss Dance, Via Sgambati 61; tel. 46 65 66. Quite a hotspot; a fair amount of dancing and kissing does indeed seem to go on here. A good discotheque.

Tongue, Via Manzoni 207; tel. 76 90 800. Rather an unfortunate name, but a very popular place in which to hang out. English, French and German spoken at the door. Dancing to screened videos, etc.

Casablanca, Via Petrarca 101; tel. 76 94 882. Discotheque and piano bar.

Cafés **Gran Café Gambrinus**, Via Chiaia 1–2; tel. 41 75 82. Opposite the San Carlo Opera House, this is the most famous of Neapolitan cafés. Founded in 1861, it has an appealing air of faded charm. Sit and watch well-dressed Naples swan by. Then have a delicious cake.

Motta, Via Toledo 152; tel. 55 20 620. Owned by the Motta coffee company, this is one of the most popular of Neapolitan cafés. Can be a bit of a scrummage.

Sports If you like football (although you will probably not hold the sport in
Football the same quasi-religious veneration as do the Neapolitans), matches are held at the **Stadio San Paolo**; tel. 61 56 23. Built in 1959, it can hold a maximum of 80,000 people. In Naples, by the way, a complimentary football ticket is a status symbol; stand by the entrance to San Paolo and watch the expression of superiority on the faces of complimentary ticket-holders when they show them to the officials.

Water sports Given its proximity to the sea, Naples not surprisingly offers a wealth of water sports. For those who want to scuba-dive, the address is **Subacquei Napoletani**, Piazza Santa Maria degli Angeli 11; tel. 41 75 79. For those who want to hire a yacht, **International Yachting Club Amatori**, Via Sermoneta 21 (in Mergellina); tel. 68 41 87. The **International Regatta** (for the One Ton Cup) is held in June.

Tennis If you would like to try your hand at tennis, there are some excellent courts in the Villa Comunale belonging to the **Tennis Club Napoli**, Via Caracciolo; tel. 38 48 01.

Racing

Horse-racing takes place at the beautifully situated **Ippodromo di Agnano**, some 10 km from the city, tel. 76 01 660. In April there's the Neapolitan equivalent of the Derby, the **Gran Premio**; and during the summer there's harness-racing.

Shopping

Coral

Naples used to be famous for her coral, tortoise-shell and lava ornament; in Victorian times, particularly, coral objects were all the rage. Now there is little in Naples that you will not find anywhere else in Italy, although you can pick up many a copy of ancient bronzes and Etruscan vases, if you like that sort of thing.

Still, corals are often a good buy in Naples, particularly necklaces, but watch out, as they will often come from Africa, not from the Bay of Naples.

Fashion

For serious shopping – particularly clothes – the street you want is the Via Chiaia. Here you will find all the famous Italian designers – Giorgio Armani, Valentino, MaxMara, etc.

Antiques

Most of the antiquarian shops are situated around the nearby Piazza dei Martiri area; at a rough count, there are some forty antique shops in this part of Naples alone. But you are unlikely to stumble upon any real bargains; there is no flea-market to speak of in Naples.

Forcella market

However, you should take the opportunity to explore the Forcella, a public market of half-Hogarthian and half-medieval animation. The Forcella is in fact a colourful Camorra stronghold and, if Naples is indeed halfway to Baghdad, this market is irrefutably its halfway Kasbah. Here, you will find counterfeit brands of malt whisky, fake bottles of Fernet Branca liqueur, ersatz phials of Chanel Number 5 ('But our perfume's much better than the French stuff – a single drop, madam, and you'll be well appreciated'), and artificial Louis Vuitton handbags ('Those costing 200,000 lire, we'll give you for just 15,000!').

But fear not; the Forcella is not controlled by the Nuova Camorra Organizzata, but by old-school spivs who have probably learned the tricks of their dubious trade through selling nylon stockings at the end of the last war. I find the atmosphere, the shouting and singing, the haggling and hassling, quite infectious.

Books

Naples has some excellent secondhand bookshops, mostly in Via Port'Alba, just off Piazza Dante. In this lively street, some of the most famous names are **Berisio**, **Cassitto** and **Guida**. Nearby, you might want to visit the wonderful **Colonnese** bookshop, at 33 Vico S. Pietro a Majella. Colonnese also publish their own books, and their shop is an Aladdin's cave of rare first editions, English and Italian. There is also an excellent selection of old postcards of Naples.

Music

You should certainly not miss the opera at **San Carlo**; the ticket office is open every day except Monday, 10 a.m.–1 p.m. and 4.30–6.30 p.m.; tel. 79 72 370.

At Capodimonte in July is held the **Iuglio Musicale**, an annual open-air music festival.

As far as entertainment in Naples is concerned, one of the best things you can do is simply walk around; there is real theatre in the streets, in the bars and restaurants. However, here are some further suggestions for the more curious.

The Lottery

Gambling – the Neapolitans are inveterate gamblers. There is often a superstitious or even religious dimension to the placing of bets: Alexandre Dumas, who spent much of his time in Naples, relates how he once heard 'a wretch praying that God would ask San Gennaro to grant him a scoop on the lottery'. There is even a sort of gambling cabbala, *La Smorfia*, in which every dream has its corresponding lottery number. Sold at most newspaper stands, it is well worth buying a copy; it is full of such curious equations as 'Blood: number 21'; 'Soul in Purgatory: 18'; 'The Madonna: 8'.

If you want to see the genuine Naples, go along to the municipal hall (or **Ufficio Lotto**), at the intersection of the Via del Grand Archivio with the Spaccanapoli, right in the heart of Old Naples. Here, every Saturday, the lottery extractions take place: at twelve o'clock precisely, a young blindfold boy pulls out the lucky numbers from a sort of revolving drum, in the august company of several *carabinieri* dignitaries and sundry bureaucrats, all of them wearing a sash striped with the colours of the Italian flag. Once the numbers have been pulled out, emotions can reach fever pitch. When I went along, uproarious applause went up, accompanied by much embracing and shaking of hands. Apparently, this was because the number extracted was 34; corresponding to a dream of a stubborn or difficult person, it is regarded by Neapolitans with the kind of dread otherwise reserved for a San Gennaro blood-failure.

Observing Neapolitan funeral customs

Still to be seen in the streets of Naples are rococo hearses of black and gold, pulled lugubriously along by a string of up to twelve black horses. As it is only the very wealthy who can afford such a kitschy send-off (such as Camorra bosses), you will be lucky indeed to see these Hammer-film stage-props. If interested, I suggest that you go along to the funeral offices of Bellomunno and Co., on Via dei Tribunali; tel. 75 93 670. Ask one of the undertakers there for the address of the house from where they will next be picking up a deceased. There will be nothing morbid or prurient in your turning up at the address: Bellomunno (the joke runs that this is in fact Neapolitan dialect for *bello mondo*, 'beautiful world') are only too keen to publicise their funerary activities. They are unique to Naples – you will not find such wedding-cake hearses in any other part of Italy. As a direct inheritance of the Spanish Bourbons, the Bellomunno funerals are of historical interest.

Attending religious festivals

Apart from the 'miracle' of San Gennaro, other unusual religious festivals include the Feast of St Anthony Abbott (17 January), when horses and other animals are blessed at the Church of Sant'Antonio, and the Return of the Pilgrims from Montevergine (Whit Monday), when in the streets near the harbour people carry staves decorated with fruit and flowers as in the ancient Bacchanalia.

Sightseeing trips

From 1 June to 30 September the not very promisingly named 'Loveboat' takes sightseers round the Bay of Naples. It leaves every day at 6, 7 and 8 p.m. from the Via Caracciolo harbour, near the US Consulate. The boat sails past Mergellina and then chugs on towards Posillipo. It is all most enjoyable, with splendid views en route. After a stop at Castel dell'Ovo, it returns to the same embarkation point. Tel. 57 51 532.

Where to stay

The Provincial Tourist Department of Naples lists for their city a total of 131 hotels; for so large and fascinating a metropolis, this is not a great number. Dozens of these hotels are close to the Central Station, around Piazza Garibaldi. In general, these should be avoided like the plague: overpriced and decidedly sleazy, some of them actually double up as brothels. And the odds are that you will be robbed of something or other. In one such 'hotel' I lost a wristwatch, camera and pocket calculator in the space of a day; complaints at the reception desk were countered only with complaints about the general, ah, untrustworthiness of Filipino room maids. This does not leave you with a particularly wide choice of Neapolitan hotels. However, the following are certainly reputable, and all of them recommended by the Tourist Office itself. If you want to make a reservation from outside Naples, the telephone code is 081.

Top range

Excelsior, Via Partenope 48; tel. 41 71 11. This is quite the best hotel in Naples. Though expensive, many of its 138 rooms look out across Vesuvius and the islands of Capri, Ischia and Procida. Conferences and art exhibitions are often held in one of its numerous *fin de siècle* salons. It's a good place to take a leisurely drink whilst watching the sun sink out in the Bay.

Royal, Via Partenope 38; tel. 40 02 44. This is a modern hotel – though on the site of the hotel of the same name in which Oscar Wilde stayed with Lord Alfred Douglas. It hasn't the style of the Excelsior, but still commands a wonderful view of the Bay.

Britannique, Corso Vittorio Emanuele 133; tel. 66 09 33. Small, stylish and not wildly expensive. Has only 86 rooms and is peaceful. Old-world charm.

Parker's, Corso Vittorio Emanuele 135; tel. 68 48 66. Excellent, old-establishment hotel inseparably linked with late Victorian and Edwardian Naples.

Mid range

Hotel Rex, Via Paleopoli 12; tel. 41 63 888. Just off the majestic Via Partenope, perhaps rather a poor man's Excelsior. Tends to the slightly bland, but is of a pleasant size (40 rooms) and very reasonable, given its situation.

Galles, Via Sannazaro 5; tel. 66 83 44. Towards the lively Mergellina area. Absolutely tiny (only 15 rooms) and an excellent hotel for the family. Takes dogs.

Muller, Via Mergellina 7; tel. 66 90 56. Modest. Excellent service.

Has a Swiss-style restaurant and, conveniently, a hotel-bus at the Central Station. Reasonably priced and far from the madding crowd of downtown Naples.

Casa Betania, Via Settembrini 42; tel. 44 48 33. Modern, with a garage. Good hotel for the family. Priced very reasonably.

Delle Terme, Via Agnano Astroni; tel. 76 01 733. Somewhat out of town (not far from the Naples football stadium) but pleasant and peaceful, surrounded by gardens. Fairly expensive, but the sulphur thermal baths are good for liver complaints.

Lago Maggiore, Via del Cerriglio 10; tel. 32 06 11. Not far from Castel Nuovo. Only 18 rooms; extremely reasonable for a mid-range hotel, and trustworthy.

Bottom range

The Tourist Office recommends the following hotels as both cheap and trustworthy; all of them are well away from Piazza Garibaldi. Curiously, they all begin with the letter 'C'.

Colibri, Via Caracciolo 10; tel. 68 18 46; 11 rooms. On the sea front near the Villa Comunale.

Crispi, Via Francesco Giorani 2; tel. 66 48 04; 10 rooms. Has a restaurant. Also near the Villa Comunale.

Canada, Via Mergellina 43; tel. 68 09 52. Excellent views of the sea. Only 9 rooms, unfortunately; but there's a lift.

I myself would like to add to this list a hotel which I consider a real find (and it too begins with a 'C'!), the **Pensione Console**, Via Mezzocannone 109; tel. 28 25 02. Plumb in the middle of Old Naples, just off the Spaccanapoli, this happy pension is run by a remarkable Neapolitan lady, Lia Console Orecchio. Absolutely brimming with goodwill and kindness, Lia will certainly make you feel at home; she may let you dry your clothes on her balcony and might even, in the mornings, offer you a cup of her excellent coffee. She prefers people to stay for longer than just one night. If you are planning to remain in Naples for a week, this must be one of the most economical – and certainly one of the safest – pensions in the city. To make the somewhat rickety lift work, put a 500 lire coin in the slot.

Where to eat
Naples on the sea

Traditionally, a first meal in Naples should be eaten on the Borgo Marinaro, a little port formed by the causeway linking the Castel dell'Ovo with the mainland. There are at least two excellent restaurants on the Borgo; in all of them, you can sit at water-level and watch the yachts bob at their moorings under the stars.

Bersagliera, Borgo Marinaro; tel. 41 56 92. A wonderful interior, with palm trees, marble floor and ornate Art-Nouveau ceiling. Fairly expensive, too. If you go as a couple, you will probably be serenaded by an ancient Neapolitan with a mandolin. The food is superb: try the house speciality, *zuppa di pesce*, an enormous plate of sundry fish, served with toast and tomatoes. It is supposed to be a first course, but suffices as a second. Wash the lot down with a bottle of Lacrima Christi.

Transatlantico, Borgo Marinaro; tel. 41 26 46. Cheaper and less stylish than the Bersagliera, but usually more animated, and less the haunt of tourists. A popular place with Neapolitans for wedding-dinners. Again, the speciality is fish. Good, formal service and sensible linen tablecloths.

Ristorante Pizzeria da Marino, Via Santa Lucia; tel. 41 62 80. Extremely popular with the locals; you would be well advised to book in advance. Excellent pizzas as well as first-class fish. Not at all expensive.

Don Salvatore, Via Mergellina 5; tel. 68 18 17. The speciality here is spaghetti *alla Cosa Nostra*, a fiery dish, I'm sure.

Ciro a Mergellina, Via Mergellina 21; tel. 68 17 80 (closed Mondays). One of the very best restaurants in Naples for fish. Not too expensive.

La Sacrestia, Via Orazio 116; tel. 66 41 86. An excellent restaurant; the specialities here are pasta dishes with *calamaretti*, baby squids.

Finestrella, Via Marechiaro 23; tel. 76 90 020 (closed Tuesdays). This is in the very elegant Posillipo area; from the terrace there is a painterly view of Ischia. Wonderful setting, and the best *spaghetti alle vongole* that I have ever had. Try also the red mullet fried in olive oil. Highly recommended.

La Fazienda, Via Marechiaro 58; tel. 76 97 420 (closed Sundays). Also in a lovely setting, with views of the Bay. Excellent fish. You should book early.

Old Naples   **Dante e Beatrice**, Piazza Dante 44–5; tel. 34 99 05 (closed Wednesdays). One of the most popular Neapolitan restaurants, but no need to book, as there are plenty of tables. Try the *zuppa di cozze*.

Pizzeria Bellini, Via Santa Maria di Costantinopoli; tel. 45 97 74 (closed Sundays). The restaurant to which all Neapolitans flock; definitely book in advance. Excellent *linguine al cartoccio*, a delicious mix of seafood and pasta.

Da Ciro, Via S. Brigida 71; tel. 32 40 72. Excellent *zuppa di pesce*. Crowded.

Antica Port'Alba, Via Port'Alba 18; tel. 45 97 13. First-class pizzas, as indeed they should be: this busy restaurant is a member of an organisation named 'Vera Pizza Napoletana'.

From the Corso Umberto to the Royal Palace   **Avellinese da Peppino**, Via Silvio Spaventa 31–5; tel. 28 38 97 (open daily). One of the best and cheapest of the restaurants near the main railway station (as with the hotels in this area, most of the restaurants should be avoided). The owner, Peppino, is a charmer, and often his friends will serenade the clients. Extremely popular with Neapolitans, though rather too hidden for tourists to have discovered – yet. Try the *rigattoni alla Bellavista*, a delicious pasta concoction made with a cheesy *ragù* sauce. Very reasonably priced: Peppino says he never takes people for a ride.

Cavour, Piazza Garibaldi 34; tel. 26 47 30. Perfectly all right, despite its none-too-salubrious situation. Crowded, so book in advance.

Al Fungo Velenoso, Corso Arnaldo Lucci 195; tel. 26 50 26 (closed Sundays). Despite its name, which translates as 'At the Poisonous Mushroom', this is an excellent place for all Neapolitan fare. Not too touristy.

Ristorante Rosolino, Via Nazario Sauro 5–7; tel. 41 58 13. Excellent Campanian specialities, as well as both national and international fare. Pricey, but good.

La Cantinella, Via Cuma 42; tel. 40 48 84. Superb risotto dishes.

Naples on the hills – the Vomero

Daniele, Via Scarlatti 104; tel. 36 44 80 (closed Mondays). Fairly expensive, but a good place in which to have lunch after you have seen, say, the Carthusian Monastery of San Martino.

Stella, Via Toscanella 64; tel. 74 00 48. Quite some distance from the main sights in the Vomero, but good for a quiet night out under the stars.

The environs of Naples

Campi Flegrei

The volcanic area north-west of Naples known as Campi Flegrei must be one of the most fascinating in Southern Italy. If you are without car, you will probably want to spend a day or two exploring on foot. As with the rest of Campania, it's best to do so from Naples.

The history of this region takes its origin in the Homeric and Virgilian myths; it was here that Hellenic civilisation first gained a footing in Italy. With its dark hills, lakes, grottoes and woods, and the overall sense of mystery that hangs over this strange and beautiful landscape of extinct volcanoes, one can see why the ancients chose the Burning Fields as a setting for the Elysian Fields, and for the Underworld. Indeed, the dark volcanic lake of Avernus (thought to be the Styx, the river of the dead) was where both Homer and Virgil chose to situate their heroes' descent into hell.

Until the beginning of the last century it was the practice to verify the overwhelming presence of carbon dioxide in one of the many grottoes here by throwing a dog into it; in about half a minute, the creature would be dead. Just about anyone who was anybody tried his hand at this dubious sport – John Evelyn, Goethe and the poet Thomas Gray. Mark Twain would have *liked* to try it, 'But now', he wrote, 'an important difficulty presented itself. We had no dog.' For better or worse, the infamous *Grotta del Cane* is no longer an igneous phenomenon – it is dead, in fact, as a dodo. However, the low craters and hot springs of the Campi Flegrei still emit steam and noxious gases; you can see them for yourself at the decidedly malodorous Solfatara Crater.

Pozzuoli

The best place from which to explore the Campi Flegrei is from Sophia Loren's birthplace of Pozzuoli (population 59,813), 12 km from Naples on an old direct road. You can take a comfortable train from the Ferrovia Cumana e Circumflegrea in Piazza Montesanto, at the end of a street directly opposite Piazza Dante. It's as well to know that this picturesque seaside town is suffering from bradyseism, a volcanic phenomenon which means a movement of the earth involving a change in the relative level of land and sea. The town, in fact, is slowly sinking by an average of 15 mm a year. You can see the effects of bradyseism on the **Temple of Serapis**; nearby volcanic activity has half-submerged the pillars of this *macellum* or city market (it was never a temple) in sea water. There are marks of marine molluscs on these columns almost 6 metres high, showing that, at one time, the market was virtually *submerged*. On 4 October 1983 there was an earthquake at Pozzuoli of 4.4 on the Richter Scale; fortunately, only one person died – of fright. But if the earth unexpectedly moves for you, I should dive into a nearby bar and order a double whisky.

Amphitheatre

From the Serapis, take the Via Solfatara to the **Anfiteatro Flavio** (open Wednesday–Monday 9 a.m.–6.30 p.m.). Built under the Emperor Vespasian in AD 67–79, this amphitheatre could accommodate up to 40,000 spectators: it is the second-largest monument of its kind in Italy, after the Colosseum in Rome. San Gennaro, incidentally, was imprisoned here by the Emperor Diocletian, prior to his decapitation. And for the record, on the ground on which you now stand, Nero once killed a bull with one blow – by seizing a lance from a guard and hurling it willy-nilly into the arena. The subterranean structures for animals and gladiators, in the middle of the arena, are in a near-perfect state of preservation. Peer down into them and imagine what it must have been like for the gladiators before they went over the top for the eventual thumbs up – or, worst luck, down.

Solfatara Crater

A pleasant ten-minute walk along the Via Solfatara, away from Pozzuoli, will take you to the awe-inspiring crater (open 9 a.m.–sunset). At the entrance, ignore the stalls displaying such signs as 'Here Lava Works', meaning 'Here we sell vastly overpriced lumps of igneous matter'. Walk on and there will shortly appear before you a low valley surrounded by mounds of grey pumice. The chalky earth beneath you, blanched an unearthly white by the sun, is stained a sulphurous yellow; constant jets of hot water are thrown from its boiling crevices. Stamp on the ground and it will ring hollow beneath your tread; a large stone thrown violently at the ground makes a report like distant artillery; the bowels of the earth, you think, might open to swallow you at any moment. Truly, this is hell: at the Bocca Grande, the Big Mouth, the temperature reaches 160°C. Though still active, this volcano hasn't erupted since the twelfth century. The experts are waiting.

Monte Nuovo

Our next stop is reached after about twenty minutes on foot along the Via Domiziana, which passes above Pozzuoli. Another product of bradyseism, this volcanic hill (140 m) is the youngest mountain in Europe – hence its name, the New Mountain; it was formed after a volcanic eruption on 29 September 1538. The ascent, by a paved path through pine forests, takes about half an hour. It is well worth it: once you reach the summit, you can descend right into the crater, taking a dirt track lined with all sorts of interesting specimens of plant life. On arrival there, you can either go to sleep, nestled comfortably among the wild fern, or (better still) take a picnic. You are unlikely to be disturbed; most people are too lazy to make the descent.

Lucrine Lake

Four kilometres further along the same road, and we reach the lagoonal lake which owes its fame to the oyster-beds cultivated in Roman times. The name Lucrine derives, they say, from *lucrum* (lucre) – a reference to the financial gain made out of the oyster culture. Sadly, the lake isn't much to write home about today, what with its wind-surfers and *Würstel* stalls.

Lake Avernus

Much more impressive is Lake Avernus, reached in ten minutes by a pine-tree path which runs along the Lucrine. Tradition once held that no bird could fly across this lake and survive, owing to miasmal exhalations from the water. The neighbouring ravines were mythically the abode of the dismal Cimmerians, a fabulous underworld people whose land, according to Homer, was on the limits of the world. The lake, once surrounded by forests that blocked out the sun, was formerly of a much more gloomy aspect; but then Agrippa came along and chopped all the trees down to make way for an enormous dockyard. If you don't get much of a *frisson* out of the lake today, you can blame it on the Roman general. The lake is of volcanic origin, its banks bordered with blocks of lava. It is at the most 34 metres deep, and still looks pretty creepy to me.

Temple of Apollo

On the east shore of the lake are the most remarkable remains. Surrounded by nettles, brambles and sugar-cane, there is a romantic air of the forlorn to this temple. In reality, though, it was a great thermal establishment built by the Romans over the mineral springs that were once so plentiful on the spot.

The Sibyl's Grotto

Now we come to one of the Campi Flegrei's great delights. A bramble-snarled path on the south side of the lake will take you to it: a battered old signpost reads '*Grotta della Sibilla*'. The grotto is an interminably long gallery cut into the rock, its roof blackened with centuries of torch-smoke – it is so dark, you will not be able to enter without a guide. Your man is Carlo Santillo: every Saturday, he works as a clerk in the Pozzuoli post office, but during the rest of the week you will normally find this wizened old fellow guarding the mouth of the cave, like Cerberus. If not, telephone him at home on 86 73 256.

Carlo is a guide of the old school; he has little time for tourist coaches, or for any lightning tours of his Grotto. Flaming torch in hand (the better to create a flickering atmosphere of doom), he will take you through the dank and cavernous chambers that lead to the Entrance of the Infernal Regions, through the labyrinth of tunnels that converge on pools of mysterious water known as the Sibyl's Bath. And all the while, Carlo will tell you (in English, if you prefer) how Virgil sent Aeneas to Hades through this or that very tunnel – 'deep in the craggy shore a cavern yawned; a pitchy lake and forests black as night,' etc. That Aeneas probably never came here hardly seems to matter – this grotto is infinitely more spooky than the Sibyl's cave over in Cumae, wonderful though that certainly is. At one point the name 'Nicolaus' will be pointed out to you, etched into the damp face of a wall – Czar Nicholas II of Russia himself, no less. Or so one is led to believe.

Baia

The next leg of our sulphurous tour takes us to Baia, about 7 km along the Via Domiziana from Lake Avernus. According to legend, this insignificant little port owes its name to Baios, the navigator of Ulysses. The celebrity of the place during Roman times was chiefly due to its brothels (Nero set up several along the coast, each staffed by a noblewoman), to its hot springs and luxurious villas. As an exclusive resort, it soon obtained a name for profligacy and loose living, and for the sort of places that we now euphemistically term 'massage parlours'.

Owing to bradyseism, most of the ancient pleasure-town now lies beneath the sea, a hidden Atlantis. But there are some interesting ruins in an Archaeological Park (**Scavi di Baia**, open 9 a.m.–dusk; closed Mondays), reached by a steep footpath to the left of the station. Here you will find the most extensive thermal establishment left us from antiquity. Unfortunately, the site is so badly signposted and kept (watch out for the wild dogs) that you will have a hard time knowing this from that; I suggest that you pick up a plan at the entrance. As you inspect the arcaded swimming pools, the old baths, circular halls and *nymphaeum* (summerhouse), enjoy the stunning views of the Bay of Pozzuoli.

Temple of Venus

Back on the road that runs through Baia, you pass on your left a great Roman rotunda that was once part of a thermal establishment. Fifteen minutes further on foot and there will eventually loom into view the enormous castle erected in the sixteenth century by the Spanish viceroy Don Pedro de Toledo. Do not climb the hill that winds its way up to this fortress because you will not be permitted entry; it houses twenty large families of *terremotati*, victims of the 1980 earthquake.

Castel di Baja

Bacoli

Continue along the road for 3 km until you come to the pleasant town of Bacoli (population 20,900). Here you should note the Wonderful Fishpond, one of the most impressive remains of Roman waterworks. To enter, you have to ask for the key at Via P. Mirabile 7 – a little old lady in black will give it to you in return for a gratuity. Descend a flight of steps and you will find yourself in an old Roman

Piscina Mirabile

reservoir with all the spooky majesty of a candlelit cathedral: 70 metres long, 25.5 metres wide and 15 metres high. The vaulted ceiling, through which shafts of sunlight sharply beam, is supported by forty-eight arched pilasters, all of them festooned with hanging ferns and ivy, like some great theatrical set-piece from one of those English Gothic novels by Mrs Radcliffe or Horace Walpole. It is highly recommended.

Cento Camerelle

From here, it is a short walk to the Hundred Little Chambers. The gates to this curious two-storeyed ruin (of which the upper part was a reservoir) are opposite a modern villa done up in the most exquisite bad taste, with plastic figurines of Snow White in the garden, and the walls painted a lurid red and green. I mention this to help you orient yourself – in these parts, the villa must serve as quite a landmark. The Cento Camerelle was probably part of Julius Caesar's villa; later it belonged to the Emperor Drusus's wife Antonia, who kept a pet eel with gold earrings.

Misenum

If you have time, you should certainly go 4 km to visit the harbour built by Agrippa in 41 BC. Today, it is the starting-point for the arduous climb to the summit of the aerial promontory known as **Capo Miseno** (155 metres), the burial place of one of Ulysses' companions, whom Virgil turned into Aeneas's trumpeter, Misenus. The view from the summit is breathtaking: before you spreads out a complicated assemblage of straits, peninsulas, bays, lakes and promontories, not to mention the Bay of Naples itself.

Lake Fusaro

Rejoining the main road from Bacoli, it is a good 45 minutes on foot to Cumae, the oldest Greek colony in Italy. For part of the way, the road skirts the edge of a lake known to the ancients as the Arthusian swamp, and now famous for its shellfish. Lake Fusaro is believed to be the crater of an extinct volcano; in 1838, it exhaled such volumes of sulphurous gas that all the oysters were destroyed.

Cumae

In Greek times, Cumae was one of the wealthiest cities on the peninsula, the centre from which all Hellenistic forms of worship spread out across Italy. It declined in importance under the Romans. Interestingly, it was at Cumae that Petronius Arbiter, general arbiter of taste to the Emperor Nero, died by opening his veins in a perfumed bath. He talked to his friends, closing the veins when the conversation became interesting, and opening them again when he was bored. A stylish way to go indeed.

Acropolis

All the most important ruins in Cumae are to be found in the Acropolis (open 9 a.m.–one hour before sunset; closed Mondays). The Acropolis is superbly situated: hard by the sea where Aeneas once beached his ships, its ruins obscured by vineyards and peach orchards, many of them in the middle of farmland, with hens and cocks squabbling in the dust. Dragonflies and butterflies flit about in great abundance.

Cumae boasts what is perhaps the most famous of ancient

Cave of the Cumaean Sibyl

sanctuaries. Excavated only in 1932, the cave is where Aeneas came to consult the Sibyl, Apollo's prophetic priestess. It is 40 metres long and shaped curiously like a Toblerone chocolate bar. Trapezoidal in design, it ends in a rectangular chamber where the prophetess spun her riddles:

> That dim cave
> Secluded, where the awful Sibyl dwells,
> Whose soul with Divination's mystic law
> The prophet-god inspires

according to Virgil. Sometimes, a wind rushes through the cave's long corridor, creating strange whispers . . .

Temples of Apollo and Jupiter

A pathway by the cave leads up to two interesting temples. That to Apollo is a Greek structure, altered in Augustan times and in the sixth or seventh century transformed into a Christian basilica. Further on, the Via Sacra takes us to the Temple of Jupiter, in a beautiful position on the summit of a hill overlooking, to the left, Lake Fusaro and the Island of Ischia. According to legend, the construction of this temple is attributed to Daedalus, who landed at Cumae after his wax-winged flight.

Benevento

Benevento (population 59,009) is the capital of the province of the same name, the smallest of the five that comprise Campania. A day's visit from Naples will well repay the effort. The countryside around, and one or two of its villages – in particular the mysterious **Sant'Agata dei Goti**, with its onion-domed Duomo – are haunting and remote.

Getting there

From Naples, Benevento lies 116 km along the A16 road. By train from Napoli Centrale (departure at 6, 7 or 8.30 a.m.), the journey takes two hours, through vineyards and gentle rolling hills. I would not recommend staying the night there; hotels are few and basic, and there are no restaurants to speak of.

Benevento is one of the oldest towns in Italy – founded, they say, by Auson, son of Ulysses and Circe. During Roman times, it grew in importance through its position at a junction of the Via Appia (which ended in what is now modern Brindisi) with the Via Latina. In Imperial times, it was the starting-point of Trajan's road to the Apulian coast. Benevento was badly damaged by bombs during the last war. More than 65 per cent of the houses were destroyed, and the Duomo received direct hits. On your walks around this enchanting town, drink a glass or two of the aromatic liqueur for which it is famous – Strega.

What to see

All the historical sights are close together; most of them are reached along the Corso Garibaldi, which traverses the town. Try to see at least the following.

The thirteenth-century **Cathedral** has a richly sculpted façade incorporating, interestingly, fragments of Roman architecture. The carved animals – lions, leopards, eagles and sundry winged beasts – around the main portal suggest a Byzantine influence.

The **Arch of Trajan**, a Corinthian marble arch erected in AD 112 in honour of the Emperor Trajan, is one of the finest and best-preserved Roman structures in Southern Italy. Reliefs represent scenes from the Emperor's life, particularly his triumph over the Germanic tribes of the Danube. When floodlit, the arch is awe-inspiring.

A tiny church dating from 762, **Santa Sofia** is situated in a pretty cobbled piazza. It has a carved portal, a plain, domed interior and charming cloisters with Moorish horseshoe arches.

The **Roman Theatre** (open 9 a.m.–sunset; closed Mondays) is one of the largest Roman theatres still surviving. Built in the reign of Hadrian and enlarged by Caracalla, it accommodated 20,000 spectators.

Caserta

Known as the 'Versailles of Naples' because of the Royal Palace built here by Charles III of Bourbon, Caserta (population 59,960) is a town where you could very happily spend an entire day, assuming that you will also visit the beautiful medieval village of **Casertavecchia** (10 km north-east), with its narrow alleys of polished cobbles and small Romanesque cathedral.

Getting there

Caserta lies 39 km from Naples along Route 87 or, if you prefer, two stops along the autostrada. Trains run every half-hour from Napoli Centrale. Do try not to visit the town of a weekend, as it will be overrun with day-trippers from Naples.

What to see

The **Palace** (open 9 a.m.–1.30 p.m.; closed Mondays) faces the station. It's an absolutely enormous heap, in the richest palatial style, and has been described as 'the overwhelmingly impressive swan-song of the Italian Baroque'. Designed by the Dutchman Vanvitelli, the building is 247 metres long, 36 metres high, and is pierced by 243 windows. One of the most sumptuous buildings of its kind in Italy, it is a monolithic testament to the vanity of kings. The **State Apartments** are chock-a-block with Venetian chandeliers, Sèvres porcelain, ormolu clocks, richly gilded frescoes, tapestries, gilded baths with gold taps, alabaster dressing tables and massive canvases depicting such ambitious subjects as 'The Death of Hector'. Of particular interest is the eighteenth-century **Court Theatre**, with its beautiful columns plundered from the Temple of Serapis in Pozzuoli.

The extraordinary **Gardens**, with their fountains fed by a Vanvitelli-designed aqueduct 40 km away, are of three kinds. There is the Italian garden, with its waterfalls and mythological statues – make sure you see the marble Diana and Acteon (Acteon was turned into a stag by the goddess and torn to pieces by his own hounds). The wood of the ancient Dukes of Caserta formed the feudal park, while the English Garden of Queen Caroline has greenhouses, cedars, tulip trees and magnolias. Join the Italians, and picnic on the Bourbon lawns.

Vesuvius and Herculaneum

Getting there

Best visited from Naples, both Herculaneum, which is about 20 km from the city, and Vesuvius are best combined in a day's visit. If you are without wheels, here's how you do it. Take the 6.45 a.m. Circumvesuviana train from Napoli Centrale to the station at Ercolano. This will leave you ample time to catch the 8 a.m. blue Sita bus from outside the station, which takes you to Vesuvius. After you have scaled the volcano, you will then have time to see the ruins at Herculaneum before they close. Remember that after midday the road up to the top of Mount Vesuvius is blocked. Take a stout pair of shoes; the walk (three or four hours return) need deter none but the frail, elderly or faint-hearted. Still, if you do demur, you are at least in good company: the poet Shelley, we are told, found the ascent too much; overcome by nausea before he reached the volcano's summit, he was revived by a dose of laudanum in a nearby church.

Vesuvius
History

Before you climb Vesuvius, Goethe's 'peak of hell rising out of paradise', a little history. The first eruption of which there is any record occurred on 24 August AD 79: this covered up and embalmed Pompeii and Herculaneum, both already half-ruined by an earthquake in AD 63. The crater that destroyed these cities was supposed to have been 12 km in circumference. The eruption was vividly described in two letters from the younger Pliny to Tacitus.

The next significant eruption occurred on 16 December 1631, when a huge cloud of smoke and ashes rose in a conical form and cast a profound gloom over Naples in the middle of the day. The earth was convulsed by violent earthquakes, whilst seven streams of lava overwhelmed the nearby towns of Bosco, Torre del Greco, Resina and Portici; 3,000 people were killed.

From 1631 up to the present day, the eruptive cycles of Vesuvius have been recorded by vulcanologists: any tremors from the volcano have been registered seismographically. The most recent eruption occurred on 19 March 1944, creating a new crater 1.5 km in circumference; twelve streams of lava were formed, but no one was killed. One of the very few British eye-witness accounts is provided by the great travel writer Norman Lewis in his book *Naples '44*:

> It was the most majestic and terrible sight I have ever seen, or ever expect to see . . . Fiery symbols were scrawled across the water of the bay, and periodically the crater discharged mines of serpents into a sky which was the deepest of blood reds and pulsating everywhere with lightning reflections.

Hardly surprising, then, that the Neapolitans will try to appease this monster with the conciliatory name *'la buonanima'*, the good soul. It has been calculated that Vesuvius erupts every thirty years; if so, why has there not been any apparent activity since 1944? More disturbing still, there are no emergency plans as to what the thousands of people living around the volcano should do in the event of an eruption. Vesuvius is an active volcano; towns that crouch under her shadow – Torre del Greco, Portici – are in very real danger of becoming latter-day Pompeiis, should the good soul so decide.

From the intersection with a road signposted *Cratere*, your walk to the top of Mount Vesuvius will take you through some interesting landscape. The lava flows eventually decompose into soil of extraordinary fertility; amid the gnarled and twisted larval blackness there are vineyards, clumps of broom, copses of oak and chestnut. It is on the foothills of Vesuvius that the plump and almost egg-shaped *Marzano* tomatoes are grown – the best, say the Neapolitans, in the world.

The last leg of the 45-minute ascent to the crater is up a steep path. At some stage you will have to pay a small fee to see the crater – you may even be charged for a 'compulsory guide', but since there is usually no guide available, I should walk on unattended.

As you tread – gingerly, in my case – around the crater's rim, the impression is of an almighty force barely controlled beneath the surface crust of things; clouds of steam rise from the mouth of the crater, as in some Victorian illustration to Dante's *Inferno*. And how insignificant the houses by the shores of Naples! – dwindling, in the great extent of prospect, down to dice. There is no protection from the dizzy, 300-metre drop, so don't walk too close to the edge of the volcano, or you may take a regrettable tumble and roll all the way down to Naples. Or, alternatively, you may tumble the other way, into the volcano itself. Charles Dickens relates how the roly-poly man with whom, one winter, he had made the ascent – a certain Mr Pickle of Portici – suddenly plunged away head foremost into the crater, 'skimming over the surface of the white ice like a cannonball'. Fortunately, Mr Pickle was all right. But it was a close shave.

Herculaneum

You need at least two hours to visit Herculaneum (open daily 9 a.m.–one hour before sunset, 'visitors will be warned of closing time by two siren-hoots'). For its dramatic views of the sea and Vesuvius, for its perfectly preserved frescoes, mosaics and sculptures, Herculaneum is of even more fascination, perhaps, than Pompeii; visitors who have time to see only one of the two towns are advised to go to Herculaneum.

History

The name Herculaneum derives from its legendary foundation by Hercules. As early as the sixth century BC, it came under Greek influence from Cumae and Neapolis; throughout its history it retained its Greekness. In 307 BC the town was taken by the Romans and, under the early empire, they built many a luxurious villa here. Herculaneum, in fact, was always a quiet residential town, without forum or amphitheatre, with none of Pompeii's commercial importance; its inhabitants numbered no more than 5,000.

HERCULANEUM

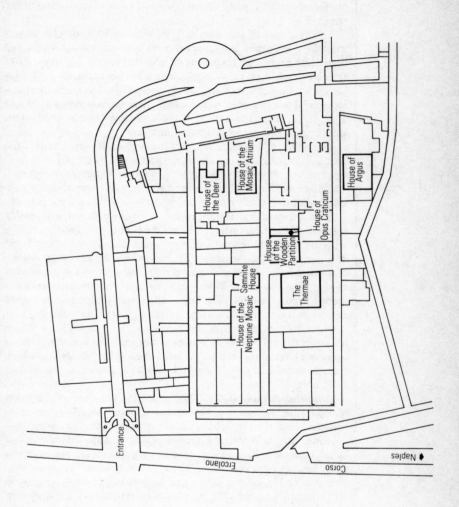

House of the Deer

House of the Mosaic Atrium

House of Argus

House of Opus Craticum

House of the Wooden Partition

House of the Samnite Mosaic House

House of the Neptune Mosaic House

The Thermae

Entrance

Ercolano

Corso

Naples

When the catastrophe of AD 79 occurred, Herculaneum was submerged by a torrent of mud and bits of lava that hardened into a sort of tufa. Excavations, sometimes burrowing to a depth of 39 metres, have consequently been laborious. As very few skeletons have been dug up at Herculaneum, it would seem that most of its citizens escaped the wrath of Vesuvius.

The discovery of the town in 1709 was due to workers sinking a shaft for a well; they stumbled upon the back stage of a theatre, and unearthed numerous fragments of sculpted marble. Charles III of Bourbon took over excavations soon after his accession and, in a largely haphazard and often quite irresponsible fashion, the theatre, a forum and five 'temples' were located, all of them between 1738 and 1765. A lull ensued and then, in 1927, more systematic excavations were begun. They are still continuing today.

The villas of Herculaneum once overlooked the sea, but over the centuries the coastline has altered, so that the ruins are now well back from the water – on the edge, in fact, of a rather unprepossessing town. The juxtaposition of modern tenements, their balconies flapping with linen, with the stately ruin of many a senator's villa is very curious.

It takes a good deal of imagination to visualise the original seaside resort. For one thing, many of the buildings now whir and flap, eerily, with the wings of numerous pigeons – and lizards everywhere flit in and out of cracks and windows. There is the spooky atmosphere, here, of a ghost-town. As you wander around the site, you will find that many of the houses are locked up – ask one of the numerous custodians to open them for you. They will probably expect some sort of *douceur* in return; Lucky Strike cigarettes go down very nicely.

What to see   There is a great deal to see: the following is a personal choice. It's an idea to pick up a map of Herculaneum at the entrance. The Roman numerals refer to the *insulae* (the large blocks of buildings into which Herculaneum is divided), and the Arabic numerals to the houses themselves.

House of Argus (II, 2). This must have been one of the finest mansions in the town; a half-broken column still lies buried in solidified laval matter. It has an idyllic garden with palm trees.

House of the Wooden Partition (III, 11–12). This house is so called because it incorporates a screen used to divide one bedroom from another. Now carbonised into a sort of charcoal, the screen has even retained its ancient hinges and lamp-brackets. The corner-shop (10) which abuts this villa contains an extraordinary clothes-press, resembling some grim instrument of torture.

House of Opus Craticum (III, 13–15). Once in the plebeian quarter of Herculaneum, this house was probably inhabited by fishermen. There is a shop with a back parlour and a workroom, and (to use the language of estate agents) two self-contained flats. In one of these, there stands a perfectly carbonised bed.

House of the Mosaic Atrium (IV, 1–2). This luxurious villa with a mosaic-paved atrium (forecourt) and terrace overlooking the now-retreated sea was once adorned with gardens, fountains, fishponds, trellised loggias and rest-rooms. The atrium floor has corrugated under the weight of the invading mud from Vesuvius, so that the mosaic now looks as though it is made of heaving waves.

House of the Deer (IV, 21). This is the grandest dwelling yet discovered at Herculaneum, containing two delicately executed paintings of deer at bay, and a figurine of an inebriated satyr, urinating willy-nilly: it causes much giggling among groups of visiting schoolchildren. The delightful gardens give views of Capri and Sorrento.

Samnite House (V, 1). To this villa a further storey was added, probably to house the servants. The ithyphallic symbol above the main portal is just like the numerous phalli which Neapolitan youths spray-gun on to the walls of their city today. The phallus was regarded as a charm to ward off the evil eye, as indeed it still is.

House of the Neptune Mosaic (V, 6–7). In a little court behind the living quarters is the famous mosaic of Amphitrite and her husband Neptune. The blues and greens are of a Mediterranean freshness. Below this villa is the best-preserved shop in Herculaneum. It contains carbonised coils of hemp and large amphorae for wine – just as they were at the moment of the catastrophe.

The Thermae (VI). In the women's baths, note the mosaic of a curiously cherubic-looking Triton, surrounded by cuttlefish and dolphins. There is also a waiting-room and a linen-room. The men's baths have shelves for clothes and a plunge-bath with a scalloped apse for a hand-basin. In the room for cold baths, note the wonderful domed ceiling, painted to represent the sea-bottom with fish on a blue background. When this was reflected in the transparent pale green of the bath, bathers would have had the illusion of wallowing in a lake.

Pompeii

No visit to Campania would be complete without a visit to Pompeii: you could happily spend four hours pottering around the ruins there, as it is from these that our knowledge of everyday life in ancient times is largely derived. In the broad pavements, you can still see the ruts worn by waggon-wheels and the stepping-stones used by pedestrians in wet weather some 2,000 years ago. On the outside walls of houses and shops (many of them curiously resembling the *bassi* of contemporary Naples) are preserved some 2,000 graffiti from over the centuries: soldiers, gladiators, prostitutes, lovers, schoolboys, travellers and poets have all recorded their comments. There are shops, public bars, taverns, villas, inns and stables – many of them more or less perfectly preserved, as though held for posterity in a photographic snapshot. But a word of warning: avoid visiting the ruins during the midday sun – it can get very hot indeed, and few of the buildings provide shade. If possible, wear flat shoes, so as to cope with the uneven paved streets.

It's a good idea to mug up on Pompeii before you actually visit the archaeological site; that way, the ruins will all the more vividly come to life – Bulwer-Lytton's romantic *The Last Days of Pompeii* and the works of Amadeo Maiuri (the archaeologist who was in charge of the most important excavations) are a good resource. Take heed, too, of the interesting notice at the ticket office: 'The Ruins Management invites all visitors to walk careful through the ruins in order to avoid unpleasant accidents. The ancient environment is in fact uncomfortable and ruined beyond all measures of safetyness.' Make head or tail of that, and you deserve a free bottle of wine at the Poste di Ristoro restaurant, near the Forum, where you can also get very good, though costly, pasta dishes.

Getting there The ruins are open daily except Monday, 9 a.m.–one hour before sunset. The best way to reach them is by train (the Circumvesuviana from Napoli Centrale); get off at Pompeii Scavi and it's a five-minute walk to the entrance near the Basilica and Forum. By road, Pompeii lies 22 km south-east of Naples along the old Torre Annunziata road.

History The origins of Pompeii are as ancient as those of Rome. The first settlement was founded there in the eighth century BC by the *gens pompeiana*, an Oscan people. Later, it came under Hellenic influence from Cumae and Neapolis. The Greeks were ousted between 525 and 474 BC by the Etruscans. Then, in 200 BC, Pompeii became a subject ally of Rome. Soon enough, the town became a favourite retreat of wealthy Romans, such as the orator Cicero, who purchased estates in the vicinity. But Pompeii under the Romans was also a prosperous industrial and trading centre; one export was a popular brand of fish sauce, and the wine trade flourished too. The first disaster struck home in AD 63, when an earthquake nearly devastated the city; the Roman tragedian Seneca relates that it killed 600 sheep and caused a temporary desertion of the city.

Then, in AD 79, came the final blow: Vesuvius belched forth a terrific column of smoke which expanded like a giant tree. A murky fog of ash and pumice dust completely obscured the light of day: the darkness, Pliny wrote, 'was not as on a moonless and clouded night, but as in a completely sealed room'. Mud and cinders buried Pompeii under 7 metres of volcanic debris; the burial was accompanied by a violent electric thunderstorm, which convulsed the sea into a mass of freak-sized breakers. Birds plummeted dead from the skies. Of the 20,000 inhabitants of Pompeii, more than 2,000 perished; not, as many think, by being swamped in lava, but through suffocation or poisoning from the noxious vapours. You can see the effects of asphyxiation on the

POMPEII

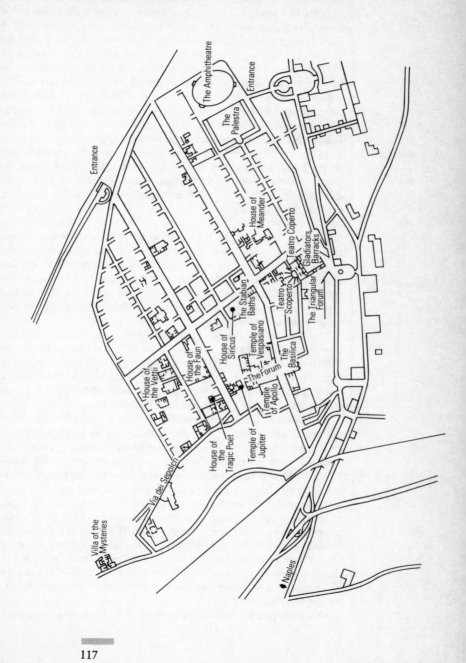

poignant expressions of the Pompeiians themselves, recreated in plaster-casts from the imprints their bodies made in the ashes – a girl burying her head in her mother's breast, a man doubled up like a foetus, his mouth a great 'O' of agony.

Pompeii remained buried for nearly 2,000 years. People feared the site, as if it were cursed, though looters carried off what they could from the buried houses, undeterred. The full extent of the dead city was not discovered until 1748, when the Bourbons set to excavating in a slap-dash way – statues were extricated, whilst the ruins themselves were left to fall down, or were simply covered up again. From that time the work has gone on; well over half the city has now seen the light of day, but excavations are far from complete.

What to see   As far as visiting Pompeii is concerned, a detailed enumeration of *all* the buildings would be madness; it would take too long and the pages of dense print might disturb the enjoyment of your visit. Accordingly, I can do no better than quote Alexandre Dumas on the subject, from his great book on Naples, *Il Corricolo*: 'I do not want to conduct you on a domiciliary excursion of Pompeii: we shall therefore visit three or four of the most important houses, enter one or two shops, maybe wander through the odd temple, cut across the Forum, inspect the theatre, read a few inscriptions, and that is that.' And whatever you do, don't forget to pick up a map of Pompeii at the entrance; it is essential to orient yourself, or else you will tread and retread the same old ground, describing circle after circle. Try at least to see some of the following.

The Basilica. Pompeii's largest public building, this was used as a law-court. The elegant tribunal is a two-level structure in the Hellenistic style with wooden staircases on the sides leading to the upper level. Innumerable phrases were scratched on the tribunal walls; one interesting graffito reads: 'I am astounded, O wall, that you do not crumble under the weight of all these writers.'

The Forum. It was here that the political, economic, governmental and religious life of Pompeii unfolded. The open space was enclosed on three sides by a double portico of white marble columns, many of them still visible. Ominously, this great courtyard is overlooked by Mount Vesuvius, the purple slopes of the destroying mountain lofty above the red and yellow ruins of the town.

Three temples grace the Forum. The northernmost is the **Temple of Jupiter** (originally with underground rooms containing the public treasury, or *aerarium*). The **Temple of Apollo** (next to the Basilica) still boasts a sacrificial stone altar; there is a splendid statue of Apollo on the right and, directly opposite, one of Diana, each in the act of shooting an arrow as though in a divinely inspired duel. The **Temple of Vespasiano** also contains an altar, decorated with scenes depicting the sacrifice of a bull.

The Triangular Forum. This square, which takes its name from the shape of the land on which it was built, is surrounded on two sides by ninety-five Doric columns; the base near the front portico was for a statue of Marcus Claudius Marcellus, patron of Pompeii and favourite nephew of the Emperor Augustus. Today, the piazza is a favourite picnic spot.

Nearby are the **Gladiators' Barracks**. Originally a colonnaded square where theatre-goers met during a play's intermission, it was during the age of Nero transformed into an arena for mock gladiator battles, before they descended into the amphitheatre for the real and bloody thing. Sixty-three skeletons were found here, one of them that of a woman whose rich jewellery suggests she might have been there on a visit to her gladiator lover, before her amorous errand was so rudely interrupted by Mount Vesuvius.

Connected to these barracks are two theatres: the **Teatro Scoperto**, which could hold up to 5,000 spectators (the boxes built over the side entrances were reserved for priestesses) and the much smaller **Teatro Coperto**, one of the finest examples of a roofed theatre or *Odeon*, which was used in ancient times for musical performances and mime.

The Amphitheatre. Built in the year Pompeii became a Roman colony, 80 BC, this is the oldest known monument of its kind. And one of the largest, too: it measures about 135 by 104 metres and could hold 20,000 spectators – in other words, the entire population of Pompeii. It was used exclusively for gladiator contests, hunts and battles with wild animals. So violent did these bloody sports become that on Nero's orders (unusual, coming from so debauched an emperor), all spectacles were banned for ten years. The notion that the people were surprised by the eruption whilst witnessing a gladiator combat is sadly (from the point of view of Hollywood drama) a pure myth.

The Palestra. This large open space had facilities for the sportive exercise of Pompeiian youth, swimming pool included. To the south-east is a latrine of considerable size.

House of Meander. Named after a Greek poet almost as famous in the ancient world as Homer, this was a most sumptuous villa; the walls are decorated with scenes from the conquest of Troy, with theatrical masques and hunting scenes. There is also a small chapel for worshipping – of all things – the wax busts of ancestors. At the time of the catastrophe, family and slaves took refuge in the room with the strongest roof, only to be killed when it fell about their heads.

The Stabian Baths. The city's largest public baths, they also contain some excellent examples of victims petrified during the catastrophe, their bones peeping through the plaster-casts. The men's dressing-room is decorated with stuccoes of cupids and trophies. Swimming alternated here with athletic exercises; around the large pool were areas where men smeared their bodies in oil and sand before boxing.

House of Siricus. This must have belonged to well-to-do people, as on the entrance to the house (where the modern equivalent of our front door mat would be) are the words '*Salve Lucrum*', 'Welcome Earnings' – a candid salute to filthy lucre.

House of the Vettii. On no account should this be missed: it gives a delightful picture of life among the merchant classes of Pompeii. At the entrance is an extremely lewd painting of Priapus, god of fertility, presumably intended to ward off the evil eye of those jealous of the owner's wealth: 'No pen', wrote Mark Twain of this example of Roman pornography, 'could have the hardihood with which to describe it.' The walls are decorated with *amorini, putti* and cherubs, most of them imitating sundry adult occupations. In a small room adjoining the kitchen is a room usually kept under lock and key containing a statue of Priapus so rude that it has the primmer tourists running for their smelling salts. The villa has a beautiful garden which brings to mind the cloistered calm of a monastery; you can still see the lead pipes that supplied the fountains with water.

House of the Faun. One of the most interesting of Pompeii's patrician villas, this is famous for its 'Welcome' ('*Have*') sign on the pavement at the main entrance. The atrium is rich in geometrical inlays of coloured marbles, with a beautiful statue of a dancing faun in the middle (the original is in the Archaeological Museum of Naples). With its clean and graceful lines, the garden is a worthy ancestor to Renaissance courtyards fourteen centuries later. This is widely regarded as one of the most illustrious private dwellings in the ancient world. The villa was discovered in 1830 in the presence of Goethe's son.

House of the Tragic Poet. This villa is so called from two representations found here of a poet reading, and of a theatrical rehearsal. It is interesting for its paintings in the atrium of such classical scenes as the Sacrifice of Iphigenia and the Rape of Briseis. At the entrance there is a mosaic of a ferocious-looking dog with the words '*Cave Canem*'.

Via dei Sepolcri. Part of the great military road from Capua to Naples, Herculaneum, Pompeii and Reggio di Calabria, this is a poignant illustration of the ancient Roman custom of burying the dead by the side of a high road. Here we find temple-like mausoleums and small funeral chapels decorated with seashells, tritons and dolphins. The poet Shelley was most impressed with these funerary monuments: 'How unlike ours!' he enthused. 'They seem not so much hiding-places for that which must decay as voluptuous chambers for immortal spirits.'

Villa of the Mysteries. Discovered in 1909, this is a vast and complex dwelling of more than sixty rooms. It contains some extraordinary murals depicting the initiation of a maiden into a Dionysiac rite, performed by twenty-nine actors. The Dionysiac Mysteries was a widespread cult in Campania, despite the severe sanctions placed on it by the Roman Senate. One can understand the sanctions – the mysterious murals even have a flagellation scene.

The islands

Capri

The picturesque outline of Capri (population 12,000), with the forbidding grandeur of its cliffs and mountains, its deep grottoes, limestone coves and weirdly shaped rocks, forms one of the most dramatic in the Bay of Naples. Sailing around the island in 1700, John Dryden, son of the English poet, used for the first time in the history of the language the word 'romantique' to describe the impression it made on him.

History

The island has attracted jet-setters, actors and sundry members of royalty ever since the Emperor Tiberius built his twelve villas here: it has a reputation for louche living, wild parties and bacchantic orgies, all of them brilliantly documented in Norman Douglas's scandal-mongering 1917 novel, *South Wind*. The latest celebrity to have died on Capri was Gracie Fields.

Kings Ferdinand I and IV used to visit Capri from Naples for the quail shooting during the spring; the birds alight on the island after their tiring flight from Africa. Gorky and Lenin lived on the island; the Italian writer Alberto Moravia has a house here, as does Graham Greene. Hans Christian Andersen, Dumas and Nietzsche, Rilke, Joseph Conrad, Turgenev, Bernard Shaw and D. H. Lawrence have all been here.

The name Capri is derived from the nickname 'Capra', meaning 'the Goat', given to Tiberius for both his fabled hairiness and his sexual appetite. Today, the Capresi are extremely proud of their randy old emperor; amid the restaurants with their notices for 'Grandes Terraces avec Jardin et Parking', you will see the odd 'Snack Bar Tiberius'. The Marquis de Sade, intrigued by the perversions of Tiberius, was an early visitor to the island.

Today, Capri is chic, chichi and incredibly expensive: you are advised to visit it from Naples, because its hotels and restaurants are overpriced and the food not particularly good.

Getting there

Boats for Capri leave every hour from the Molo Belverello under the Castel Nuovo; there are also services to Ischia and Procida, and connections between the three. The Tourist Office is at the end of the dock at Marina Grande; tel. 83 70 634. Be forewarned: in the summer months, Capri is for the Neapolitans rather like Coney Island for New Yorkers – it can get very crowded indeed.

What to see

On arrival in Capri, the first thing you should do is visit the famous **Blue Grotto**: this is the island's biggest money-spinner (some 5,000 people visit the grotto in the month of August alone), and probably rather an overrated experience. However, to have seen Campania without visiting the *Grotta Azzurra* is like to have been to Egypt without seeing the pyramids; it is essential tourism, even though no less a person than André Gide couldn't wait to get out of the cave.

A tourist-laden boat whisks you from the Marina Grande to the grotto. At the entrance, swarms of grasping 'fishermen' (many of them in fetching white nautical caps) demand an extra fee for transferral to their rowing-boats which then glide into the curious aquamarine of the grotto – it has been compared to a candle held at the back of a bowl of copper sulphate. The water, a beautiful fluorescent blue, reaches a depth of 20 metres and you will be fed some mumbo-jumbo about how it once served as a *nymphaeum*, a swimming pool, for Tiberius. You will also be told that a mysterious and narrow passage at the back of the cave leads to Tiberius's villa above, which would indicate that the emperor crawled on all fours through the tunnel to reach his natural swimming pool. Well, as Norman Douglas wrote in his wonderful book on Campania, *Siren Land*: 'Tiberius and his frail cortège, after scrambling on their stomachs for half a league through this dank and dismal drain, certainly deserved, and perhaps needed, a bath.' All I can say is, *'Evviva la Grotta Azzurra!'*

Anacapri   After the grotto, take the bus or funicular to the resort of Anacapri (literally 'over Capri'), on the high eastern plateau of the island. It's more peaceful up here, less overrun by tourists. The thing to see is the villa of the Swedish author and physician Axel Munthe, **San Michele** (open 10 a.m.–sunset). Crouched under the shadow of an old castle sacked by the pirate Red Beard, and built on the site of one of the goatish Tiberius's villas, this whitewashed nineteenth-century house commands some absolutely stunning views of the sea. From the terrace – where, incidentally, Queen Victoria of Sweden's two dogs Tom and Fellow are buried – you should watch the sunset. The villa itself is crammed full of antiquities, many of them phoney and rather vulgar; look out, though, for the splendid Medusa's head in Munthe's study.

Near San Michele is the *seggiova* (chair-lift) which takes you up to **Monte Solaro**. From its summit you are afforded a spectacularly panoramic view of the Apennines to the east and the mountains of Calabria to the south. The journey is strongly recommended.

Returning to the charming little piazza of Anacapri, with its ritzy cafés and their diamanté clients, take the Via Tiberio to the **Villa Tiberio** (open 10 a.m.–one hour before sunset), an arduous 40 minutes' walk. The overgrown ruins are very badly signposted, so that you hardly know which room is which: it seems to consist largely of a number of vaulted chambers, stairways, terraces and corridors. On the highest point is the small chapel of Santa Maria del Soccorso, from where there are glorious views over the cliffs from the belvedere. It was from this point that Tiberius threw his enemies into the sea. According to Suetonius, a party of sailors was stationed below, and when the bodies were hurled down they whacked at them with oars and boathooks, to make sure they were completely dead. On a happier note, the gigantic statue of the Madonna and Child outside the chapel was brought to the site by a US naval helicopter.

Returning to the piazza again, it is a short walk from here to the fourteenth-century Carthusian monastery, the **Certosa San Giacomo**, and the **Garden of Augustus**. The Certosa – also built on the site of one of Tiberius's numerous *dependances* – gives a rare sense of how Capri must have looked in the Middle Ages, with its cool and angular Gothic chapel. The conventual buildings themselves are now part of a music conservatory, hence the ubiquitous sound of tinkling pianos.

The nearby Garden of Augustus, named after the emperor, consists of a wonderful series of belvederes, stacked one on top of the other. In one corner is a statue dedicated to Lenin, who fled to Capri after the abortive St Petersburg rising of 1905. From the gardens there is a fine view of the peculiar-looking **Faraglioni**: sheer sugar-loaf rocks emerging from the deep blue waters of the sea which, since time immemorial, have been a symbol of Capri.

Ischia

With a population of 39,162, Ischia is the largest of the Neapolitan islands, about 46 km in circumference. Its name derives from *Iscla*, a corruption of *insula* (island) which, in Neapolitan, became Ischia. Unlike Capri, which has more than its fair share of British tourists, Ischia is almost entirely geared to the German market; elderly Germans flock here for its famous health spas, therapeutic sands, mud baths and thermal waters. If you are suffering from rheumatic or arthritic complaints, from metabolic diseases such as gout or obesity, from nasal, pharyngeal or bronchial catarrh, or from gynaecological or dermatological ailments, Ischia is perhaps the place for you. Otherwise, there is not an awful lot to see. The climate is genial and the scenery almost everywhere singularly beautiful, but there is little of any monumental importance; you will probably not want to spend very much more than a morning here.

What to see

Ischia Porto is the major port, with the greatest concentration of hotels, boutiques and clothes shops, and a long and excellent beach. **Cassamicciola Terme**, an expensive spa town where Heinrich Ibsen lived, has a not very attractive sprawl of modern hotels. **Lacco Ameno** is grander though dull (I'm not sure that it really deserves its epithet Ameno, meaning pleasant or agreeable, since its waters are among the most radioactive in Europe). **Sant'Angelo** has a central piazza and an uncrowded beach. The **Castle** of Ischia, a pile of ruined fifteenth-century edifices, is privately owned.

I would strongly recommend that you take a mule up to the top of **Monte Epomeo**, an extinct volcano. This you do by taking the bus from Lacco Ameno to **Fontana**, the highest village on the island. Here you can hire one of the beasts for about 30,000 lire; ask for

Raffaele, a weather-beaten man in a beret. His mule, Celentano, is young and quite sprightly, although she does insist on frequently stopping for a good munch of grass whilst, rather like Robert Louis Stevenson on his donkey in France, you sway about in the saddle. The climb up to Monte Epomeo takes you through some unusual volcanic scenery, with splendid views en route. At the summit, you overlook Cassamicciola, which was practically destroyed by an earthquake in 1883: 3,000 people were killed in the space of 15 seconds.

Procida
Small (population 10,015), unexploited and ramshackle, Procida is in many ways the most curious of the Neapolitan islands. In the tortuous streets of its vaguely Byzantine centre, you will see vegetable-laden donkeys clopping past the fishermen as they mend their nets. The tiny houses are almost Arab in appearance – whitewashed, flat-roofed dwellings with curtains for doors. Many of the houses along the harbour, though, are a veritable explosion of liquorice allsorts colours: pink, mauve and yellow, with fishing boats painted a flaking white and blue moored virtually at their front doors.

Rich in oranges, lemons, grapes and melons, Procida is, in effect, the market-garden of Naples. The soil is predominantly volcanic and, according to Pliny, the island is a fragment torn off in an earthquake from neighbouring Ischia. There is good bathing at the **Lido di Procida** and at the **Marina di Chiaiolella**, on a bay to the southwest, partly enclosed by the little island of Vivara. There are no hotels to speak of in Procida; a shame, really, since it would be a nice place in which to relax for a while.

From the Marina Grande, where the boat deposits you, it's a good 20 minutes' walk to the main square, the Piazza dei Martiri. Here there is a tablet commemorating twelve of the inhabitants executed after the uprising of 1799, when the short-lived Parthenopean Republic was set up in Naples; they include a sailor, a lawyer, a surgeon and a chemist. The nearby **Castle** – now unfortunately a prison – commands superb views of Ischia and Monte Epomeo.

The Via San Michele climbs up to the unusual abbey church of **San Michele**, full of superstitious amulets, human bones and trinkets. The ceiling is painted with Luca Giordano's Saint Michael defeating Lucifer. There is also a wonderful sixteenth-century painting of the saint's legendary expulsion of the Saracens from Procida in 1535; note his flaming sword, celestial armour and billowing red cape.

The Sorrentine Peninsula and the Amalfi Coast

Sorrento
Sorrento, 47 km from Naples on Route 18, is, with 15,040 inhabitants,

one of the largest and most popular of Campanian resorts. Here, near the rocky cliffs that describe the southern arc of the Bay of Naples, the Sirens tempted Ulysses and his crew; the name *Sorrentum* is said, poetically, to derive from these deceiving sea-creatures. In Roman times, Sorrento was a favourite resort of rich Romans: Agrippa, Augustus and Antonius all had villas here.

Today, the town retains a pleasantly faded air of nineteenth-century aristocratic tourism – its comfortable, old-fashioned hotels once housed such luminaries as Ibsen, Wagner and Nietzsche. But one's overall impression of Sorrento now is, I'm afraid, one of a total orientation to mass tourism: restaurants with names such as 'Snack Bar 2000', 'Big Ben Pub', 'The English Inn' (serving, of all the most inedible things, *pizza mit bolognese sauce*) depressingly abound. You can buy 'Sex-Instructor' T-shirts ('First Lesson Free'), though Sorrento is also famed for its inlaid woodwork, lace and straw-pleating.

For better or worse, however, Sorrento is the ideal, the essential, place from which to explore such delightful spots as Amalfi, Ravello and Positano. Although there are several good hotels, I suggest that you stay in the eastern Sant'Angelo edge of the town, which is less spoiled by tourism.

What to see

The main square is the pretty **Piazza Tasso**, built over a 50-metre ravine with the ruins of an old watermill at the bottom. The statue is of the poet Torquato Tasso, born here in 1544. He was arrested for vagrancy, spent seven years in prison and finally, after disguising himself as a shepherd, went completely mad. The Sorrentines are very proud of Tasso.

From here, walk down the Via Tasso until you come to the lovely church of **San Francesco**, with its thirteenth-century Moorish-style cloisters. Classical concerts are performed here in July. In the gardens of the nearby **Villa Comunale** stands the splendid **Albergo Imperiale Tramontano**. Here, in 1881, Ibsen wrote his play *Gli Spettri*, otherwise known (to the British that make up 80 per cent of Sorrento's tourists) as *Ghosts*. The hotel incorporates the remaining room of the house in which Tasso was born.

Nearby is the famous **Correale Museum** (April–September: 9.30 a.m.–12.30 p.m., 4–7 p.m.; October–March: 9.30 a.m.–12.30 p.m., 3–5 p.m.; Sunday: 9.30 a.m.–12.30 p.m.; closed Tuesdays). This contains a collection ranging from Greek and Roman sculptures to manuscripts of the ubiquitous Tasso, Neapolitan paintings, furniture and porcelain.

A wonderful walk is to be had along the Via del Capo (it runs out of Piazza Tasso) to the **Capo di Sorrento**, a superb place for a sunset swim. On your way, you will pass the villa where Maxim Gorky lived from 1924 to 1933, but beware of the sign *'Cani Mordaci'*, biting dogs: the villa is very obviously not open to the public. Beyond this, on the right, a dirt track takes you down to the sea and to the ruins of the

Roman **Villa of Pollio Felix**, also known as the **Baths of Queen Giovanna**. The ruins of this once-sumptuous Roman house have a delightful *nymphaeum*, or bathing pool. The views here, with Vesuvius smoking away in the distance, are quite magical: it is an excellent spot to fall asleep, take a picnic, read a book, smoke a cigarette, drink a bottle of wine. You are far away, at any rate, from packaged Sorrento.

What to do

There isn't much to do in Sorrento during the summer, but if you happen to be there on Good Friday, don't miss the famous *Cristo Defunto* religious festival. During this, the Sorrento faithful wend their way through the streets wearing very odd-looking black gowns and hoods with slits for eyes – like the members, you think, of some spin-off Ku Klux Klan faction. The celebrants all carry symbols of the Crucifixion and Resurrection: a pair of pliers, a wine-soaked sponge, a cock (as in the one that crowed), flails and goblets of wine. Pagan, probably; but quite fun.

One thing you might do in Sorrento is hire a motorbike; it is the ideal way to see the Amalfi coast. But do wrap up well: on the more mountainous stretches of the coast it can get quite cold. And if hiring a lightweight *motorino*, don't carry on your back any form of rucksack – when driving uphill, the weight of it can topple you over backwards. It happened to me and it really isn't much fun. The best place from which to hire is the **Antares** agency, Corso Italia 287; tel. 87 72 983.

Where to stay

Most of the eighty-three hotels in Sorrento are expensive: one of the best is the **Bellevue Siren**, Via Marina Grande 1; tel. 87 81 024. An eighteenth-century establishment perched atop a cliff, it has the air, inside, of a rambling mansion, chock-a-block with fine furniture and paintings. Several rooms command views of Vesuvius.

Of comparable elegance (and price) is the four-star **Excelsior Vittoria**, Piazza Tasso; tel. 87 81 900. The terrace is lined with busts of ancient Romans. Caruso stayed here; a room is named after him.

More reasonably priced is the excellent two-star **Hotel Savoia**, Via Fuorimura 50; tel. 87 82 511. The 26 rooms are mostly equipped with baths, and the management is friendly.

Over in Sant'Angelo, I would strongly recommend the four-star (though far from expensive) **Villa Garden**, overlooking the sea on the Corso Marion Crawford; tel. 87 81 387. The view from some of the rooms is wonderful, though the restaurant is decorated in a somewhat nightmarish fashion.

Also in Sant'Angelo, try the **Hotel Milton**, on the nearby Via Cocumella; tel. 87 82 969. It has three stars but at a two-star price.

Where to eat

One of the best restaurants in Southern Italy is probably the **Don Alfonso**, way above Sorrento in the hills of Sant'Agata; tel. 87 80 026. The owners rear their own poultry, make their own olive oil and grow all sorts of unusual organic vegetables.

Others, more moderately priced, include the **Kursaal**, Via Fuorimura, tel. 87 81 216, famed for its huge antipasto buffet, and **La**

Favorita O'Parrucchiano, Corso Italia, tel. 87 81 321, excellent for local Campanian cooking, with dishes served in a giant, multi-level conservatory.

Sant'Agata sui Due Golfi

Whether by car or by bike, we now leave Sorrento on the breathtakingly scenic Strada di Capodimonte, heading for Amalfi. After 10 km, we arrive at the delightful mountain village of Sant'Agata sui Due Golfi, so called because it commands superb views of the two gulfs of Salerno and Naples. The **church** has an exquisite sixteenth-century Florentine altar of inlaid marble, brought here from a Neapolitan church in 1845.

The cat that smoked

Opposite the church is a strange café named the **Bar Orlando**, run by the distinguished-looking Alfredo Cliento. A generous man, he may make you a present of his faintly lunatic book *Jolly il Gatto che Fuma: Storia di un gatto prodigio* (Jolly, the Cat that Smoked: the history of a cat prodigy). Alfredo's cat – now sadly dead, though everywhere there are photographs of his beloved Jolly, even a statue of the creature atop a cappuccino machine – was in fact so extraordinary a prodigy that he could even smoke a cigarette whilst flying through the air. A sign outside the bar reads '*Vedermi per Credere*', See me to Believe me. People from all over Europe used in the past to seek out the legendary smoking cat – everybody, says Alfredo with a sigh, except Queen Elizabeth II of England. But no matter; early one morning, Alfredo caught the plane to London and threw a copy of *Jolly il Gatto che Fuma* over the gates of Buckingham Palace, in the hope that the good monarch would read it. I should certainly have a chat with Signor Cliento over a cup of his excellent coffee; he is not only a mine of information about cats (quoting the French poet Baudelaire's thoughts on the slinky creatures), but also about the local history of Sant'Agata.

Five minutes uphill from the Bar Orlando takes us to the **Deserto**, a suppressed Franciscan monastery (near the O Sole Mio Hotel) commanding a superb view of Capri and the two bays. The bell-tower is inscribed with the rather terrifying warning: TEMPUS BREVE EST.

Positano

There is sufficient time, though, to rejoin the 154 road to Amalfi until we arrive, 8 km further on, at Positano. With a population of some 3,133, this bustling little town derives its name from Poseidon. During the Anjou dynasty, Positano was an important harbour and still disputes with nearby Amalfi the honour of being the birthplace of Flavio Gioia, inventor of the compass. (The dispute is pointless, since Gioia probably never existed.)

Today, Positano is known as 'the poor man's Capri', even though the wealthy – including the film director Franco Zeffirelli – have many a sumptuous villa here. But with its Moorish-style white and pink houses falling from terraces among bougainvillea-festooned gardens, all of them overlooking a small bay with a majolica-domed church, Positano is an impressive contender with Capri for beauty. Although there is little in Positano of any monumental interest, you may well want to spend some time here. 'Positano bites deep,' wrote John Steinbeck. 'It is a dream that isn't quite real when you are there and becomes beckoningly real after you have gone.'

Grotta di Smeraldo

Another 8 km along the road to Amalfi and we pass above a fairy-tale cavern with deep gorges and rock formations on the grotto floor visible through the stalagmite-punctured emerald water. If you have already seen the Blue Grotto over in Capri, you may as well give this one a miss. Otherwise, it is open in the summer, June–September, 8 a.m.–6 p.m., unless the sea is in the slightest bit turbulent, in which case you will not be permitted entry.

Amalfi

Cutting across the Capo di Conca, beyond which opens a wonderful vista of the Amalfi coastline stretching to the Capo d'Orso, we come after 4 km to one of the great delights of Southern Italy, Amalfi town itself.

History

Almost twice as populous (population 6,258) as Positano, Amalfi is sometimes referred to as a miniature Athens of the Middle Ages, for the magnificence of this city is entirely medieval – it was not known to the Greeks or Romans. In the seventh century Amalfi was governed, like Venice, by its own set of Doges. At that time, it was recognised as the first naval power in the world – the Emperor of Constantinople even established a court here for the regulation of all controversies in naval matters.

Amalfi merchants traded with all parts of the world; the city sent out settlers to Byzantium, Asia Minor and Africa. In the Holy Land the Amalfitani founded hospitals and churches, one of which, dedicated to St John, became the Order of St John of Jerusalem, the Knights Hospitallers. Their symbol, the Maltese cross, is now to be seen on just about every Amalfi street corner.

In 1113 Amalfi fell to the Norman Roger II; since then, its Maritime Republic, which once vied with Genoa and Pisa, declined irrevocably. Webster's Jacobean tragedy, *The Duchess of Malfi*, is based on the life of the unfortunate Joanna of Aragon, consort in the fifteenth century of the Duke of Amalfi.

In Edwardian times, Amalfi was a favourite wintering haunt with the British. Although the town has succumbed to package tourism, there is still about it an air of faded glamour. And there is extraordinary beauty. Encircled by craggy mountains and sheer precipices of wild magnificence, the town's tiled cupolas and pastel-washed houses huddle together in a higgledy-piggledy picturesque. Writers have for centuries waxed lyrical about Amalfi; the last to do so was Margaret Drabble in the *Sunday Times*:

> Amalfi clusters, the cliffs aspire, the sea extends. It is a living view, of living rock and living light. It changes minute by minute of an evening as the light changes, like a moving painting, like a wall of slowly evolving time, a perfectly composed combination of safety

and danger, distanced, marginally landscaped by man, inviting the artist.

The Duomo On that particular verdict it is hard, I think, to improve.

Amalfi's Cathedral, dedicated to Sant' Andrea and approached by a lofty flight of steps, must be one of the most beautiful religious monuments in Southern Italy: half-Saracen, half-Romanesque, it has a tall bell-tower of 1276, inlaid with glazed and coloured tiles. The mountains and monasteries in the background blend in quite naturally with the soft golden-brown marquetry of the façade. (I'm not so sure about the fountain in the Cathedral square: it spouts drinking water from a frog's bottom and a nymph's nipples – hardly holy, but there's no accounting for tastes.)

The interior of the Cathedral is handsome Baroque; down in the crypt are the remains (everything but the head) of St Andrew the Apostle, brought over from Constantinople in the thirteenth century. A miraculous oil called, believe it or not, Manna of St Andrew, is believed to seep from the bones. Not surprisingly, this leakage attracts numerous devotees: in 1218, for example, St Andrew's tomb was visited by St Francis of Assisi. The impressive bronze statue of St Andrew is supposed to be the work of one of Michelangelo's students; the two smaller statues on either side are attributed to Bernini's father.

As you leave the Cathedral, turn right into the **Cloister of Paradise**. This jewel of Saracen-inspired architecture was built in the thirteenth century as a cemetery for the city nobility; the interlacing arches of geometrically designed white marble are delightful. The monks here have put up an interesting sign: 'The cultured person marvels at works of art; the poorly educated person deforms them with his signature.' So don't take a pen to the cloister walls.

Seaward of the Cathedral lies the **Municipio**. In this rather sad and faded building moulders the famous **Tavole Amalfitane**. This ancient script – written, the custodian tells me, in a most appalling dog-Latin – may not be much to look at, but the maritime laws that it enumerates were recognised in the Mediterranean until 1570.

Shopping Amalfi is famed for its high-quality paper; if you want to buy some, visit the old paper-mill (founded 1500) in Via Casamare, near the *carabinieri* headquarters. Antonio Cavaliere, the owner, has been making paper for over half a century. His exquisite writing paper is faintly watermarked with the Maltese cross.

Where to stay Up the road, along the sea-front, stands the famous **Hotel Luna**. A tablet by the entrance tells of how Ibsen here wrote his play *La Casa di Bambola*, otherwise known as *The Doll's House*. If interested, ask the hotel-owner to show you the letter which Ibsen wrote to the Barbaro family in 1894, thanking them for their hospitality; the same family, incidentally, runs the hotel today. Ibsen stayed in Room 15, which overlooks the sea: it has been lovingly preserved. In the hotel gardens are some beautiful eleventh-century cloisters; in 1220, St Francis of Assisi prayed in them. Today, they are an excellent place to sip a dry Martini.

Strangely, Amalfi does not have many hotels; you can always, of course, try the Luna, but it will break you financially. However, you might want to try the three-star **La Bussola**, with moderately priced rooms offering colourful views of the marina; 16 Via Lungo Mare, tel. (089) 87 15 33.

Also recommended are the two-star **La Conchiglia**, at the end of Via Lungo Mare, tel. (089) 87 18 56, and the two-star **Hotel Amalfi**, Via Truglio, tel. (089) 87 24 40. The latter, clean and attractive, is nearly always overbooked. But a real find, otherwise.

Where to eat

There are numerous good-value *trattorie* in Amalfi. Among the best is the **Taverna degli Apostoli**, Largo Augustariccio, tel. (089) 87 29 91. A vaulted restaurant at the foot of the Cathedral (fifty years ago it was the town prison), its speciality is fish *a l'acqua pazza* – literally 'mad water' – based on tomatoes, onions, pepper and celery.

The **Trattoria da Bararacca**, Piazza Ferrari, tel. (089) 87 12 85, is the oldest restaurant in town. The food is excellent – perhaps not surprisingly so, as twenty-one relations work here preparing the fish dishes.

Ravello

One of the loveliest places in Campania, the small medieval town of Ravello is set high on a mountainside above Amalfi – 'closer to the sky than it is to the seashore,' wrote André Gide. The setting is wild and romantic, criss-crossed with winding, rustic streets, and planted everywhere with flowers. Though only 6 km from Amalfi, the 2,415 inhabitants of Ravello seem quite apart from their sister town.

Ravello began as a wealthy offshoot of the Amalfitan Maritime Republic, later gained independence and its own bishop, and had a period of splendid prosperity in the thirteenth century, when its inhabitants are said to have numbered 36,000. Today, it is a mere village, though with some thirteen churches, four monasteries and numerous palaces. The American writer Gore Vidal is an honorary citizen of Ravello, and lives there for most of the year.

What to see

Founded in the eleventh century, the **Cathedral Church of San Pantaleone** is a fascinating hybrid structure with a thirteenth-century campanile and a pair of 1179 bronze doors with fifty-four panels depicting Old Testament scenes. These doors – the delicacy of their workmanship is extraordinary – are normally kept shut behind wooden partitions; you have to pay the custodian to open them. This custodian, by the way, is quite a card; he looks pretty well barnacled to the church (he's been here for twenty years now) and claims to be a good friend of Jacqueline Kennedy, Gore Vidal's half-sister. Don't believe a word of it, but just listen to his banter: 'Hello! Postcards, you like? German, you speak? Very good prices for you. Hello! English, you speak? . . .' And so on, ad nauseam. I have to admit to finding this wily old shark more interesting than the pulpit with glorious Byzantine mosaics and richly carved cornices and capitals. An ampoule of the blood of St Pantaleone, patron of Ravello, is kept in the chapel: it liquefies on the anniversary of his martyrdom, 27 July 290. Obviously he has a bit of competition, here, from the Neapolitan San Gennaro.

On the south side of the Cathedral stands the thirteenth-century **Palazzo Rufolo**, one of the most magnificent residences on the Amalfi coast (open 9 a.m.–4 p.m.). It has an exquisite Saracen-style cloister, with delicate fern-leaf decorations. Its chambers have been inhabited by Charles II of Anjou, Robert the Wise, Pope Hadrian IV, perhaps Boccaccio and certainly Wagner, who was here inspired to write parts of *Parsifal*. The verandah commands a superb view of the jagged coast, the emerald-green of the Mediterranean.

The nearby **Villa Cimbrone** (open 9 a.m.–4 p.m.), a mansion restored by an eccentric Englishman at the end of the nineteenth century, has a magnificent garden, laid out on the most advanced point of the rocky ridge upon which Ravello lies. The drop beneath the gardens is so sheer, it may bring on a mild attack of vertigo.

Salerno and Paestum

Salerno

Taking Route 163 out of Amalfi, we come after 23 km to Salerno. With a population of 157,681, this is a major town and port – the capital of the southernmost province of Campania, in fact – and beautifully situated on the Gulf of Salerno. It is a rather sad place, Salerno: the main streets have a dusty, down-at-heel look; the blocks of flats have about them a makeshift and shabby air. The town was much devastated in the fighting of 1943 and considerably damaged, too, by a landslip in 1954. Consequently, Salerno is not in the slightest geared to tourism; it seems telling that the Tourist Office, in Piazza Amendolo (tel. [089] 22 47 44), is almost always closed. But no matter; the florists next door will give you all the information you want.

History

The shabbiness notwithstanding, I find Salerno an absolutely fascinating place. It probably derives its name from its position on the salt (*sal*) sea where the River Irnus (now the Irno) entered it. The town has a marvellous medieval quarter, its narrow streets running up against dead ends and cobblestoned courtyards. The main thoroughfare here is the **Via dei Mercanti** – the street of shopkeepers: it still preserves artisan and commercial traditions, the shops selling leather goods and bits of junk.

This medieval centre was once world-famous; it held the first university ever founded, set up in the ninth century by four 'masters', a Greek, a Jew, a Saracen and a Latin. The Medical School enjoyed its greatest period of brilliance between the eleventh and thirteenth centuries. It was once the most famous in Europe: St Thomas Aquinas mentions it as being pre-eminent in medicine, as Paris was in science and Bologna in law. Accordingly, William the Conqueror's son came here to heal a wound he had received as a Crusader in the Holy Land.

What to see

There are good reasons for spending a day or two in Salerno. It has not yet been run over by tourism. It has a stupendous cathedral, and is one of the best places in Southern Italy for the *passeggiata*, that civilised evening stroll in which everybody in a town or village participates, contentedly ambling arm-in-arm. It is also an excellent point of departure for the Greek ruins at Paestum.

The **Cathedral of St Matthew**, founded in 845 and rebuilt by Robert Guiscard between 1076 and 1085, is more interesting than anything you'll find in Sorrento. The bronze doors of the portal were made in Constantinople and, from 1079, the church has housed the remains of St Matthew, the bones brought back from Capaccio in 955. (It is strange to think that the bones of both St Matthew and St Andrew – now in Amalfi – should be within such close distance of each other.) You'll find these bones in the crypt, the entrance to which is by a curious ancient bas-relief of a boat from which men are unloading bales of hay. The saint's tooth is kept in a separate reliquary.

The beautiful Cathedral courtyard is surrounded by twenty-eight marble pillars – some Roman, some plundered from the Greek temples at Paestum. Around the walls are fourteen ancient sarcophagi, converted by the Normans into Christian sepulchres.

The interior has suffered at the hands of restorers after severe earthquake damage in 1688; but don't miss the two twelfth-century pulpits, and the paschal (Easter) candlestick. In their decorations, these show both Arabo-Sicilian and Byzantine motifs.

Behind the Duomo, on the Via S. Benedetto, is the curious **Museo Provinciale** (open 9 a.m.–1.30 p.m.), occupying two floors of the Lombard-Romanesque convent of S. Benedict. It contains some interesting local finds – a huge hippopotamus's femur, the jaw of an *elephans antiquus*, and a bronze head of Apollo from the first half of the first century BC.

Where to stay

Salerno is not particularly well served for restaurants or hotels. But you might want to stay at the **Plaza** in Piazza Ferrovia 42, tel. (089) 22 44 77. It has three stars, and pretty well all the mod cons.

But for those who don't mind a bit of healthy squalor, try the **Albergo Italia**, Corso Vittorio Emanuele 84, tel. (089) 22 66 53. This is a fairly rudimentary establishment, but there's nothing wrong with it. Some of the light bulbs could do with changing, though.

Where to eat

As far as I'm concerned, there's only one Salerno restaurant worth eating in – and it's very, very good: the **Trattoria da Sasà**, Via Diaz 42, no telephone. There are no fussy decorations, just large tables with large white tablecloths and napkins. The young and very lively owner, Salvatore, will usually insist on showing you the fish before cooking it.

The speciality here is *spaghetti alla marinaia*.

The last leg of our Campanian tour takes us to Paestum. The archaeological site lies some 40 km south of Salerno along the coastal (Route 18) road. You can take a bus to Paestum from Salerno at Piazza Concordia, down by the sea-front. There's one every hour.

Paestum

The ancient city of Paestum, whose name, like Positano, probably derives from Poseidon, was by the Greeks actually called Poseidonia. It now stands on a lonely, silent and desolate plain, with jagged mountains looming large in the background. Everywhere, the Doric temples are entangled in wild herb bushes and flowers – appropriate, perhaps, as in Roman times Paestum was famous for its violets and roses, the flowers of which were used in a lucrative scent industry. Paestum artichokes, too, are famous; in this solemn wilderness, once notorious for malaria, they now grow in abundance. The grazing buffaloes here produce the mozzarella cheese served in local restaurants. It is all very scenic. In 1883, Baedeker's guide described it: 'The temples are adorned with a luxuriant growth of ferns and acanthus, enlivened solely by the chirping grasshopper, the rustling lizard, and gliding snake.' Nothing very much has changed.

Founded by the Greeks in 600 BC, Poseidonia fell to the Romans in 273 BC; under Augustus it fell into total desuetude. It was rediscovered in the eighteenth century during the building of a coach-road.

What to see

The excavations (open 9 a.m.–4 p.m.) are entered off the main road by the **Porta della Giustizia**, next to the Ristorante Nettuno. The first ruin to appear before you is the **Basilica of Hera**, the oldest of the Doric temples, dating from 565 BC. In front of the temple is a large, rectangular, sacrificial altar, and next to it a pit into which the remains of the sacrifices were cast. Curiously, the fifty columns diminish from base to top in a curve, lending them an air of the bulbous.

The Temple of Neptune, considered by many to comprise the most beautiful Doric buildings in the world, is the third best-preserved Greek temple in Europe, after the Theseion in Greece and the Temple of Concord at Agrigento in Sicily. The view from the middle of the temple towards the sea is suitably dramatic: 'The effect of the jagged outline of the mountains through groups of enormous columns on one side, and on the other the level horizon of the sea, is inexpressibly grand,' wrote Shelley. The roof has completely vanished.

The Forum. This rather resembles a paddock or some kind of football pitch; only by a strenuous stretch of the imagination can one see how this might have been the Greek market-place. The adjoining **Temple of Ceres** is a fine example of the majestic style of Greek architecture; during the Middle Ages it was used as a Christian church.

In the splendid **Museum** (open 9 a.m.–4 p.m., closed Mondays) are sculptures, painted pots, terracottas and very early tomb paintings. Most remarkable is the cycle of paintings from the so-called **Tomb of the Diver**, perhaps the only extant examples of Greek mural painting.

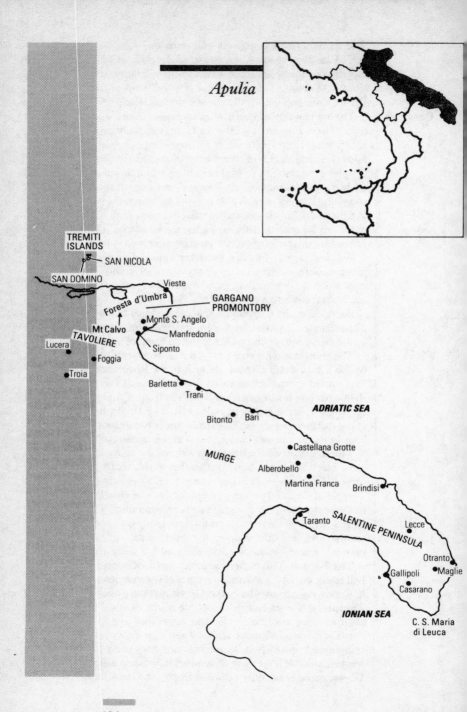

Apulia

TREMITI ISLANDS
SAN NICOLA
SAN DOMINO
Vieste
Foresta d'Umbra
GARGANO PROMONTORY
Monte S. Angelo
Mt Calvo
TAVOLIERE
Manfredonia
Siponto
Lucera
Foggia
Troia
Barletta
Trani
ADRIATIC SEA
Bitonto
Bari
MURGE
Castellana Grotte
Alberobello
Martina Franca
Brindisi
Taranto
SALENTINE PENINSULA
Lecce
Otranto
Gallipoli
Maglie
Casarano
IONIAN SEA
C. S. Maria di Leuca

Apulia

Introduction

Apulia (Puglia in Italian) is situated in the far south-east of the Italian peninsula; lying to the east of the Apennines, it forms the entire 'heel' of Italy from the northern 'spur' in the Gargano promontory to its southernmost tip in Cape S. Maria di Leuca. The region falls into four well-defined areas. The **Gargano Massif** is rugged and austere, with great craggy mountains dominated by the barren hump of Mount Calvo. Just inland is the **Tavoliere**, a vast and sometimes parched plain of wheatfields surrounded by hills, the most extensive tract of flat country in the whole of Italy. Further south comes the **Murge**, a vast plateau between the spur and the heel, consisting of a series of upland plateaus descending in terraces towards the Adriatic coast. Finally, there is the **Salentine Peninsula**, a flat area characterised by numerous outcrops of rock in the red soil.

Apulia is divided into five provinces: Foggia, Bari, Brindisi, Taranto and Lecce. All are great producers of wine; annually, they turn out some 11 million hectolitres, about one tenth of the wine consumption of the entire European Community. Often, the wine is potent. Before embarking on an exploration of Apulia, you might want to try a bottle of Malvasia di Lecce, a sparkling white wine that is powerful as well as explosive. Osbert Sitwell relates how a bottle was uncorked with 'immense noise, as of a mine being exploded, while a torrent of sparkling liquid splashed like a golden fountain over a passing lorry. It was like the launching of a battleship; the hubbub was indescribable.' An exaggeration, to be sure; but your wine will certainly effervesce.

Industry　Wine, wheat, sheep, olives, almonds and figs: such are the chief interests of the Apulian farmer. But along the coast Apulia is heavily – and many would say disastrously – industrialised. The Taranto steelworks – so advanced, they are the envy of the USA and even of the USSR – have caused serious pollution, destroying the shellfish beds from which the population used largely to earn its keep. Built in 1960, the steelworks now cover three times the surface area of Taranto city itself and are much resented by the locals. A common enough complaint is, 'But we aren't on the Ruhr. We're in Apulia.' The trouble is that the steel plants have not produced any noticeable metalworks around them, only vast areas of abandoned farmland.

Collectively, they are a perfect example of what Southern Italians mean by a 'cathedral in the desert'.

But fear not, Apulia is otherwise one of the most fascinating of all the Italian regions – for the austere beauty of its landscape, the magnificence of its churches and castles, the oriental appearance of its whitewashed towns. You could happily spend a fortnight visiting.

Architecture

It is here that you will find the celebrated architectural style 'Apulian Romanesque'; under the Norman kings and their Hohenstaufen successors this found expression in the creation of some of the most beautiful churches in all Italy. A typical Romanesque church, a fusion of styles both Oriental and French, has a broad and majestic façade, often of an extreme simplicity, with a large rose window in the centre. The sides are usually adorned with blind arcading, highlighted geometrically with strange wavy or zig-zag patterns of a distinctly Saracen or Byzantine stamp. For during the eleventh century, there were Sicilian Muslims living in Apulia.

Numerous Apulian towns are crowned with splendid castles built either during the reign of Frederick II (1197–1250) or in the time of the Angevin kings who ruled Southern Italy from Naples until the sixteenth century. One of the most famous of these castles is in the seaside town of Otranto (from the shores of which you can see the mountains of Albania) – Sir Horace Walpole used it in his Gothic chain-rattler of a novel, *The Castle of Otranto*.

Peculiar to Apulia too are its *trulli* – curious houses of a conical design, igloo-like in their brilliant coats of whitewash. The greatest concentration of *trulli* is at Alberobello, which must rank as one of the most magical places in Southern Italy.

History

Apulia's past is not so different from that of the rest of Southern Italy. The Greeks were the first to settle, founding Taras, now Taranto, at the end of the eighth century BC. It flourished under Roman rule, when the ports of Apulia (linked directly to Rome by the Via Appia, which terminated in Brindisi) became of paramount importance. The Romans laid out roads, canals and allotments on a logical grid-iron pattern – hence the name Tavoliere, which means chess board.

After the fall of the Roman Empire, Apulia was fought over by Lombards and Byzantines. In 843 the Saracens took the city of Bari. With the Norman invasion, from the first Crusade (1096) until the last (1270), Apulia began an immense trade with the Levant: goods came from Constantinople, Cairo, Alexandria, Palestine, Syria, Phoenicia and Tripoli. But with the rise of the feudal nobility, and the intervention of foreign powers in the struggles for the throne of Naples, Apulia went to the bad. Under the Spanish viceroys, in particular, it was reduced to one of the poorest regions in Italy.

Only in the period between the last wars was the problem of restoring prosperity to Apulia properly tackled. In Mussolini's day Bari was given a modern function as the main port for trade with Africa, thus restoring the city to its former days of Levantine glory. And in 1939 the great Apulian aqueduct, the largest in the world, was finally completed.

But water is in short supply in Apulia; rainfall is light and the region fully deserves the epithet which Horace gave it – *'siticulosae'*, thirsty. Apulia also gets extremely hot, and is best avoided during the dog-days of July or August. But there are 748 kilometres of coastline, and some lovely sea in which to cool off. As for accommodation, you should stay at a provincial capital or a well-known resort; elsewhere, hotels are few and far between.

Getting there

There is no international airport in Apulia (a curious fact, given the importance of the region's petrochemical and steel plants); flights from Brindisi and Bari only connect with Rome and Milan. Roads, however, are well maintained across the region. The main axis of Apulia's highway system is the Foggia–Bari–Taranto *autostrada*, which links across the Apennines to Naples. Apulia has an excellent railway network; the most famous train is the *Espresso del Levante*, which shuttles between Lecce and Milan. All the different regional centres of Apulia, the provinces and main towns, have excellent railway connections.

Foggia

This busy city (population 141,711) is the ideal place from which to explore the Tavoliere, and is conveniently located for day trips to the wonderful medieval towns of **Lucera** and **Troia**. It is reached from Naples by rail or by road on Route 90.

Foggia is not in itself wildly interesting, but there are some attractions you should not miss.

What to see

The twelfth-century **Cathedral of Santa Maria Icona Vetere**. Just off the Piazza del Lago, this is a curious hybrid of the Baroque and Norman. The somewhat overpowering campanile was erected following reconstruction after an earthquake of 1731, but the crypt and lower part of the walls are Romanesque. Aerial bombardment in 1943 revealed an interesting Pisan-style arcade along the church's lower flanks, dating from the fourteenth century. The interior of the Cathedral houses the Byzantine icon after which the church is named; it was found, they say, in 1073, by a shepherd, at the bottom of a pond.

The Civic Museum (open Monday–Friday 9 a.m.–1 p.m., Saturday 9 a.m.–12 noon; closed Sunday). Beautifully laid out, the museum has sections devoted to archaeology, science and popular traditions; the ethnographic section has some quaint-looking looms and spinning-wheels. There is a wonderful collection of stuffed birds. As you leave the museum, don't miss the curious Romanesque doorway (on the outside walls) with carved eagles from Frederick II's thirteenth-century palace.

At this point you should make a detour along the nearby Via San Eligio (it cuts through a lively marketplace) to the weird and wonderful **Church of Calvary** (1693). Today, only five of the little domed structures that arch over the path leading to the church doors survive; originally there were seven. Walking under them you were supposed to purge yourself, symbolically, of the Seven Deadly Sins. Architecturally, this is not a particularly common Baroque device, and so all the more worth a visit.

Where to stay

Foggia is short on hotels – as a city it is not geared to tourism. However, I recommend the following.

Hotel Palace Sarti, Viale XXIV Maggio 60; tel. 0881-23321. In the first category, this is likely to set you back a bit, but it is quite the best hotel in town.

Hotel Asi, Via Monfalcone 20; tel. 0881-23327. A modest hotel, reasonably priced, with a slightly old-world atmosphere.

Locanda Centrale, Corso Carioli 5; tel. 0881-71862. Highly recommended for those on a low budget. For a start, the hotel actually lives up to its name, being only a five-minute walk from the station. It is kept spotlessly clean, the old-fashioned rooms are both enormous and airy, and the owner, a rather worried-looking woman whose ancestors were Albanian horse-rustlers, will tell you all you need to know about Apulia.

Where to eat

Eating out in Foggia is frankly a disappointment. There is only one good restaurant, but it is very good: **Ristorante del Cacciatore**, Via Pietro Mascagni 12; tel. 0881-20031 (closed Sundays). You should try the delicious *tagliatelle verdi*.

Lucera

Eighteen kilometres north-west of Foggia along Route 17 lies Lucera (population 31,314). Buses leave Foggia station every ten minutes; there is no train. Perched on top of a hill overlooking the Tavoliere, this is a haunting town of dusty narrow streets, the atmosphere almost Middle Eastern; indeed, it was here that Frederick II kept 20,000 Saracen soldiers from Sicily under his surveillance. An enlightened monarch (though the Arabs sarcastically referred to him as the 'Sultan of Lucera'), he allowed his captives to build mosques and follow their own customs and trades. Sadly, none of the mosques survives, but one can well imagine their presence here, centuries ago.

What to see

The **Cathedral**, erected by Charles III of Anjou in 1305, stands on what was the site of the principal Saracen mosque. Declared a national monument in 1874, it is one of the great architectural creations of medieval Apulia. The façade (there are some dangerous-looking fissures in the intricate biscuit-brown brickwork!) is of an elegant simplicity, with two antique marble columns supporting a Gothic canopy. Walk behind the church and inspect the massive buttresses and tall lancet windows; it is all distinctly French in design, and haunts one like the great Gothic churches of Normandy. And the hundreds of sprigs of purple foxglove peeping out of the stone only enhance its majestic, forlorn air.

The interior is Lombard in design; the nave, with its soaring pointed arches, is most impressive. The frescoes and stained glass are of a graceful French Gothic. It is hard to believe that one is in Italy.

Behind the Cathedral, in Via de Nicastri, is the fascinating **Civic Museum** (open Tuesday–Friday 9 a.m.–2 p.m.; Saturday–Sunday 9 a.m.–1 p.m.). It is located in the old family home of the Baroness De Nicastri; one or two of the rooms still retain her seventeenth- and eighteenth-century furniture, and are extremely rare examples of how the Southern Italian nobility once lived. In the other rooms are prehistoric flints found in the Gargano, Roman oil-lamps, Arab teapots and some exquisite Roman mosaics.

Lying to the north-west of Lucera is an interesting **Roman amphitheatre**. Built in 27 BC, when the Roman Senate awarded Octavius the honorific title of Caesar Augustus, it was later used almost exclusively for throwing Christians *ad bestias*. It is the earliest amphitheatre known to have been dedicated to the Emperor Augustus.

A ten-minute walk from the amphitheatre will take you to the **Castle**. This mammoth construction is well named 'the Key of Apulia', both for the breathtaking views it commands of the vast and flat expanses of the Tavoliere, and because it is the largest castle in Apulia. The *enceinte* is nearly 1 km in circumference and it is topped with no fewer than twenty-four towers. This palatial fortress is almost entirely the work of Frederick II. Within its walls he indulged to the full his passion for all things Arabic; dressed in sumptuous Muslim robes and escorted by an entourage of lions, his habits became those of an Asiatic monarch.

Troia

From Lucera it is 18 km due south by Route 160 to the little town of Troia (population 8,782). If you are coming from Foggia, do not on any account take the train: Troia's station is nowhere near the town.

Perched 439 metres above sea level on a hill, this is an eerie place. In the evening the air is thick with swooping bats and swallows, and the streets are lined with old men, sitting on chairs outside shopfronts reading newspapers, not saying a word to one another. The view of the Tavoliere from up here is breathtaking, the farmland rolling away to the distant horizon flat as the baize on a billiard-table.

What to see

Troia is famed for its **Cathedral**. Founded in 1017, it is one of the most harmonious examples of the blending of Romanesque styles in Apulia – Lombard, Byzantine, Saracen and Pisan. The great rose window, of an astonishing elaboration, is surmounted by a semi-circular frieze of animals (oxen, elephants, porcupines and apes), carried by porphyry pillars resting on lions. The surface of this strange façade glows with yellow and green stones, and the fantastic bronze doors are embellished with an array of saints of Byzantine aspect. The interior, however, disappoints: there is too much Baroque.

Manfredonia and the Gargano Promontory

Driving 36 km north-east from Foggia on Route 89 you will eventually come to the sea at Manfredonia (population 45,520). Resting at the foot of the Gargano Promontory, Manfredonia is of a mean and somehow dismal aspect; much of it was destroyed by the Turks in 1620. However, it is an excellent – indeed the *only* – starting-point for excursions into the Gargano. And if you stay in Manfredonia, you can always bask on the town's excellent sandy beach, which extends for miles. Apart from the impressive **Castle**, built by King Manfred in 1256, the beach is the town's main asset.

Where to stay

As far as hotels go, there is not much to choose from.

Hotel Gargano, Viale Miramare 18; tel. 0884-27621. A three-star hotel, it overlooks the sea and is in the nicer end of town.

Albergo San Michele, Via degli Orti 10; tel. 0884-21953. One-star category and reasonably priced, it is across from the station and has pleasant rooms.

Albergo Santa Maria della Grazia, Via degli Orti 6; tel. 0884-22465. For those on a low budget: rudimentary but fine.

Where to eat

Eating in Manfredonia is poor. I suggest you try the trattoria in the **Albergo San Michele**; it is representative of most of the restaurants here – not bad, but nothing to write home about.

Monte S. Angelo

You need only stay one night in Manfredonia. One of the most exciting trips out of the place, 16 km along a winding road, is to the town of Monte S. Angelo (population 18,388). Approaching this tiny town, the scenery changes dramatically from the chess-board flatness of the Tavoliere to the jagged rockiness of the Gargano Massif. With its craggy, bleached, limestone cliffs and rocky coves and grottoes, this is one of the most ravishingly beautiful areas in Southern Italy. Tourism has arrived, but it hasn't wrecked things – yet.

What to see

The **Sanctuary of San Michele** is one of the oldest and most celebrated in Europe. At the time of the Crusades it became an obligatory stopping-point on the way to the Holy Land. If possible, try not to visit it on a Sunday; on days of worship it is so packed you will barely find room to move. I attended Mass one Sunday and *carabinieri* officers were having to fend off the excited worshippers. The sanctuary of St Michael was said to have been consecrated by the Archangel himself, who appeared to Norman knights in the eleventh century.

Another word of advice when visiting the sanctuary: do not, for heaven's sake, wear a pair of shorts – the priests will turn you away with such disdain you may not want to come back again. The words inscribed over the doorway of the sanctuary are warning enough: '*Haec est domus specialis in qua noxialis quaeque actio diluitur* (This is no ordinary house; here all sinful actions are washed away).'

The entrance to the sanctuary is by the lofty hexagonal campanile built by Charles I of Anjou in 1273. On your right is the altar of St Francis of Assisi, beneath which is a 'T' said to have been carved into the rock by the saint. A flight of eighty-six stairs (note the way the pilgrims have traced the shapes of their hands into the stone on the walls) takes us down to the **Grotta dell'Arcangelo**, the heart of this mysterious sanctuary. The vast recesses, hewn out of the rock, are dank with water, and everything here has the appearance of extreme age: spooky and dim. A 'Tourist Guide of the Shrine' puts it this way: 'The irregular rocky roof reverberates mysterious veining which in certain places, for its calcerous character, gives orgy to a constant dripping.'

Behind the main altar is a rather indifferent statuette, made from white Carara marble, of the Archangel. It is a replacement of the one that King Ferdinand I stole in 1460, melting its silver ornaments to mint commemorative coins. Behind the altar is a tiny well from which water, said to possess curative powers, is ladled in a silver stoup.

Directly opposite the entrance to the sanctuary is the **Tomba di Rotari**. Nobody knows for sure whether this is a baptistry, campanile or mausoleum. Probably the building dates from the end of the twelfth century. Above the doorway there are charming (and very crude) medieval reliefs depicting the Passion. Next door is the medieval church of **S. Maria Maggiore**, with a beautiful main doorway; to visit it, you must tip the custodian.

A short walk up the nearby Via Reale Basilica takes us to the ruins of the Norman **Castle**, begun by Robert Guiscard and continued by Frederick II. From its bastions, you are afforded a wide view of the Gargano.

One thing you might do whilst in Monte S. Angelo is make a trip to the primeval **Foresta d'Umbra** (Forest of Shade), a thickly wooded interior of beech, pine and oak where the light barely penetrates. A good place to take a picnic is by the lake and deer preserve in the middle of the forest, where the roads from Monte S. Angelo, Vieste and Vico del Gargano intersect.

Siponto

Three kilometres south-west of Manfredonia is Siponto, once a Roman colony and in Norman times an important commercial centre until malaria wiped out all the inhabitants in 1223. Little remains of this depopulated town except the remarkable **Santa Maria di Siponto**. The back of this church, standing all alone in the middle of a grove of pines amidst some small pre-Roman ruins, overlooks the not very mystical Foggia–Manfredonia railway line. But no matter; this is a beautiful twelfth-century cathedral, built above an underground church dating from the fifth century. The interior seems quite oriental, with a central white cupola upheld by four rectangular piers. On the walls are mosaic fragments found nearby in an early Christian basilica. The crypt is an extraordinary forest of sixteen stone columns with Byzantine capitals which, together, form a Greek cross.

Vieste

North of Manfredonia, the road begins to climb round the coast. Sixty kilometres along Route 89 you come to Vieste (population 11,820), a delightful fishing village where you may want to stay for a couple of days. It's the best place from which to visit the Isole Tremiti, a group of small limestone islands 22 km off the Gargano Peninsula.

Vieste boasts some of the best beaches in Apulia; the **Castle**, perched high on a summit, offers a tremendous view of the *costa garganica*; and the Baroque **Duomo** has an unusual copper weather-vane atop its spire. But Vieste is not famed for its monuments; rather, it is the atmosphere of the place that draws the crowds. Its white-washed houses, stacked along broad flights of terraced stairways, are Arabic in aspect and there is a colourful population of people selling necklaces, leather goods and shells.

Where to stay

Hotel Scialara, Lungo Mare Enrico Mattei; tel. 0884-76684. Three-star, situated very pleasantly on the sea-front.

Hotel Merinum, Lungo Mare Enrico Mattei; tel. 0884-76721. Similar to the Scialara in terms of quality and situation.

Hotel Aurora, Piazza S. Maria della Grazia; tel. 0884-78001. Some way from the sea, but as a two-star hotel perfectly all right.

Albergo Lido, Via Silvio Pellico 17; tel. 0884-76709. Down by the sea. One-star only but strongly recommended for those on a tight budget; it has airy double rooms with sinks and showers that often work.

Where to eat

La Pentola, Via Barbacane 1; tel. 0884-77539. The speciality here is fresh grilled fish; the service is good and the restaurant peaceful when the television isn't blaring.

La Teresina, Corso Cesare Battisti 55; no telephone. Delightfully situated near the town public gardens. The thing to have here is grilled sole (*sogliola*).

The Isole Tremiti

Famed throughout Italy for their natural beauty, clear waters and mild climate, the islands can be reached only from Vieste between July and September, during the peak tourist season. It is best to book a boat or hydrofoil at Gargano Viaggi, Piazza Roma 7; tel. 0884-78501. You could quite happily spend a day on the islands; accordingly, boats generally leave Vieste at 9.30 a.m. and return at 6 p.m.

In classical mythology these islands are the *Insulae Diomediae*, on which the companions of Diomedes were metamorphosed into herons. Today, some of the elderly inhabitants of the islands still speak the Neapolitan dialect, since they are descended from those Neapolitans whom, for various reasons, Ferdinand II had exiled there.

San Nicola

All boats deposit you at the port of San Nicola, one of the three main islands. Most interesting here is the **Church of Santa Maria a Mare**, founded in 1045 and successively rebuilt throughout the fif-teenth, seventeenth and eighteenth centuries. The monastery has a sorry history: fortified by Charles II of Anjou, in the fourteenth cen-tury it was invaded by pirates who slaughtered all the monks; in 1567 the monastery, now a sort of fortress, barely managed to fend off an assault from Soliman II; and in 1783, Ferdinand I of Naples completely suppressed the place.

San Domino   The largest of the Tremitis, San Domino is accessible by boat from San Nicola. Its broken coastline has spectacularly beautiful bays and inlets, with grottoes to rank with those on the island of Capri. San Domino was the scene of the death of Julia, granddaughter of Augustus.

Barletta   Sixty-three kilometres east of Foggia on Route 16 (about halfway to Bari) lies the town of Barletta (population 75,728). This is a dusty and ramshackle place, though its obvious indifference to the financial benefits to be accrued from tourism gives it a charm of its own. It is full of reminders of the Crusades, of Richard the Lionheart and, of course, of Frederick II.

What to see   The most famous monument here is the enormous **Colosso**. You will find this fifth-century bronze statue of the Byzantine Emperor Valentine at the junction of the Corso Vittorio Emanuele with the Corso Garibaldi. Over 5 metres tall, it is probably more than 1,500 years old. Aesthetically, the statue is extremely crude; but the Emperor, holding aloft in his right hand a cross, has a majestical power which is quite overpowering.

The colossus stands outside the twelfth-century **San Sepolcro**, a good Romanesque church more interesting for its interior, which is built in the Burgundian Gothic style with cross-vaults on the aisle-ceilings. By the altar there is a lovely sixteenth-century Byzantine-style Madonna with a tender, almost sensual expression.

A right turn from Corso Garibaldi takes you to the old town: a maze of winding streets. You will eventually come to the Cathedral, a curious hybrid of architectural styles: the main portal is sixteenth century, though the rest of the church dates from the twelfth century. It was enlarged and added to in the fifteenth century.

Above the left-hand doorway is a eulogy in medieval Latin to the church's royal donor, Richard the Lionheart of England. But it cuts a sad spectacle, Barletta's Cathedral: for ten years it has been under so-called restoration, hence the birds that wheel about the belfry, the smashed windows, the graffiti. No one seems to know when the church will open to the public. And the same applies to the massive thirteenth-century **Castle** across the way, which has been under restoration for no less than eighteen years.

At the intersection of Via Cavour and Corso Garibaldi, we come to the wonderful **Museo e Pinacoteca Comunali** (City Museum and Art Gallery); open Tuesday–Sunday 9 a.m.–1 p.m. The treasures here are housed in a run-down Dominican convent, and why they cannot be moved to the empty and abandoned castle is a mystery. Still, there is a marvellous bust here of the Holy Roman Emperor Frederick II (the only known likeness), made in around 1194 but now missing the nose. There is a good deal of bric-a-brac (most of it covered in dust and tagged with yellowing labels) to do with the Risorgimento, but best of all is the gallery dedicated to De Nittis, one of the greatest of Italian painters from the 1800s. De Nittis was born in Barletta and studied in Paris (where he died at the age of thirty-eight) and London, where his work came under the 'Japanese influence' so popular with Impressionists of the time. All these wonderful pictures – delicate oils and watercolours of clouds, chrysanthemums and cats, of *haut bourgeois* society ladies, and of Westminster Bridge in the smog – have been donated to this sad and dilapidated museum by De Nittis's widow. I strongly recommend a visit.

On the last Sunday in July, one of Apulia's most colourful pageants takes place in Barletta: the **Disfida**, which re-enacts a battle of 1503 between fifteen French and thirteen Italian knights. If you miss the fun, visit the **Cantina della Disfida** (open Tuesday–Saturday 9 a.m.–1 p.m., 4–6 p.m.; Sunday 8 a.m.–1 p.m.), a dungeon-like museum with puddles of water seemingly everywhere. The exhibits are of pots, pans, furniture, flags and pageant-like drapes from the epoch.

Trani

Thirteen kilometres beyond Barletta lies the little circular port of Trani (population 40,700), constructed by the Venetians in the fourteenth century. It is certainly picturesque: the blue and white fishing boats bob at their moorings; the elegant eighteenth-century palaces fan out in a crescent along the water's edge; the street lamps are made of wrought iron; in the tumbledown artisans' shops there is much mending of fishing-nets and, not so nice, manufacturing of coffins.

What to see

Trani is a spacious town, full of light. The nearby **Villa Comunale**, laid out on what were in the Middle Ages the walls and fortifications guarding the port, is itself a delight, the best place from which to see the eleventh-century **Cathedral** perched in a dramatic position on a spur of land jutting out into the sea. From this vantage point the church actually looks as though it is rising out of the sea. The patron saint of this church is Nicholas the Pilgrim, an idiot boy who spoke only two words – *'Kyrie Eleison'*.

The façade, made of dazzling white stone, is of the utmost simplicity and elegance; this is one of the most majestic churches you are likely to find in Apulia. The rose window is surrounded by six animals on projecting consoles; the central of the three simple Romanesque windows below is flanked, surrealistically, by toy elephants. The tall Lombard campanile is one of the most perfect in Apulia; the twelfth-century bronze doors, adorned with figures of Christ and the Apostles, are by the same Barisano of Trani who designed the extraordinary bronze doors of the Cathedral at Ravello (there is a relief of St George slaying the dragon in the panel at the bottom of the left-hand side).

The impressive interior has been religiously restored to its pristine

Romanesque design; the walls are of such a dazzling brilliance that they look as if they have been scrubbed white with pumice stone. The interior is all the more impressive because bare of ornament – there is nothing but an enormous purity of volume, space and light. By the main altar are fragments of twelfth-century Christian mosaics depicting Adam and Eve, and a serpent curled in an 'S' around the Tree of Knowledge; and a creature half-man, half-horse, blowing a trumpet.

From the crypt, you descend into the cavernous depths of the **Church of Santa Maria**, full of Gothic tombs and Lombard sarcophagi. It also contains the damp, cobwebbed and rather smelly Hypogeum of St Leucio, built to house the relics of the saint. Until recently, mounds of skulls were kept here. It is certainly not the sort of place in which I would care to stay the night.

Adjacent to the Cathedral lies the Via Ognissanti, which runs through the medieval heart of Trani. There is still an air of the antique about this street, lined as it is with small furniture-restorers' workshops. (It is worth remembering that under Frederick II a large and prosperous Jewish community thrived in Trani; mostly, it was engaged in the manufacture of silk. Numerous street names in Trani's medieval quarter recall it: Via La Giudea, Via Sinagoga, Via Mose di Trani.) Halfway down the Via Ognissanti we come to the **Ognissanti** itself, a twelfth-century chapel once part of a hospital used by the Crusaders.

Bari

History   'Fish-famous Barium' is what Horace called this city: the epithet still holds good. For Bari has always had strong links with the eastern Mediterranean and in its bustling *trattorie* you are likely to eat the finest fish that ever flounced in nets. Since 1930 Bari has every September hosted the Fiera del Levante, an important fair for the exchange of goods between European markets and those of the Near or Far East. Little, it seems, has changed: Bari was an important commercial centre under the Roman Empire and was in the eleventh century Italy's most important Adriatic port, rivalling even Venice in terms of trade.

Today, this bustling city (population 357,274) has earned itself the nickname 'il Milano del Mezzogiorno', the Milan of the South. Bari is indeed the only city in Southern Italy where people actually look as though they are getting on with things.

Bari is an important centre of religious worship, and has been so ever since 1087, when a ship berthed at the port bearing the remains of St Nicholas, Bishop of Myra in Asia Minor. The body had been stolen by sixty-two (no less) Bari sailors. With pious pomp and circumstance the saint was buried two years afterwards in the crypt of the present Church of S. Nicola, where it lies today.

St Nicholas is the patron saint of children, sailors and Orthodox Russia. He is also the original Father Christmas – a title awarded him after he saved three girls from becoming prostitutes by throwing alms in at their window. Or so the legend has it. Another story relates that the saint had resurrected three children who had been cut up by a butcher and stoppered in a bottle of brine.

Today, Bari is made of two quite distinct cities: the modern quarter, broadly laid out to a chess-board plan with wide thoroughfares and straight avenues, of which the Via Sparano is the widest and the most chic; and the Old Town, which stands a world to itself on a peninsula, criss-crossed with an intricate cat's-cradle of winding streets and tumbledown dwellings – an Oriental city in miniature.

The *Citta Nuova*, New Town, resembles the newer sections of any other progressive Italian city, though it contains some wonderful turn-of-the-century cafés and Art-Nouveau department stores. But the Bari which will interest you the most is the *Citta Vecchia*. When visiting, do hang on to your wallet or handbag: if either is snatched, you will not have the remotest hope of catching the thief – the streets so resemble a rabbit warren, you will only end up, should you decide to give chase, in a blind alley. The invading Saracens discovered this soon enough when they were lured into dead-ends and attacked from the roof-tops above.

What to see
The Castle

First on the list of monuments to visit in the Old Town is the Castle, dominating the Piazza Federico di Svevia down by the sea-front. Built between 1233 and 1240 by Frederick II, its massy ramparts and angular keeps, their corner angles sharp as a knife, nevertheless date from the sixteenth century. A bridge over the moat (now a municipal garden with benches and flower-beds) leads to a courtyard separating the outer walls from Frederick's original fortress, a castle within a castle. From here a Saracen archway richly carved with plants takes us into the medieval heart of the castle – a simple courtyard pretty well bare of ornament, apart from four solitary palm trees.

On the west side of this courtyard is a delightful **Museum** (the Gipsoteca) containing plaster-cast reproductions of sculptural and architectural ornaments from Romanesque churches in Apulia. It is worth inspecting the reproduction gargoyles here, since the originals are often perched on top of churches out of eye-sight.

The Duomo

Opposite the castle stands the Cathedral. Begun in 1170 to replace the Byzantine structure demolished by William the Bad in 1156, this is one of the most noteworthy medieval churches in Apulia. Its austere façade is Romanesque in spirit, though mouldings with grotesques and a frieze of Byzantine inspiration outline the roof. The rose window is a modern replica.

A solemn and austere beauty marks the interior; the clean lines of the nave perfectly complement the dark and sombre timber roof, a pre-Gothic construction. The nave contains remains of a fourteenth-century marble pavement with a rose design that geometrically reflects the design of the rose window itself.

Down in the crypt, not very tastefully Baroqued in the eighteenth century, hangs a much venerated (and much repainted) Byzantine icon of the Madonna. She has an unusually dark complexion and the curator will tell you that, since the icon is *indisputably* the work of St Luke, this is unquestionably how the Virgin must have looked.

Ask the curator to show you the recent excavations below the church, which have brought to light an early Christian basilica dating from the ninth century. The remains present a picture of cavernous gloom; there is even a tiny cemetery for unbaptised babies. If you have time, ask to see the beautiful eleventh-century *Exultet* roll on parchment, kept in the Curia across the road from the church. The script, which was once unfurled in front of the kneeling faithful, is decorated with Byzantine illuminations.

S. Nicola | Behind the Duomo we take the Via del Carmine down to the **Church of S. Nicola**. (On Sundays, the surrounding streets are full of families grilling fish in the open; the aroma of fried sole will certainly bring on an appetite.) This church – the first of the great Norman churches in Southern Italy – is a medley of the styles so typical of Apulian art: Byzantine, Lombard and Saracen. The façade, said to resemble the churches of St Nicholas and St Stephen in the Norman city of Caen, is of an almost military austerity: indeed, the tower on the right (like the one on the left, unfinished) comes from a Byzantine fortress originally on the site. The steep gables on the central part of this grim, Lombardian façade point upwards to form a sharp triangle, bringing to mind the shape of a bishop's mitre – just about all, on the face of it, that's faintly ecclesiastical about this church. Note the miniature sphinxes above the main portal, the beasts on jutting corbels, the monstrous allegorical symbols. Two magnificently stylised, though sadly worn, bulls support the columns on either side. Before entering, you should not miss the wonderful **Porta dei Leoni** on the north side of the church: the door is decorated with scenes of chivalry, the knights on horseback suggesting French origins.

The **interior** is arranged with Lombard simplicity on the Latin cross plan. The austerity is badly marred, though, by the nightmare Baroque ceiling of fretted gold: the ornamental tastes of the seventeenth century clash violently with the bare and conventual solemnity of the Norman design. Still, the nesting birds seem to like it up there – watch out for droppings. As you enter, it is worth gazing upwards to see how the second transversal arch is severely stilted, fanning abnormally outwards: the distortion is the result of a fifteenth-century earthquake.

In the apse stands what is perhaps the masterpiece of Apulian

sculpture, the magnificent episcopal throne. The little men at the feet
– quite overwhelmed, it seems, by the weight of the marble – symbolise, in the traditional medieval iconography, the wickedness of the
world and the eternal struggle between the flesh and the spirit before
the Last Judgement.

The **crypt**, with windows of translucent marble and twenty-eight
stone columns, is where we find the bones of St Nicholas. They are
kept in the altar, and you are bound to find black-clad women here,
muttering their prayers to the hallowed remains, for the bones are said
to exude a sort of manna, a 'healing oil'. It is probably only the product
of condensation; crypts are clammy places.

The **treasury** is well worth a visit; ask the young Dominican
Father, Padre Giovanni, to unlock the doors, and untold treasures
await you. Foremost among them is the crown of King Roger the Norman of Sicily, whose coronation took place here in 1131. There are
pieces of rotten wood that formed the urn in which St Nicholas's
bones were reputedly contained, and numerous objects to do with
Russian Orthodoxy, many of them brought over to Bari by the last
Czar Romanov, Nicholas II himself. The Russian connection is of
vital importance. The cult of St Nicholas has always united Catholic
and Orthodox believers, and the modern chapel in this church, dating
from 1966, is the only place in the world where, for the first time in
history since the 1054 schism of the two churches, the Orthodox lit-
urgy may be heard within the walls of a Catholic place of worship.

Padre Giovanni, a charming fellow with a wry sense of humour,
will no doubt be keen to tell you of the Prince of Wales's visit to the
church in 1985, when he was feverishly kissed by a Bari fishwife, and
of the choir from Jesus College, Cambridge, that came here in 1987 to
perform Benjamin Britten's *Saint Nicholas*, a cantata for children.

From the Church of St Nicholas, you can make an interesting
excursion through the cramped and dusty streets of the Old Town.
Turn into Piazzetta Sessantadue Marinai, named after the sixty-two
sailors who stole the remains of the saint. From here, after you have
passed under an arch, walk down the Strada Martinez. At the end of
this street, on your immediate right, is a pagan temple. Only eight columns stand but, with a touching devotion, the local population have
turned the temple into an open-air church, the **Santa Maria del
Popolo**. Plants and other votive offerings have been placed at a tiny
image of the Virgin and the place is an altogether perfect example of
the curious fusion of pagan and Christian which one so often finds in
Southern Italy.

The harbour

From here it is but a short walk to the Molo San Nicola, a small fishing harbour where you can watch boys smashing squid against the
rocks.

*Palazzo della
Provincia*

The rather ugly grey and white building in the distance (the one
with a tall clock tower) is the Palazzo della Provincia, which houses

the **Pinacoteca Provinciale** (open Tuesday–Saturday 10 a.m.–1 p.m., 4–7 p.m.; Sunday 8.30 a.m.–12.30 p.m.). Containing paintings by Vivarini, Veronese and Tintoretto, and landscapes by Poussin, Corot and Salvatore Rosa, the gallery is certainly worth a visit.

The exhibits are arranged in terrible taste – indifferent twentieth-century abstracts hanging side-by-side with medieval paintings of the Virgin – but you should look out for Giovanni Bellini's picture *San Pietro Martire*, which shows the saint with a dagger through his head and a sword through his heart, though for all that he doesn't seem to bat an eyelid. There are some wonderful paintings by the Bari-born Francesco Netti, Italy's most illustrious Impressionist.

What to do   Bari ranks with Naples as a cultural centre of Southern Italy. The two-month opera season starts at the **Teatro Petruzelli** (Corso Cavour; tel. 080-218132) in January. The opera house is anyway worth seeing out of season, as it is considered the best in Italy after the Scala of Milan and the San Carlo of Naples. There is a concert season at the **Teatro Piccinni** (Corso Vittorio Emanuele; tel. 080-213717) and all performances are listed in the monthly tourist brochure *Eccobari*, available from the **Tourist Office** in Corso Vittorio Emanuele 66; tel. 080-219951.

If you are lucky enough to be in Bari on 8 May, you should not miss the annual festivities in honour of St Nicholas. A procession of boats leaves from the Molo San Nicola and sets out to sea, where a great icon of the saint receives homage from the people of Bari.

Bari is excellent for shopping – all the best shops are on the Via Sparano. You should pay a visit to the extraordinary **Mincuzzi** department store, a flamboyant though rather faded Art Nouveau affair – a still point in a changing world if ever there was.

Where to stay   **Grand'Hotel & Oriente**, Corso Cavour 32; tel. 080-544422. All
Top range   rooms (of which there are 175) with televisions, baths and telephones, but the style of the place is 'Liberty', Italian Art Nouveau, so called after the London department store of the same name. It has a distinctly old-world elegance.

Grand'Hotel Leon d'Oro, Piazza Moro 4; tel. 080-235040. Fits the same description as the above, though not so soignée.

Mid range   **Hotel Plaza**, Piazza L. di Savoia 15; tel. 080-54007. Modern, clean and bang in the centre. Has 40 rooms.

Hotel Victor, Via Nicolai 71; tel. 080-216600. Good service, though slightly bland. Has 65 rooms.

Windsor Residence, Parallela M. Amoruso 62–7; tel. 080-510011. Self-consciously Art Deco in design, but otherwise clean and comfortable.

Bottom range   **Hotel del Corso**, Corso Vittorio Emanuele 30; tel. 080-216100. Clean, simple and unpretentious, though 5,000 lire for a shower does seem a little excessive. And the management are likely to take violent exception (as I found out to my detriment) to anyone choosing to wash clothes in his or her hotel room. But otherwise this is one of the most reasonably priced hotels in Bari. Also, it's very central – a five-minute walk from the Old Town.

Pensione Romeo, Via Crisanzio 12; tel. 080-237263. Friendly; most rooms have baths.

Where to eat **Alla Vecchia Bari**, Via Dante Alighieri 47; tel. 080-216496. The best restaurant in Bari, excellent for all Apulian fare. Decorations are unpretentious, and the service formal.

Al Pescatore, Piazza Federico II di Savoia 6; tel. 080-237033. The best fish in town. You can sit outside and admire the view of Bari's castle, just across the road.

Taverna Verde, Largo Adua 19; tel. 080-540309. Situated on the Lungo Mare near the Molo San Nicola, this is extremely popular with the locals. Tables spill out on to the piazza; book early.

Stoppani, Via Roberto di Bari 79; tel. 080-5213563. One of the most famous Art Nouveau cafés in Southern Italy, this is the ideal place to limber up with a drink before visiting any of the above restaurants. They also make their own, very expensive, chocolates.

Bitonto If you have not already had your surfeit of Apulian Romanesque architecture, you should make a short trip (18 km on Route 98) to the small town of Bitonto. If you are without a car, take the hourly train from Bari's Stazione Ferrovia Nord, next to the main train station. The Bitonto **Cathedral** is blackened with age and sprouting vegetation but is nevertheless, with its mellow golden stones, one of the most beautiful churches in Southern Italy. Built in 1200, the façade, enlivened by sculptured lions and griffins, has a superb carved portal. The lofty interior boasts a fine pulpit dating from 1229, with an interesting relief panel thought to show Frederick II with one of his wives and his two sons.

Brindisi Leaving Bari on the coastal Route 16, we eventually come after 155 km to Brindisi (population 81,893). I shouldn't stay the night here; the place is bound to disappoint, teeming as it is with back-packers about to take the ferry to nearby Greece. Sleazy restaurants with names like 'Trattoria Acropolis' do not help matters.

What to see Still, with a couple of hours to spare, you should try at least to see some of the following.

The **terminal columns of the Via Appia Antica**. These stand – peculiar anachronisms in modern-day Brindisi – at the top of a long flight of steps down by the sea at Lungo Mare Regina Margherita. One is complete, the other collapsed in 1526 and half of it was removed to Lecce, where it now supports the bronze statue of that city's patron S. Oronzo. But where is the Appian Way, the famous Roman road which these columns mark the end of? You'll find it – straight as a ruler – by the nearby Trattoria Le Colonne. A notice by one of the columns, affixed to the wall of a house, tells us that this is where Virgil died, 21 September 19 BC, on his return from Greece.

The Archaeological Museum in Piazza Duomo (open Monday–Saturday 9 a.m.–1 p.m.). This is quite fun. There's a colossal bronze foot; there are Roman anchors dredged up from the sea nearby; there's an impressive marble bust of the Emperor Trajan, and numerous cinerary urns with Latin inscriptions. The Duomo next door is not worth visiting.

On your right-hand side as you come out of the Museum are the Gothic arches of the **Portico dei Cavalieri Templari**, the Gate of the Knights Templar. Brindisi was an important Crusader port.

Walking up the nearby Via Giovanni Tarantini, we come to the **Church of San Giovanni al Sepolcro**, a circular construction erected by the Crusaders on their return from the Holy Land. The portal is flanked by two incredibly worn Romanesque lions. The church has great charm, though I'm not sure how long it will be before it collapses: it looks as if it has been badly knocked sideways.

Lecce

Continuing along the coastal Route 16, after 35 km we come to Lecce (population 83,050). After the stout Norman castles and restrained Romanesque churches you have so far seen, Lecce will come as a surprise. It is a city of Baroque – of a Baroque run wild under the influence of the Spanish court, its viceroys and clergymen. Indeed, during the seventeenth century, Lecce had as many monks and nuns as it had laymen, which is why this is a city primarily of churches. But Lecce is also a city of palaces and piazzas; balconies are adorned with grinning caryatids or festooned with foliage; cornices swirl round columns; Baroque window frames are laden with great swags of flowers; and doorways are upheld by stone trophies and heraldic crests.

This explosion of all things ornamental largely occurred in Lecce between 1660 and 1720, more or less coincident with the activities of Sir Christopher Wren in England. The colour of the local stone (*'Pietra di Lecce'*) is a warm golden brown and it is so malleable you can virtually cut it with a knife – nothing was too intricate or decorative that it could not be fashioned out of this stone. It would have been impossible to produce the Lecce Baroque out of marble. The whole of this town is a monument to the mason's art – it is an enormous fruit bowl.

Oddly, Lecce was not discovered by foreigners until a British architect, Martin Briggs, stumbled upon its delights in 1902. He wrote a book about Lecce called, appropriately enough, *An Unknown City*. It is still fairly off the beaten track; indeed, Lecce must be the only Southern Italian city never to have put Garibaldi up for the night. But many a newcomer has fallen in love with this Florence of the Italian South.

It is the perfect place from which to explore the Salentine Peninsula. If you have the time, put up for at least a couple of nights here.

What to see

We start our tour of Lecce in **Piazza Sant'Oronzo**, once the city's ancient marketplace and civic square. This is dominated by a huge bronze statue of the patron saint, Oronzo, perched atop an ancient Roman column from Brindisi. The **Tourist Office** (tel. 0832-24443) is worth mentioning here, as it is housed in the middle of the square in Lecce's elegant sixteenth-century former town hall, or *sedile*. Adjoining this on the right-hand side is the charming **Chapel of San Marco**, the lion of St Mark (symbol of Venice) hung in a lunette over the doorway as testament to the large colony of Venetian merchants who traded with Lecce in the sixteenth century.

Roman amphitheatre

Lying in the same square, below ground level, are the remains of a Roman amphitheatre (the entrance is by the Bank of Italy). Built in the first century BC and excavated only in 1938, it is most interesting for its depictions of gladiatorial contests chiselled into the slabs of stone that now line the entrance to the arena proper – gladiators fending off lions with spears; gladiators gored by bulls.

Santa Croce

North of the square, a narrow street takes us to the Church of Santa Croce, the supreme expression of the Lecce Baroque. It took 150 years to build, and the façade positively *pullulates* with detail: fantastic monsters, human-shaped caryatids around the great rose window of wedding-cake fanciness, smiling little angels that flit to and fro along the front of the huge balcony.

Antonio Zimbalo (nicknamed '*Zingarello*', Gypsy) was responsible for the upper and more opulent half of the church. Though his efforts were firmly rooted in Renaissance Classicism, he was without doubt Lecce's most extravagant architect. Much of the city as it stands today is the product of his design.

The **interior** is surprisingly simple, with two rows of unfussy Corinthian columns supporting the plain, unlavish walls.

To the left of Santa Croce stands the impressive **Palazzo del Governo**, once a monastery. The façade is far less elaborate than that of the adjoining church. This time, Zimbalo designed the lower half.

The Duomo

We now make our way down Via Vittorio Emanuele to the Piazza del Duomo, the administrative centre of Baroque Lecce. This is a rare example of a completely closed square in Italy; there is nothing quite like it, perhaps, in Europe. The Cathedral in front of you, rebuilt between 1659 and 1670 by Zimbalo, is an example of how even the decorations in Lecce have themselves been decorated; consequently, it lacks both grace and solemnity. No doubt the decorative overloading was there to lure poor folk into the church. The interior dates mostly from the eighteenth century and is uninteresting. The bell-tower, a great exclamation mark of a building, is also the work of Zimbalo; it is 68 metres tall.

The Seminary

To the right of the Cathedral is the magnificent Seminary built between 1694 and 1709, designed by Giuseppe Cino, a student of Zimbalo. The decorations around the windows swirl like icing on a cake, but enter the spacious courtyard and you have the perfect example of Lecce Baroque at its most mad: a seventeenth-century **well**. From afar, the decorations on this are so detailed that it looks as if it might be sprouting giant clumps of broccoli. Go closer, though, and you will see that the stone pomegranates have actually been split open to reveal the seeds inside.

Next to the Seminary is the **Palazzo Vescovile**: at one time, its ground floor was occupied by shops, hence the open porticos, and the arcaded front.

The Rosario

A walk down Via G. Libertini takes you past the Church of Santa Teresa and the Church of Sant'Anna to the weird and wonderful Church of the Rosario, Zimbalo's last work. Note the stone vases of fruit and flowers, the giant acorn-like objects, and the carved peacocks that peck at melon, pear and fig. The whole church is a riot of birds and flora. Today, the cloisters have been taken over by a tobacco company – appropriate, when one thinks that the monks here used to make a famous snuff, the *'polvere Leccese'* (Lecce dust) which Napoleon used from the beginning of his career until his last days on St Helena.

Museums

On Viale Gallipoli towards the station stands the excellent **Museo Provinciale** (open Monday–Friday 9 a.m.–1.30 p.m., 3.30–7.30 p.m.; Sundays and holidays 9.30 a.m.–1 p.m.). In this beautifully laid out museum you will find Bronze Age belts and buckles, terracotta children's toys, Roman coins and Attic vases. Upstairs on the third floor is a wonderful thirteenth-century gospel cover inlaid with gold and blue-and-white enamel.

Interesting, too, is the **Missionary Museum of Chinese Artefacts**, Via Monte S. Michele 1 (open Monday, Thursday and Saturday 9 a.m.–12.30 p.m., 4–7 p.m.). A must for any Sinophile, this contains twelfth-century Chinese coins, a Buddhist altar, a bronze statuette of Kublai Khan, and tools, amulets and weapons from the 'aboriginal peoples of Formosa'. There is also a fascinating Natural History and Marine Fauna section, with over 200 specimens of crustaceans and some 250 stuffed birds.

Where to stay

Grand Hotel, Viale Quarta 28; tel. 0832-29405. My favourite hotel in Lecce: near the station (but a good ten minutes' walk from the Baroque centre), this is a faded Edwardian establishment. Once a private house, it was opened as a hotel in 1930. It has 73 rooms, most of them quite spartan. Three-star, but not at all expensive.

Patria Touring, Piazza G. Riccardi 13; tel. 0832-29431. Three-star, plumb in the middle of the historical centre. The 92 rooms are inside a converted eighteenth-century *palazzo*.

Risorgimento, Via Augusto Imperatore 19; tel. 0832-42125. Three-star and strongly recommended by the Lecce Tourist Office; it has 107 rooms.

Soggiorno Faggiano, Via Cavour 4; tel. 0832-42854. A pretty ramshackle affair, for those on a low budget. Central, near the post office.

Where to eat

Gambrino, Piazza G. Riccardi 13; tel. 0832-29481. Situated inside the Hotel Patria, this is my favourite Lecce restaurant. It has good traditional cooking, unfussy though elegant decorations, formal service and enormous white napkins. It is very reasonably priced.

Gamboro Rosso, Via M. Brancaccio 16; tel. 0832-41569. A *trattoria* with first-class local cuisine, cheap and always popular with the locals.

Gallipoli

Among your trips from Lecce to the Salentine Peninsula, you might include the city of Gallipoli (population 17,114), 50 km across the peninsula on a minor road to the other side of the Apulian coast. If you have no car, you must go by chuff-chuff train (incredibly slow) from Lecce.

Named from the Greek *Kallipolis*, 'beautiful city', Gallipoli does indeed have a distinct air of the Greek, with its low, whitewashed, flat-roofed houses, and with shops everywhere full of olive oil, still one of the town's principal trading commodities. Prior to the First World War, Gallipoli exported vast quantities of oil to Russia, for use in icon lamps.

What to see

Gallipoli is pretty, but there is not a great deal to see. The fifteenth-century **Duomo** will disappoint after Lecce, but it contains many excellent paintings by local artists. The fourteenth-century **Castello**, a circular bastion jutting out into the water, was where rebel barons held out against Charles of Anjou for seven months; and it was sufficiently strong, too, to resist bombardments by the English and Bourbon fleets in 1809.

But best of all in Gallipoli is the totally eccentric **Museo Civico** (open 8.30 a.m.–1 p.m., 4–6 p.m.; closed Wednesday and Saturday afternoons). Inside, this resembles some great eighteenth-century lumber-room piled high with strange junk – the enormous vertebrae of a whale; Peruvian and Albanian banknotes; cannonballs; two unexploded sea-mines; the *'dente incisivo di ippopotamo'*, incisor teeth of a hippopotamus; eighteenth-century frock coats and silk and velvet waistcoats, all badly smelling of camphor.

Casarano

From Gallipoli you absolutely must make the 15 km journey inland to the tiny town of Casarano, birthplace of Pope Boniface IX, who reigned 1339–1404. The minuscule **Church of Casaranello** is one of the strangest and most beautiful you are likely to come across in Southern Italy, containing the only known early Christian mosaics in Apulia. The mosaics occupy the vault of the chancel and the cupola: in the former are geometric designs with animals and in the latter is an intricate design of the night sky, the dome dotted with stars rather as in the inside of an Egyptian tomb. The mosaics are wonderfully fresh – blues, sea-greens and bright blood-reds. The Byzantine icon of the

Madonnna, on the second arch to the left of the aisle as you enter, is quite without compare elsewhere in Italy – its iconic equivalent was once only to be found in the Church of Santa Sophia in Constantinople. There is a delightfully crude depiction of the Last Supper, with Judas the only disciple minus a halo.

Otranto

This beautiful fishing town and resort (population 4,151) was once the capital of Byzantine territory in Apulia. It is 55 km south of Lecce on Route 611. If you are going by train, you have to change at the dreary manufacturing town of Maglie.

What to see

The **Duomo**, founded by the Normans in 1080, has a very fine basilican interior with a beautiful mosaic pavement, the entire work tessellated by a single priest in about 1165. It consists of a long Tree of Life, extending the whole length of the nave, with intertwining branches full of birds, animals and fish. It is all very allegorical; the design extremely primitive but always simple and brightly coloured. A chapel to the right of the main altar looks quite pretty from afar, until you realise that it contains numerous skulls of those 800 inhabitants of Otranto slaughtered by the Turks in 1480. There was a time when arrows protruded from not a few of the eye-sockets.

The 800 martyrs are commemorated by the **Church of San Francesco**, which stands on the outskirts of the city on top of a hill. The church was built in 1614 in honour of Francesco, a Calabrian priest who had repeatedly prophesied the Turkish invasion: 'O Otranto, unhappy city, how many corpses I see lying in your streets; how much Christian blood I see you drowned in.' His visions were not heeded; three months later, the terrible day came. A large sixteenth-century painting in this church shows the gruesome executions, a *pasha* sitting calmly on top of an Ottoman cushion whilst his men systematically slice off the heads of the faithful with their scimitars.

From the church it is a short distance to the **Grotto Zinzulusa**, the most interesting marine cave in Apulia, full of stalactites and stalagmites.

Otranto's **Castle** was built by Ferdinand of Aragon in 1485–98 to resist any further invasions by the Turks. It was the subject of Horace Walpole's famous 'goblin tale which thrilled so many a bosom', as Sir Walter Scott called *The Castle of Otranto*. But there is nothing remotely Gothic about the castle, with its great round towers.

From the castle it is a short walk along the Via San Petro to the minuscule **Byzantine church** of the same name. This was Otranto's first cathedral, built in the tenth century; amazingly, it survived the ravages of the invading Turks. There are some wonderful mosaics on the walls. This is the hidden jewel of Otranto – most tourists do not bother to visit it.

Travelling to the very tip of Italy's heel will prove a waste of time – the sanctuary on top of the Cape of Santa Maria di Leuca is uninteresting.

Taranto

Lying at the northern extremity of the gulf that bears its name, Taranto (population 227,242) can be reached either from Lecce (86 km along Route 7) or from Brindisi (68 km along Route 7). If you are travelling by train, Taranto is connected only with the Naples–Brindisi line.

Taranto is the best place from which to explore the Murge of Apulia and the peculiar whitewashed *trulli* that characterise so much of the area. Three days there would more than suffice, but it is a great and fascinating city – you may want to spend longer.

History

Legend tells us that the origins of Taranto date to 1,200 years before the founding of Rome, when Tiras (or Taras), son of Neptune, was brought by dolphin to the site of the present city, at what is today the mouth of the River Tara. Hence the modern name Taranto. In all likelihood, the name does not, as some scholars have maintained, derive from the species of large spider (*Lycosa tarantula*) whose bite induces a contagious hysteria of melancholy madness which was apparently prevalent in Southern Apulia. The city may, however, have *given* its name to the noisome creature, which in turn gave its name to the *tarantella*, a traditional dance of the region.

But there is no accounting for myth, and we can at least be certain that the real founders of Taranto were emigrants from Sparta in 701 BC, and that the prosperity of their new-found colony came from its strategic position on the Ionian Sea, and from the plentiful supply of fish. Taranto was long one of the most important cities in Magna Graecia; the sophisticated elegance of Greek Tarentine life can today be gauged by the exhibits in Taranto's splendid Museo Nazionale.

In 272 BC the city fell into the hands of the Romans. With the decline of the Roman Empire in the west, Taranto went rapidly downhill: in 967 the Saracens razed the entire city to the ground. From the ruins rose what is now the Old Town, a Byzantine village that passed from the Normans to the Swabians, and from the Swabians to the Angevins.

During the Napoleonic Wars, Taranto's strategic position against the English Mediterranean fleet was realised by the French; in 1801 they set about fortifying it. One of the military engineers, an artillery officer, was Choderlos de Laclos, author of that steamy book *Les Liaisons Dangereuses*.

Although British aerial bombardments of November 1943 destroyed the entire Italian fleet at Taranto, the city is still an important *Arsenale Militare*, naval yard; everywhere you walk, sailors stroll about in spotless white uniforms. But as with Taranto's fishing industry, the city's importance as a naval base is fast diminishing with the

156

rapid expansion of the Italsider steel works, which now employs some 25,000 workers.

What to see

Taranto stands partly on the mainland and partly on an artificial island formed by cutting through the narrow peninsula that once closed the inner 'sea', the Mare Piccolo, from the outer 'sea', the Mare Grande. The **Old Town**, where we start our tour of this fascinating city, is bounded on both sides by the Small and Great Seas. The grimy streets in this part of Taranto are busy with barefoot urchins, the dark byways full of mystery. You will be reminded of Naples and it is advisable to leave your camera behind in your hotel room.

S. Domenico Maggiore

Walking down from Piazza Fontana, we come to the Church of San Domenico Maggiore. Built by Frederick II in 1223, the building has undergone frequent alterations, but the Gothic portal and Romanesque central window blend harmoniously with the high Baroque double stairway – this latter, incidentally, an architectural feature of many a regal *palazzo* in seventeenth-century Palermo. Among the church's paintings is an unusual 'Circumcision' by Marco Pino of Siena. There is a ghastly plaster-cast model of a recumbent Christ in the fourth chapel. The ceiling has been restored; it was completely blown away during that November night of bombing.

The Cathedral

A few hundred yards further on, and the wonderful Duomo will suddenly loom large. This is dedicated to the patron saint of Taranto, the seventh-century Irishman St Cathal of Munster, who, on returning from the Holy Land, was persuaded by the Tarentines to remain as their bishop. The church was begun in 1071. The façade is Baroque, the cupola Byzantine in style. The strange Saracen designs along the outside wall of the nave and transept are worth inspecting.

The church is divided into three naves by sixteen marble columns with Roman or Byzantine sculptured capitals. Note the lovely capital of the second column on the left: purely Byzantine in inspiration, with birds pecking at fruit. The seventeenth-century ceiling of dark wood and fretted gold is impressive; life-size figures of the Immacolata and San Cataldo (as the Italians refer to the Irishman) hang from the woodwork and they look as though they have levitated themselves up there, hovering like giant bees among the rafters.

The medieval nave is long and graceful, pierced only by tiny lancet windows, which account for the gloom. Before leaving, you should have a look at the **Chapel of San Cataldo**, to the right of the main altar. It is a riot of marble inlay, an orgy of rococo, a 'jovial nightmare in stone', as the great Norman Douglas described it. Indeed, it almost puts the convoluted ornamentation of the Lecce Baroque to shame. But then this is the most important Christian building in Taranto, a city that claims to have been converted to the ways of Christ by St Paul himself.

The Bridge

Walking to the **New City** from the Old, you eventually come to the Ponte di San Francesco – a swing-bridge connecting both 'cities'. It

157

overlooks the great shipping canal, the main link between the Mare Piccolo and Mare Grande. It is usually only opened for warships. From this bridge, you are afforded a good view of the **Castle** built by Ferdinand of Aragon in 1480 and occupied today by the Italian navy. Way out in the distance lie the islands of **San Pietro** (to the right) and **San Paolo** (left), which delineate the outer confines of Taranto harbour.

National Museum

Cross the bridge into Piazza Archita, Taranto's main square, and nearby, at Corso Umberto 41, is the Museo Nazionale (open Monday–Saturday 9 a.m.–2 p.m.; Sunday 9 a.m.–1 p.m.). Second only to the antiquities collection in Naples, this museum has the finest examples of Magna Graecian art in Italy. Excavated mostly from the city's necropolis, these include sculpture and mosaics, imported and local pottery, jewellery, terracotta figures, coins and prehistoric materials. You should try at least to see the **sarcophagus** cut from a single block of marble, containing the skeleton of a Greek athlete, whose teeth are absolutely perfect and who is a favourite with visiting schoolchildren; the **Head of Aphrodite**, from the mid-fourth century BC; the **sleeping Hercules**; and the fantastic Greek **nutcracker** in the shape of two hands.

Near the museum are the delightful **Giardini Publici**, majestic gardens with lush verdure and lofty palm trees. This is the ideal place to read a paper or take a picnic; from the terraces you get the best view of the Mare Piccolo, with numerous warships anchored in the dockyards at your feet.

What to do

If you are lucky enough to be in Taranto on Good Friday, you should not miss the **Holy Week Festival**, which has its roots in medieval Spanish ceremonials. The celebrants dress up in long white robes with pointed hoods and altogether look like a cross between members of the Ku Klux Klan and the Spanish Inquisition.

Where to stay

Top range

Mare Grande Park Hotel, Viale Virgilio 90; tel. 099-860183. Four-star; expensive but elegant.

Hotel Principe, Via Solito 27; tel. 099-334470. A new hotel and very sumptuous with it; three-star.

Hotel Pisani, Via Cavour 43; tel. 099-24087. Tucked away in a quiet cul-de-sac, this is close to the Museo Nazionale. Low-key and unpretentious; excellent value.

Mid range

Hotel Taras, Via Falanto 1; tel. 090-26728. Only 35 rooms and a little outside the centre, but clean and friendly.

Hotel Sorrentino, Piazza Fontana 7; tel. 090-407456. An excellent establishment, the rooms commanding fine views of the sea. Slightly ramshackle but family-run and you will feel quite at home there.

Bottom range

Albergo Ariston, Piazza Fontana 15; tel. 090-407563. Clean, with well-kept rooms. There are numerous long-term clients here, so book in advance.

Pensione Bella Taranto, Via P. Amadeo 60; tel. 090-22505. Bang in the centre of the New Town. Large modern rooms; no singles.

La Barcaccia, Corso Due Mari, opposite the Castle (tel. 090-26461). Slightly pretentious decorations, with a lot of brass anchor stuff, but this is where you will find the best fish in Taranto. The owner, Arturo, bones these fish with amazing dexterity: one is not surprised to find that he was himself born into a Taranto family of fishermen.

Da Gesu Cristo, Piazza Rammellini; tel. 090-26466. On one of the tiniest squares in the Old Town, from the outside this looks like a fishmonger's, which for much of the time it in fact is. But inside there's a small restaurant. Slightly grimy, but plenty of local colour.

Inland on the minor 172 road, 35 km from Taranto, is the charming town of Martina Franca (population 39,234). Only two trains leave Taranto for Martina Franca: at 8.45 a.m. and at 12.45 p.m. Whether travelling by car or by train, you will pass through the heart of Apulia's *trulli* district – the landscape is primitive, broken up into smallholdings of olive groves, vineyards and orchards, separated by low stone walls.

Martina Franca doesn't itself possess any *trulli*, but the place is one of the South's best-kept secrets: a perfectly preserved eighteenth-century Apulian provincial town, the elegant houses white-stuccoed but with Baroque doorways and windows, and with bulging wrought-iron balconies. Squares are encircled, gracefully, with old cast-iron streetlamps. Whilst in Martina (called 'Franca' because it enjoyed immunity from tax under Philip of Anjou) you should not neglect to try a glass of the fortified white wine – *bianco neutro di Martina* – for which the town is famous. Much of it eventually finds its way into bottles of vermouth and spumanti.

After passing under the graceful Porta Sant' Antonio, by the Piazza XX Settembre, Martina's principal square, turn to your immediate right and you will come to the eighteenth-century **Palazzo Ducale**. Although this has today been converted into the town hall, you are free to wander around the elegant rooms on your own. If you want a very obliging guide, though, ask for Signor Montedenaro, who works in the *Nascite e Matrimoni* (Births and Marriages) department. The palace was supposedly designed by Bernini, and one can well believe it: the rooms are hung with graceful chandeliers of Venetian glass, and the walls and ceilings painted with biblical scenes and episodes from Greek and Roman mythology – the destruction of Troy, paintings of Daphne, Jove and Apollo. It is highly recommended.

From the Ducal Palace, walk up the Via Vittorio Emanuele until you come to the (extremely lofty) **Church of St Martin**. This has a wonderfully fanciful Baroque façade, adorned with heads of angels, trumpets, cannons, drums and flags. A sculpted figure of the saint and beggar, over the main door, dominates.

Continue down the Via Garibaldi until you come to the charming **Café Tripoli**. Founded in 1911, this is a perfect and very elegant example of a turn-of-the-century Southern Italian bar, with wonderful old woodwork, ancient 'Cinzano' signs and speckled mirrors. It is here that you should take your glass of Martina's fortified wine.

Nearby, at Via Monte d'Oro 4, stands the **oldest house** in Martina Franca, dating from the 1300s. It was only in the seventeenth century that all the houses in Martina were whitewashed, as a protective layer of paint was superstitiously believed to ward off the plague which was at that time sweeping across the countryside. The walls of this ancient little house are painted, then, with successive coats of whitewash, and you can see the layers, like strips of *mille feuille*, flaking off the one from the other, century after century. It is a little like dating a tree by counting the number of rings in the trunk.

Alberobello

A ten-minute train ride will take you from Martina to this small town (population 9,361), which has a quarter wholly composed of *trulli*. It is all quite magical, of a fairy-book charm. In former times the area was thick with oak woods, which is why the town derives its name from Silva Arboris Belli.

Trulli houses

The *trullo* is a circular single-storey hut built of dry stone blocks with a conical roof of overlapping slates. Usually these houses are whitewashed, and the roof is decorated with arcane symbols and hieroglyphs – sometimes, but not always, with a cross. Mostly, they are quite pagan-looking, hinting at the symbols of black magic. Nobody seems to know who first built these simple dwellings, or why they should be peculiar only to the region of Apulia. Some say they were constructed by Byzantine monks; others that they were originally primitive tombs copied from similar constructions in Syria and Mycenae. Whatever the verdict, most of the inhabitants of Alberobello will be content to show you the insides of their dwellings, but do not buy any of the straw shoes which they smilingly fob off as 'Apulian Artefacts' – they are made in Taiwan.

The Grottoes

Twenty-eight kilometres north of Alberobello, along a twisting minor road, are the Castellana Grotte, perhaps the most spectacular series of caverns in all Italy. Sixty-five metres below ground level the grottoes interconnect with chambers rich in stalagmites and stalactites, alabaster in colour. The grottoes themselves are a good twenty minutes' walk from Castellana station (follow the signs for *Grotte*), but you should not miss this opportunity to fathom the mysterious underbelly of Apulia.

There are two different tours. The first is for a kilometre's distance only, lasting one hour; guides operate at evey second hour from 8.30 a.m. to 7 p.m. The second is for three kilometres and lasts two hours; tours are conducted from 9 a.m. to 5 p.m. I strongly suggest that you take the longer option (though it will cost you 25,000 lire) – it is a magical mystery tour, with fossils in the shapes of giant wolves, owls, slithering serpents, the Madonna and Child, Milan Cathedral and the Leaning Tower of Pisa. At one point it seems as though you are walking through some underground version of the Grand Canyon, with fossils in the shape of cacti. The high point is the *Grotta Bianca*, perhaps the most beautiful cavern in the world on account of its brilliant crystalline formations. It is like the Snow Queen's palace, the roof bristling with thousands of needle-sharp icicles.

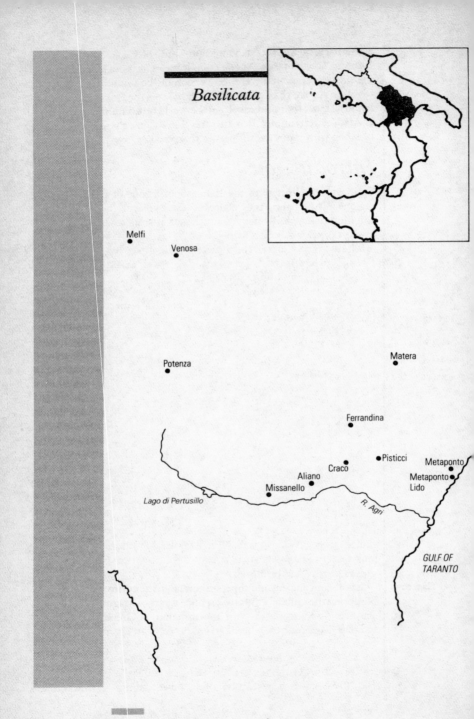

Basilicata

Melfi

Venosa

Potenza

Matera

Ferrandina

Pisticci

Craco

Aliano

Metaponto

Missanello

Metaponto Lido

Lago di Pertusillo

R. Agri

GULF OF TARANTO

Basilicata

Introduction

Basilicata, the 'instep' of the Italian boot, is one of Italy's smallest regions. It is also the poorest. The villages here, primitive communities hedged in by centuries of custom and sorrow, were immortalised in a book which was, in 1945, the first to awake Northern Italy to the plight of the Southern Italian peasant – Carlo Levi's *Christ Stopped at Eboli*. Prior to its publication, Basilicata was a land outside history and time, abandoned to the ravages of earthquakes, and to outbreaks of malaria. Levi wrote of a 'closed world shrouded in black veils, bloody and earthy, that other world where the peasants live and which no one can enter without a magic key'.

But Basilicata is still, when all is said and done, a land outside time. Tourist facilities are improving, but much of the region is difficult of access, with over 90 per cent of it mountain. Wedged between Campania to the west, Apulia to the east and Calabria to the south, the region is a world to itself, an island. In the forests, wild boar and wolves are not uncommon; the land is barren and hostile to cultivation; industries remain undeveloped; and there is much illiteracy, if no longer malaria. Poverty apart, much of Basilicata's landscape is impressive – great white hills of eroded clay like enormous icebergs, a terrain that geologists compare to the Valley of Goreme in Cappadocia, Turkey. It is so impressive, in fact, that I once met a priest there (undoubtedly mad) who was seriously thinking about asking Sergio Leone to come to Basilicata to film one of his 'spaghetti westerns'. But one can see why: in particular around the village of Aliano, where Levi set *Christ Stopped at Eboli*, the mountains look as though they have been transported wholesale from the Grand Canyon. Otherwise, Basilicata is a land of golden wheat fields and olive groves, earthy and primeval.

History

It is also an ancient and superstitious land; the entire southern coast bordering the Gulf of Taranto was once a part of Magna Graecia, and the area is magnificent with the remains of Greek theatres and temples. **Metaponto**, where the mathematician Pythagoras retired, has many unspoilt, sandy beaches which, once you have pottered about the temples, are well worth lying on. Moving into the arid hinterland of Basilicata, the town of **Matera** will strike you, from afar, with the force of an apparition: of an almost biblical aspect, its clay hillsides are honeycombed with *sassi* – peculiar cave-like dwellings hollowed out of the rock, now abandoned. It was here, in the parched and lunar landscape, that Pier Paolo Pasolini shot much of his brilliant film *The Gospel According to Matthew*. All in all, you could comfortably spend three or four days in Basilicata.

The name of this region has been changed several times. The classical one of Lucania was resurrected in the Fascist period, but on 27 December 1947 the Italian Constitution officially reverted to the name Basilicata, after the *basilikos*, Byzantine administrators of justice, who once ruled the area. Elderly people here will still talk about *'Lucani'* instead of *'Basilicatesi'*, particularly those who are still nostalgic for Mussolini. I should stick to Basilicata – a name that poetically brings to mind the superabundance of basil that grows here.

In Basilicata, you will not always come upon efficient or comfortable hotels except in the provincial capitals; many of the most interesting villages are without even a restaurant. Be prepared to rough it.

Getting around

Basilicata is served by two major rail lines: one runs along the coast between Reggio di Calabria and Taranto, stopping at Metaponto for a bus connection to Matera; the other connects Naples with Taranto, stopping at Potenza and Ferrandina (a real one-horse town, and even the horse has gone), where buses connect to Matera. By car, the shortest and most convenient route (which more or less follows that of the railway) from Naples to Potenza is via Salerno, Battipaglia and Auletta. Or you can go via Avellino and from thence along the Via Appia (SS 7) to Potenza. There are no airports in Basilicata.

Wine

Basilicata produces a splendid wine from the Aglianico grape (*ellenico* i.e. from Greece, like the civilisation itself down here) – the Aglianico del Vulture. Ruby-red in colour, garnet when old, it has the faint aroma of strawberries or raspberries. The wine very nicely accompanies poultry or game and it might be an idea to drink a bottle or two of the stuff should you want to venture into the *sassi* of Matera at night – the caves are full of wolves and howling dogs.

Potenza

The 603,000 inhabitants of Basilicata are divided into two provinces: Potenza and Matera. The city of Potenza (population 56,597), capital of the region, is not worth visiting. Badly hit by the 1980 earthquake, many of its undistinguished buildings are supported by great forests of wooden scaffolding – a sad and dingy place.

Melfi

The nearby towns, however, of **Venosa**, birthplace of the poet Horace, and Melfi, a beautifully preserved Norman centre, are certainly worth visiting. Melfi boasts the **Abbazia della Trinità**, an impressive ruin of an unfinished Norman church, with half-built bell-towers and nothing but the sky for a roof. In days gone by, the Trinità was much frequented by barren women; in it there used to be a vestibule containing a round Roman pillar, worn smooth by female figures passing close between it and the wall in the belief that they would thus become pregnant.

Matera

Capital of the second of Basilicata's two provinces, Matera (population 44,513) is the best place from which to base excursions to the rest of Basilicata. There is no train station, but four SITA buses run to and from Metaponto's train station; and there are two per day running to and from Potenza. Matera, with its grandiloquent air of decay, is one of the strangest places you are likely to visit in Southern Italy; and the *sassi* will haunt you long after you have left, will linger on in the mind.

What to see
The Cathedral

The Cathedral, reached along the Via Duomo from Matera's busy Piazza Vittorio Veneto, is one of the finest churches in Southern Italy of the Apulian–Romanesque style. Completed in 1270, it now imperiously overlooks the *sassi* in the gorges way down below. The west end has a large rose window supported by angels, the creatures bent double under their magnificent, holy load. You should have a look at the door here, surmounted by a tiny carved relief of a monk with the word 'Abraham' inscribed above it.

Inside are Romanesque columns and a thirteenth-century Byzantine fresco of the Madonna (first chapel on the left). Unfortunately, some fairly radical architectural surgery was inflicted on this medieval interior when the Italian Baroque was in its heyday; the ceiling fairly drips with gold. But no matter; at the end of the north aisle is a famous sixteenth-century Nativity, a model crib teeming with a host of sculpted figures, sheep included. It is one of the most celebrated of Basilicatan works of art, for the manger and the miniature caves are clearly modelled on the *sassi* of Matera. To illuminate the model, you must drop a coin in the appropriate slot.

The caves

From here we begin our tour of the extraordinary *sassi* scattered about in two principal areas: the **Sasso Caveoso** and the **Sasso Barisano**. Only 700 or so people live in these caves today, but looking at their dank and dingy interiors, one can well imagine how the *sassi* were once a breeding-ground for so many diseases. In *Christ Stopped at Eboli*, Carlo Levi relates how his sister, visiting Matera in the late 1930s, found 'children naked or clothed only in rags with wrinkled faces like old men, reduced to skeletons by hunger'. Malaria, dysentery and trachoma were the diseases.

From Via Ridola, descend to the Sasso Caveoso. There are stupendous views en route of the dramatic canyon formed by the Gravina River, and you soon come to **Santa Maria d'Idris** and **San Pietro Caveoso**, just two of Matera's 120 *chiese rupestre* – primitive chapels carved into the hillsides by monks in the eighth and thirteenth centuries. In both are traces of a neolithic village, and on the walls some fine Byzantine frescoes. In the fifteenth century, the monks abandoned their caves and local peasants moved in; even today, much to the annoyance of Matera's Tourist Office, many of these churches are 'privately owned' – that is, they are now used as stables.

As you walk about the Sasso Caveoso, don't hesitate to employ for a small fee the services of one of the barefoot ragamuffins who double up in these parts as tour guides. They will spin you a lot of untruths but will take you to churches and *sassi* otherwise inaccessible. Accompany them as they show you tombs, caves, excavations and Byzantine frescoes. One of the best tours is across the Gravina River (not easily forded – the stepping-stones are slippery and the current swift) to the other side of the canyon where you climb a fairly precipitous mountain-face to visit a fascinating network of cave-churches and *sassi* – ask to see **Sant'Agata** and **La Madonna delle Tre Porte**. Do *not* attempt this journey on your own; the path is ill-defined and if you set off in the afternoon, night will fall before you have even begun to ford the river. Night fell, in such a way, on me – and panic-fear, it must be said, soon got a hold.

Churches   Returning to Piazza Vittorio Veneto it is a short walk to the curious **San Giovanni Battista**. Built in the early thirteenth century, it has a fine carved portal with delicate foliate decorations of Byzantine inspiration. A Saracen arch is embedded in the door recess. Inside, a hotch-potch of architectural styles prevails: early northern Gothic, Apulian–Romanesque, Arab.

Taking the Via Corso, you come first to **San Francesco**, a thirteenth-century church, badly Baroqued in the seventeenth century, containing an even older rock-chapel; and then to the bizarre **Purgatorio**. A Baroque nightmare, this is the largest church in Southern Italy dedicated to the dead – rather a common theme in both Basilicata and Apulia. The convex façade, with its ghoulish paraphernalia of winged egg-timers, skeletons, skulls, scythes and *memento mori*, dates from 1747.

The Museum   A short way on, we reach the Museo Nazionale Ridola (open Tuesday–Saturday 9 a.m.–2 p.m.; Sunday 9 a.m.–1.30 p.m.). Housed in a now deconsecrated eighteenth-century convent, the museum is actually the private collection of Domenico Ridola, a turn-of-the-century Materan doctor. It contains finds from the neolithic hills nearby, arrow-heads, flints, pots and pans. And there are many treasures from Matera's *Grotta dei Pipistrelli* (Cave of the Bats): stone objects, decorated bones, fossils, painted and 'graffito' pottery. The museum is beautifully laid out.

The Carlo Levi   At the end of the Via Ridola stands the Fondazione Carlo Levi
Gallery   (open Tuesday–Saturday 9 a.m.–2 p.m.; closed Sunday). Within the walls of a converted eighteenth-century school are held some thirty-five of Levi's superb oil paintings – all of them portraying scenes from Basilicatan life such as are found in *Christ Stopped at Eboli*. The view of the *sassi* from the terrace of this building is quite stunning.

What to do   During the last week in June occurs the **Festival of Santa Maria**

della Bruna. This climaxes on 2 July with a Procession of Shepherds and the Procession of the Madonna on a cart, both of them accompanied by medieval warriors and clergy on horseback. The cart is ritualistically torn to pieces by all the Materans, as they search for precious relics.

Where to stay

Hotel President, Via Roma 13; tel. 0835-214075. Probably as bland as the old 'Jolly Hotel' on whose site this now stands, but clean, comfortable and modern. Three-star.

Hotel Italia, Via Ridola 5; tel. 0835-211195. Opposite the Purgatorio Church. Every room has recently been refurbished with cooker, fridge and bathroom, so you can cook for yourself. Highly recommended.

Albergo Roma, Via Roma 62; tel. 0835-212701. For those on a budget – clean and friendly (mind you don't bang your head on the low-slung entrance), but it often fills up with Basilicatan locals. So book in advance.

Albergo Moderno, Via De Sariis 11; tel. 0835-212336. Only check into this place if you are desperate. As a hotel it is perfectly safe (and dirt cheap) but on the whole it is a sad, dark and smelly place. It does not, in other words, live up to its somewhat optimistic name.

Where to eat

Il Terrazzino, Vico S. Giuseppe 7; tel. 0835-222016. A restaurant in a converted *sasso*, this is where you will find some of the best Basilicatan cooking. The mustachioed patron paces up and down among his clients rather like an adjudicator at public examinations; but the food more than makes up for his overweening presence.

Trattoria Sorangelo, Via Lucania 48; tel. 0835-216779. The best restaurant in Matera for *cucina casalinga*, home-made local cooking such as the Materans themselves eat. Always popular; book early.

Osteria Paternoster, Via Lombardi 3; no telephone. Beneath street level and rather cavernous with it, but the good food is standard family fare. And cheap.

Aliano

One of the most interesting excursions to be made from Matera is to the tiny village in which Carlo Levi, exiled by the Fascists as a political prisoner, wrote *Christ Stopped at Eboli*. Aliano (population 1,706) lies some 60 km further inland from Matera, between the towns of Craco and Pisticci, and is fairly inaccessible. (Matters are further complicated by the fact that Levi changed the name of the village to Gagliano.) By bus (there is no railway) you will have to change some four or five times. But I am only trying to put you off because Aliano is still unspoilt, and will not survive tourism.

The village has not changed much since Levi lived there. Old women, their faces baked almost black by the sun, balance large earthenware pots on their heads, as in Africa; donkeys, burdened with great bushels of firewood, clip-clop down the cobbled streets; ancient men, clad in the dusty black corduroy of the Basilicatan peasant, seem hardly to move from their morning-to-evening place at Aliano's one and only bar. As Levi wrote: 'The seasons pass today over the toil of the peasants just as they did three thousand years before; no message, human or divine, has reached this stubborn poverty.'

Aliano is perched dramatically on top of a ridge of limestone at a height of 500 metres above a ravine. Its scattering of ramshackle dwellings, baked by the sun the colour of mud, cling for dear life to the spur of a jagged saddle of chalk, a great wound in the earth. The landscape all around is weird and distinctly lunar; it is here that you find Basilicata's famous *calanchi* – boulders and escarpments of calcareous stone. You do not have to be familiar with *Christ Stopped at Eboli* to appreciate the otherworldliness of this scenery.

Where to stay and eat

The trouble is that there are no hotels in Aliano. The nearest is in the village of Missanello – the **Hotel Ristorante La Gola**; tel. 0971-955160. And there is only one 'restaurant' in Aliano, the **Ristorante Bar Centrale**, Via Roma 38; tel. 0835-668239. It is rudimentary, but the food is surprisingly good and, as with all the inhabitants of Aliano, the patrons are possessed of an antique respect for any foreigner who has strayed off the beaten tracks of tourism.

If you are seriously thinking about visiting Aliano, I suggest that on arrival you contact Don Pierino di Lenge, the young and dynamic parish priest. He knows all there is to know about Carlo Levi (he lovingly tends the writer's tomb in the municipal cemetery) and may be reached on 0835-668074.

What to see

Padre di Lenge has recently founded in Aliano a charming **Museo di Civiltà Contadina** (open Friday and Saturday 10 a.m.–12.30 p.m., 5–7 p.m.; Sunday 9.30 a.m.–12.30 p.m.). This Museum of Peasant Culture, next door to the house in which Levi was confined, is piled high with the sort of rustic objects to be found in the pages of his book: wooden cheese sieves, milk churns, ploughs, pewter pots, pestles and mortars. All very ramshackle and charming.

Metaponto

On the coast 60 km from Matera, along the minor roads 7 and 407, is one of the great city states of Magna Graecia. Founded by Athenians in the seventh or eighth century BC, it was later destroyed, as was much of Basilicata, by the Saracens. Such ruins as remain, though, are well worth seeing. Unfortunately, they are several kilometres apart, and not always easy of access. If you are without a car, I suggest this itinerary.

What to see

Exit from Metaponto station and follow the road in front of you for 3 km and then turn right on the coastal highway for Taranto. Follow it for another 3 km until you come to the **Antiquarium** (open October–March, Tuesday–Saturday 9 a.m.–1 p.m., 3.30–6.30 p.m.). It is worth investigating the contents of this superbly laid out museum before wandering about the ruins themselves; they include interesting maps and aerial photographs of Metaponto, a good collection of Greek artefacts from the area, including terracotta fertility symbols from the first half of the sixth century BC and the stone torso of an archer.

In the grounds of the Antiquarium stands the beautiful **Tavole Palatine**, a sixth-century Doric temple dedicated to Hera. One cannot help but notice, here, the odd juxtaposition of temple and telegraph pylon: a meeting of worlds apart which is periodically enhanced by the jet planes that soar across Metaponto from the Italian air base at Bari.

From here take the bus outside the Antiquarium which leaves every half-hour back to the station and get off at the yellow sign on the left-hand side of the road pointing to the Parco Archaeologico. Thirty minutes on foot down a dirt track through fields will take you to the **Tempio di Apollo Licio**, one of the oldest temples in Magna Graecia, dating from the early half of the sixth century BC. Archaeologists have deduced that it had thirty-two columns and stood some 6 metres high. The adjoining **Theatre**, currently being excavated by the German Institute of Florence, was the first to be constructed from a mound of dirt rather than dug out of a hillside, as was normally the practice. Most delightful about these ruins is the scenery in which they stand – surrounding fields of artichokes, muddy streams in which croak thousands of frogs, the smell everywhere of thyme and basil, of saxifrage and lemon.

If you feel like a swim, I suggest you walk from here to the nearby Metaponto Lido. A fairly unspoilt resort area, it boasts some splendid beaches and tennis courts.

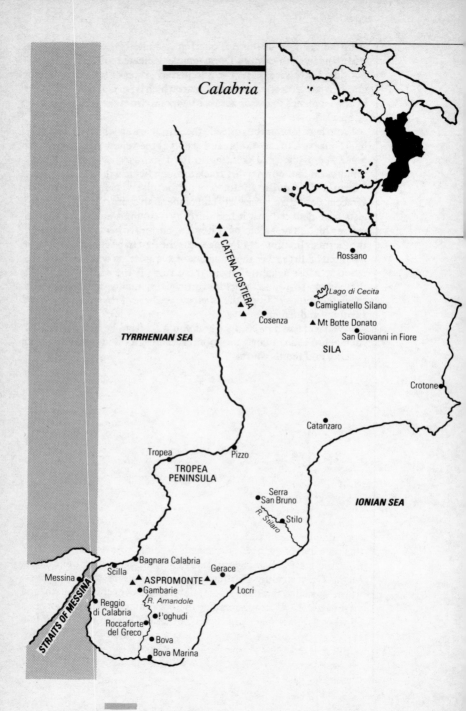

Calabria

Rossano

Lago di Cecita
Camigliatello Silano

▲ Mt Botte Donato
San Giovanni in Fiore

SILA

CATENA COSTIERA

Cosenza

TYRRHENIAN SEA

Crotone

Catanzaro

Tropea   Pizzo

**TROPEA
PENINSULA**

Serra
San Bruno

IONIAN SEA

R. Stilaro
Stilo

Bagnara Calabria

Scilla

Gerace

Messina

ASPROMONTE ▲▲

Locri

STRAITS OF MESSINA

Gambarie
R. Amandole

Reggio
di Calabria

Roccaforte
del Greco

Ŀoghudi

Bova

Bova Marina

Calabria

Introduction

Calabria is the toe of the Italian 'boot'. It forms a long and narrow peninsula dividing the Ionian from the Tyrrhenian Seas. Measuring 250 km in length and at its narrowest only 30 km in width, Calabria was probably at the back of Napoleon's mind when he said of Italy that she had one capital defect: her length was disproportionate to her breadth.

Napoleon was of course thinking in terms of political and military strategy but the defect has proved a hindrance to travellers too. Until the beginning of the twentieth century, Italy stopped short of Naples; further south and all was African darkness – dangerous and remote. And Calabria was, above all, dirty: 'The poverty, filth, ignorance and degradation of the inhabitants', pontificated the Edwardian traveller Augustus Hare, 'is indescribable; and emigration of the effectual males to America only increases the evil.'

Certainly in the eyes of Northern Italians, Calabrians are still a rough and ready people ('Arabs'), but mass emigration, at any rate, is now a thing of the past. The work of the Cassa per il Mezzogiorno, Italy's relief fund for the deprived South, has resulted in a considerable improvement of the Calabrian's lifestyle. Hydro-electric systems have brought money to the region, and there is a large and lucrative trade in oil – the olive groves of Calabria are among the best in Italy. But the region is primarily agricultural – and poor.

In days bygone, the danger for travellers in Calabria was often the bandits. The eccentric English traveller Crauford Tait Ramage wrote of Calabria in the 1820s that 'it is harassing to be constantly in the expectation of being either robbed or murdered'. Today, need one say, this is no longer the case; and there is absolutely no danger to tourists from the fearful 'Ndrangheta, the Calabrian version of the Sicilian Mafia. Only wealthy Northern Italians need fear the 'Ndrangheta, whose speciality is kidnapping; Calabria is 92 per cent mountain, and victims are easily sequestered at the bottom of a ravine or gorge. It happens often enough: the landscape, according to the Edwardian travel-writer Norman Douglas, 'is an incredibly harsh agglomeration of hill and dale, and the geology of the district . . . reveals a perfect chaos of rocks of every age, torn into gullies by earthquakes and other cataclysms of the past'.

Little has changed. Although a feature of the Calabrian coastline is the occasional Aragonese castle, symbol of direct (and notably corrupt) Spanish rule from 1559 to 1713, the region is less rich in monuments or works of art than Apulia or Campania; countless medieval towns have anyway been destroyed by earthquakes. But this is more than compensated for by the rugged beauty and variety of Calabria's natural scenery.

On the west, the region is traversed as far south as the Vale of Maida by the Catena Costiera range of mountains. The northern boundary with Basilicata culminates in Monte Pollino (2,248 m). In the centre the region expands into the granite plateau of the Sila, a vast and beautiful area of woodland with emerald-green lakes. In the extreme south rise the Aspromonte group of mountains, wild and savage.

In Calabria, we are in the primitive heart of the Italian South. But you could happily spend two weeks here; you will feel the better for it, invigorated by the mountain air, the seaweed-scented winds off the Ionian Sea.

The best beaches are along the west coast – particularly around the Tropea Peninsula, which also has some of the most scenic hinterland; Tropea itself, a delightful old town, is well worth investigating. Resorts on the east coast of Calabria are few and far between, and beaches are bleak and rocky. The camping parks and youth hostels here – part of the tourist and commercial world of the Mediterranean – have nothing to do with the rough reality of Calabria; as an independent traveller, you will want to avoid them. Still, there are some interesting remains at the sleepy east-coast town of Locri: Greek temples and theatres – just about all that is left in Calabria of Magna Graecia.

Of Calabria's three provincial cities, only Cosenza and Reggio are worth visiting; Catanzaro is a sad and gloomy place, interesting only for its decorative *fin de siècle* pharmacist shops. Cosenza, on the other hand – a tumbledown city with a romantic medieval castle – is the best place from which to branch out into the Sila, and from which to visit Rossano, a beautiful medieval town. Reggio itself has little to offer, apart from two famous bronze statues of Greek warriors in the city museum, but the city is nevertheless surrounded by some of the most stunning scenery in all of Southern Italy. And there are villages where the inhabitants speak a Greek dialect derived from the ancient language spoken by the Greeks who emigrated to Calabria between the seventh and sixth centuries BC. Besides, Reggio is important as an embarkation point for nearby Sicily. Another major town which you would do well to avoid is Crotone, perched on a dreary promontory off the Ionian coast and badly polluted by emanations from nearby industries.

History

The history of Calabria is first of all that of Magna Graecia, from the cities of which flowed the Hellenic culture that has left so indelible an imprint on western civilisation. In the second millennium BC, Greek traders came to Calabria and began to barter with the indigenous inhabitants. These were the Greeks who first introduced the vine and the olive to Italy. That is the reality; the myth tells of how Italos, grandson of Odysseus and Penelope, conquered the Calabrian toe of Italy and introduced into his new kingdom the civilities of ancient Greece.

After the Greeks came the Byzantines (who, in the seventh century AD, first applied the name Calabria to the region); and then the Saracens, followed by the Normans and the Aragonese. All have left their architectural marks on Calabria, scattered and widely dispersed though they are.

The main route from Naples to Calabria (a distance of some 328 km) is along the coastal SS 18 – the spectacularly beautiful Autostrade del Sole, in the concrete foundations of which is believed to lie many a Mafia or 'Ndrangheta victim. The motorway travels all the way down to Reggio di Calabria. There are express trains running to and from Naples to Reggio; travelling time is about five hours. You can fly from most European airports to Lamezia, near Cosenza.

Places to stay in Calabria are for the most part situated along the west coast, much of which is separated from the motorway by mountains (and from the sea by the railway line). I strongly advise that you seek a hotel near the motorway; inland, accommodation is, to put it mildly, sparse. And spartan.

Before you depart for Calabria I recommend that you invest in a copy of Norman Douglas's classic of 1915, *Old Calabria*. There are some superb chapters on the Sila, Calabrian brigandage, cave-worship and mysterious flying monks. Douglas, following in the footsteps of the novelist George Gissing, was one of the first English-speaking tourists to explore Calabria; even today the region is largely unknown to the British.

If you are planning to travel about by train, be warned. A friend in Rome told me that Calabrian trains are of a 'Biblical slowness', though I found their speed properly primordial. To pass the time on these lightning intercities, take on board a bottle or two of Calabria's famous Ciro wine – a strong red of high reputation praised by Pliny, no less. 'Purest nectar' was how Norman Douglas described its liquid ruby red.

The Tyrrhenian Coast

Cosenza The sub-provincial capital of Cosenza (population 102,086) is divided into two sections – an old and a new. The new is a busy town of civil servants; a centre for figs, oranges, honey and liquorice. It is particularly famous for the traditional manufacture of *mattonelle*, 'little bricks' – coloured tiles with which so many public buildings in Southern Italy are richly adorned. Apart from that, very little else seems to go on in Cosenza. The old town, built precariously on a steep hillside above a mere runnel of a river (the shallow Busento), looks as though it has for innumerable centuries been sound asleep.

Which is to say, it is fascinating. You climb up the narrow winding streets between ramshackle houses so close as almost to block out the sun. From their iron balconies hang heavy flags of linen, their brilliant white a contrast to the dingy cat-infested streets below. Everywhere, the ill-paved streets look down into subterranean family bedrooms, dimly aglow with the spectral flicker of black-and-white television sets. Now and again one catches a glimpse of the stern medieval Castle way up above – the site of Louis II of Anjou's marriage to Margaret of Savoy, illuminated today for the benefit of nobody knows who.

What to see It is quite a haul up to the **Castle** (open 9 a.m.–1 p.m., 4–7.30 p.m.), but worth the effort. Parts of the building are without a roof, but there are some interesting vaulted ceilings, with fireplaces surmounted by baronial coats of arms. You can walk around the fourteen bastions, from which there are stupendous views of Cosenza. The abandoned iron gratings that you see lying about everywhere are parts of the prison that the Castle became under the Bourbons.

Descending from the Castle you will soon come to the beautiful **Duomo**. Consecrated in 1222 in the presence of Frederick II, it is a mixture of styles Romanesque and Gothic. The façade, with its large rose window, is one of the most graceful in Calabria. The Cathedral is ideally complemented by the surroundings – the houses that fan out around a perfect half-moon piazza, resembling the props to an opera set.

The simple but pleasant Gothic interior has an exquisite tomb (to the left of the main altar) containing the remains of Queen Isabella of Aragon, who died in 1270 when she fell from her horse. The intricately carved stonework shows the queen kneeling to adore the Madonna and Child, one of the most exquisite of all Italian medieval works of art.

Behind the Duomo is the **Archbishop's Palace**. It contains a stunning Byzantine reliquary crucifix, presented by Frederick II when he attended the consecration of the Cathedral. It is worked in gold and enamel and adorned with Greek lettering.

Where to stay There are only six hotels in Cosenza. Among the best are:
Centrale, Via Dei Tigari 12; tel. 0894-7368182. Three-star, with 48 rooms. Clean and modern.
Imperiale, Viale Trieste 50; tel. 0894-27000. Two-star, with 67 rooms. Comfortable.
Excelsior, Piazza Matteoti 14; tel. 0894-74384. My favourite hotel in Cosenza – wonderful run-down Edwardian charm. Enormous

rooms (watch out for any roosting pigeons) and marble corridors that seem to go on for ever. One-star, if that.

Where to eat

There is a shortage of decent restaurants in Cosenza. Good news, then, that **La Giocondo**, Via Pave 35, tel. 0894-29810, is quite a find. Cheap, with excellent service and, even better, local food. Decorations unpretentious.

The Sila

Now that we are in Cosenza, a journey to the nearby Sila Massif is an absolute must. Dark with climbing softwood, the Sila (known locally as the Black Mountain) must be one of the most unusual parts of Southern Italy. As Norman Douglas wrote of this Calabrian forest some seventy years ago: 'Were it not for the absence of heather with its peculiar mauve tints, the traveller might well imagine himself in Scotland. There is the same smiling alternation of woodland and meadow, the same huge boulders of gneiss and granite which give a distinctive tone to the landscape, the same exuberance of living waters. Water, indeed, is one of the glories of the Sila – everywhere it bubbles forth in chill rivulets among the stones and trickles down the hillsides to join the larger streams that wend their way to the forlorn and fever-stricken coastlands of Magna Graecia.'

One can hardly improve on that. Suffice it to say that the Sila, a corruption of the Latin *silva* or forest, is divided into three main parts – La Greca, La Grande and La Piccola. The area's two main villages are Camigliatello Silano and San Giovanni in Fiore; both are in the Sila Grande and are easily reached from Cosenza. In the dog days of summer, Calabrians take to the breezy heights of the Black Mountain to cool off. You could do the same. If you want to stay in the Sila there is plenty of chalet-style accommodation.

Getting there

From Cosenza station (the *old* station, not the new) opposite the Excelsior Hotel, the tiny train to San Giovanni leaves at 5.58 a.m., 6.58 a.m., 8.01 a.m. and 9.02 a.m. These are the only trains. Once in San Giovanni there are connections for Camigliatello at 12 noon and 1.44 p.m. only. Given the inconvenience of these public transport hours, you may want to hire a car – telephone the Cosenza Automobile Club, Via A. Tocci 2, on 0894-75035. But the train is worth taking; it will trundle you through some of the most spectacular scenery in Italy – gorges and lateral valleys, lakes and forests of silver birch. You feel, like Alice in Wonderland, as though you had shrunk to become a passenger on a toy railway.

San Giovanni in Fiore

San Giovanni (population 17,162), 35 km east of Cosenza, looks rather shabby. But it is well worth visiting for the peculiar costumes still worn by the women – a white linen scarf with a square top fastened at the back of the head with a gold safety-pin; a black velvet blouse; and strange greasy ringlets of hair hanging from either side of the head like the locks of an Orthodox Jew. The town itself, of a distinctly Alpine aspect, grew up in the twelfth century around the **Badia Florense** (a ponderous abbey of stone and timber), founded

175

by the abbot Gioacchino, who enjoyed quite a reputation, after his return from the Holy Land, as a local prophet. Dante wrote about him:

. . . and, shining by my side,
Joachim the Calabrian Abbot, great
In gift, through whom the spirit prophesied.

Camigliatello A summer and a winter resort 25 km from Cosenza, Camigliatello **Silano** is reminiscent of the lumber towns of New England – it hardly seems Italian at all, even though it is equidistant from the Ionian and Tyrrhenian Seas. From here you can take an hour's pleasant walk down to **Lago di Cecita**, which is typical of the lakes in the Sila – bosky scenery, the distant clanging of cow bells. Or, if you are more ambitious, you can climb to the top of **Monte Botte Donato** (1,930 m), the highest peak in the Sila. It will take you about two and a half hours.

Where to stay If you want to stay in Camigliatello, I suggest the **Hotel Aquila and Edelweiss**, Viale Stazione 13; tel. 0823-978044. As you might guess from the name, the hotel is popular with Germans, and with other Alpine folk familiar with the famous flower. As the hotel brochure puts it: 'We cater for those who climb to ask the pine wood of the zone pure air, oxygen and coldness.'

While in Cosenza, you should on no account miss making the day-trip to the little town of Rossano, on the Ionian coast (see p. 178).

Pizzo Some 80 km from Cosenza, further down the coastal Route 18, is Pizzo (population 9,000), a charming town chiefly engaged in catching swordfish. For some reason Pizzo is not much frequented by tourists. I consider it one of Calabria's most beautiful spots. The whitewashed houses, the lively marketplace and piazza, the narrow winding streets, its dramatic position over the sea – all this makes Pizzo a breezy, happy town, the perfect place in which to wind down for a day or two. And there are some very respectable beaches too.

What to see Pizzo is famous among Calabrians for its ghoulish **Castle**. Built in 1486 on a promontory overlooking the sea, this is where Napoleon's brother-in-law, Joachim Murat, ex-King of Naples, was tried by court martial in 1815 and shot, five days after he had attempted to regain his throne. It is a dramatic story. 'Officers,' Murat addressed the firing-squad, 'I have commanded in many battles; I should wish to give the word of command for the last time, if you can grant me that request.' Permission granted, he called out, 'Soldiers, form line,' as six drew themselves up ten feet away. 'Prepare arms, present.' Lifting to his lips a miniature gold revolver belonging to his wife, Murat himself called out, 'Fire!' He fell back against a door and three soldiers, placed on a roof above, finished him off by firing a volley into his head.

Murat, a vain man, would not have appreciated the messy state of his head. According to Calabrians, his last words to the soldiers were,

'*Mirate al petto, salvate il viso* [Aim for the heart, spare me my face].'
Today, this expression is often used ironically in Pizzo, much as we
might say, 'Give us a break!' Curiously, Murat's words were the very
ones which Paul Newman, playing an American novelist, used in the
1963 Hitchcock pastiche *The Prize*, when he was besieged by hundreds
of photographers at the Nobel Prize awards.

For a couple of hundred lire, the custodian of Pizzo Castle will
gladly show you the spot where the hapless Murat bloodied the courtyard. He is buried in the **Duomo di San Giorgio**, which contains
several interesting marble statues – among them a sixteenth-century
John the Baptist and a regal figure of St Catherine of Alexandria.

Where to stay **Hotel Murat**, Piazza della Repubblica 41; tel. 0963-231006. Bang
in the middle of the main square, slightly run-down but has a certain
faded charm.

Hotel Grillo, Via Riviera Prangi; tel. 0963-231632. Two-star, with
120 beds; bland but comfortable.

Where to eat **Ristorante La Ruota**, Piazza della Repubblica 36; tel. 0963-
232427. The best restaurant in Pizzo. Fish is the speciality but the
oven-baked pizzas are excellent too. There are tables outside.

Pizzo is a convenient town from which to make a day-trip to the
fascinating village of **Serra San Bruno**, which lies some 40 km
inland along the minor 182 road. A bus – the only one – leaves Pizzo
for Serra at 6.15 a.m. (see p. 179).

Tropea We now head south along the coastal Route 522 until we arrive after
30 km at the small fishing town of Tropea (population 6,955) – even
more beautiful, perhaps, than Pizzo. '*Nobile Tropea*', the Calabrians
call the town, and with good reason, since it must be one of the most
picturesque in all of Southern Italy. Huddled on a cliff above the sea,
Tropea is also that rare thing, a seaside resort which is quite unspoilt.
It is the Italians themselves who take their holidays in Tropea, as one
can tell from the dozens of black-clad women who line the cobbled
streets, selling from their rickety stalls huge bunches of dried
aubergines and peppers, oregano and fennel.

What to see True, there is a Lunar Park (and I recommend the remarkably
seedy House of Horrors), but even this is quite overshadowed by the
precipitous rock – once an island – on top of which stand the remains
of the **Benedictine Monastery**. The path that ascends to this edifice
is lined with old fishermen's caves.

Apart from Tropea's splendid beaches – clean, golden, aquamarine
blue – the town's principal attraction is the **Norman Cathedral**. At
the back of this graceful, sandstone church hang two most extraordinary objects – unexploded American bombs. According to the notice,
they fell harmlessly on the town during the last war: '*Cosi la Madonna
protegge miracolosamente i suoi figli* [Thus the Madonna miraculously
protects her sons].'

Throughout the old town of Tropea are numerous **palaces** con-

177

structed by the lesser nobility and the rising middle class. Many, though in a sad state of neglect, are models of eighteenth-century design; often, the courtyards flaunt faded coats-of-arms with such Latin mottoes as 'Non Commovebatur', with an image underneath of a lighthouse standing steadfast on a rock in a stormy sea. Many of these *palazzi* are crowned with grotesque masks and gargoyles to ward off the evil eye.

Where to stay

Rocca Nettuno, Via Annunziata; tel. 0963-61612. Three-star, the best hotel in Tropea, huddled on top of a 40-m-high rocky plateau overlooking the sea. The gardens boast 'prickly pears growing between picturesque ponds'.

Hotel Residence Triangolo al Tondo, Via Tondo 5; tel. 0963-61796. Two-star, modern, not particularly stylish but cheap. All rooms are equipped with refrigerators and cooking facilities. Excellent for the family.

Hotel Miramare, Via Liberta 77; tel. 0963-61570. Two-star, bang by the sea in an attractive (though dilapidated) eighteenth-century *palazzo*. According to the brochure, 'All comforts rooms with bathed-showers, running waters, warming in times of winter.'

Where to eat

Al Timone, Piazza Duomo: unfortunately, the very hospitable owner, Muscia Annuziato, has no telephone. Directly opposite Tropea's (potentially combustible?) Cathedral, this is absolutely one of my favourite restaurants in Southern Italy. Try the spaghetti *all'inchiostro di seppia* (with squid's ink): the pasta looks as though it has been unkindly smeared in axle-grease, so weirdly black are the strands. But it's scrumptious.

So far, we have been travelling down the Tyrrhenian coast; given the elongated shape of Calabria, you will at some stage have to cross the hinterland to explore the eastern coast.

The Ionian Coast

Rossano

The small town of Rossano (population 25,321), north of Cosenza and about a two and a half hours' bus journey from there, should definitely not be missed. Buses leave Cosenza at 6.30 a.m. only, but it is well worth the early rising.

Perched dramatically on a hill overlooking a ravine, Rossano boasts one of the most delightful churches in all Calabria – the ninth-century Byzantine **San Marco**. The five tiny drum-shaped cupolas and the three palm trees that stand at the entrance give this church a distinctly Oriental appearance, like something out of the *Arabian Nights*. Inside, all is dazzling whitewash. If the church is closed (it nearly always is), knock at the door of Via Marco 37 and ask to speak to the curator.

The **Duomo** itself is not very interesting (although it boasts a beautiful Byzantine Madonna above the main altar), but on no account should you miss the adjoining **Museo Diocesano** (open daily 9 a.m.–12 noon, 4–6 p.m.). This glorious lumber room is piled high with ecclesiastical treasures – portraits of Pope Urban VII, silver monstrances and reliquaries, chalices and goblets, a bone belonging to St Martin.

Most splendid of all, though, is the **Codex Purpureus**, a sixth-century Greek manuscript illustrating the life of Christ on purple-dyed vellum. It is made of 185 pages, one of which is turned every year. When I visited, page 18 was on display, which means that, before the turning of the last page, we shall all be dead! Still, you can always buy a book with reproduction plates, worth it just to have a look at the por-trayal of the Last Supper: the disciples are lying in a circle around the table, eating with their fingers from a single large bowl in true Eastern fashion. Leonardo da Vinci's famous depiction of the Last Supper, with the disciples seated in front of individual plates around a rectan-gular table, is historically wrong. As indeed are most paintings of the Last Supper.

We left the Tyrrhenian shore at Tropea, which is the best place from which to cross to the Ionian Sea, cutting 109 km inland on Routes 18, 536, 182 and 110 until you arrive at the interesting town of Stilo.

Serra San Bruno

But not before you come, after 70 km, to the remote and severe mountain village of Serra San Bruno (population 6,700). The severity is in the colour: grey stone, everything grey. But the houses of Serra often have graceful seventeenth-century balconies, the curlicued ironwork adorned with bright red roses. A river runs through the town, the Fiume Garuso, and in the summer months you will often see cattle-drovers goading their livestock across the waters. The town has some prosperity from its craft of woodworking; houses are some-times timbered, the dark brown wood carved and decorated with skill.

What to see

Serra was founded in the late eleventh century by Bruno of Cologne, who gave his name to the famous **Carthusian monastery** which now stands a little way outside the town, built on land granted St Bruno by King Roger the Norman in 1090. The sixteen monks here live a life of absolute self-denial; their days are spent in study, prayer and tilling the fields. They rarely talk to one another as they have all taken the vow of silence. Women are unfortunately not allowed to visit the monastery (I don't see what's wrong with disguising your-selves as men in order to enter), and visiting hours are deliberately awkward: Monday–Friday 10.30–11.30 a.m.; Saturday 3.30–5.30 p.m.; closed Sunday. Before leaving Pizzo it is best perhaps to tele-phone the monastery (0963-71253) and ask for an appointment. It more than repays a visit, for it is the subject of a strange and hitherto unsolved mystery . . .

In the meantime, stroll down Serra's main street, the Corso

Umberto, and admire some of the churches that line the way; all have very distinct Baroque façades of carved granite (a local stone). First on the left, the **Chiesa Matrice** (1795), which contains four marble statues, the work of a certain Dutchman signing himself 'David Müller 1611'. The carved eighteenth-century pulpit is a good example of the skill of Serra's local wood craftsmen. Next is the **Addolorata** (1794), which has a very peculiar elliptical façade that curves itself right the way round the sides of the church. Then the **Assunta**, which dates from the thirteenth century though the Baroque façade with campanile and clock-tower was added in the eighteenth. To have so many churches in so short a street is an indication of how religious a place Serra became after the founding of the Carthusian monastery.

We reach the monastery by following the Corso Umberto down to the end, until it becomes a forest path winding its way through pines. Ten minutes later and the **Certosa di San Bruno Monastery** looms large, although it ought to be said that, as a result of the terrible earthquake of 1783, little of the original building survives. The façade of the former abbey church of 1595 remains – bleak and one-dimensional, like part of a strange Hollywood set, its massive stone pinnacles turned outwards by the tremors. The bones and skull of St Bruno, kept in a 1900 chapel, are taken out, twice a year, in procession. The monks here are buried anonymously, one on top of the other, with only a sheet to divide the corpses. No names on the crosses.

The promised mystery is that, out of a sense of remorse, the pilot of the B29 plane that dropped the atom bomb on Hiroshima is supposed to be living in this monastery; his name is Lehmann Leroy. Everyone in the village of Serra will tell you so, for they have all seen him – a tall guy with a beard, though most of his face is hidden by the white hood of the Order of St Bruno. When the Pope visited the monastery on 5 October 1984, he was rumoured to have granted the B29 pilot an audience, and to have listened to his confession. The enigma is further complicated by the fact that the Sicilian nuclear physicist Ettore Majorana, who vanished under mysterious circumstances in March 1938, was supposed recently to have died in this monastery. Prior to his disappearance, Majorana had carried out some important research into nuclear fission; people say he committed suicide as he feared the consequences of his work. If both Lehmann Leroy and Ettore Majorana, indirectly connected one to the other through Hiroshima, indeed both took vows within the walls of this monastery, the coincidence fairly taxes one's belief.

But do not, for the love of heaven, say anything about these mysterious brothers to any of the monks who show you around the monastery. I made the mistake of doing so and the *padre* suddenly turned from mild-mannered guide to crotchety old man. Besides, the story may be the result of hearsay, of journalistic fabrications. But I think not; when I asked the sexton in Serra's municipal cemetery whether he thought there was any truth in the rumours, he smiled and said, *'Voce del popolo, voce di Dio* [Voice of the people, voice of God].' This old Calabrian proverb means that if everyone holds to the truth of a rumour, then it must be God's honest truth and nothing but.

Past the monastery, continue along the avenue until you come to a clearing in the woods. A tiny lake, the waters of which are believed to have miraculous curing powers, marks the spot where St Bruno died. It is a delightful part of Serra – leafy and tranquil. The trees here – *abete bianco*, silver firs – are such as you find elsewhere only in the Black Forest.

Stilo

Passing through some of the most wild and darkly dramatic scenery in all Italy, you will soon arrive (after 37 km) at Stilo (population 3,306). This is an attractive town of twisting, narrow streets and higgledy-piggledy terracotta tiled houses. It is dramatically situated on the flank of Monte Consolino, overlooking the Stilaro River (in summer, usually dried up). 'So many and so exquisite are the beauties of Stilo,' wrote Edward Lear, 'that to settle to drawing any of them was difficult.'

What to see

And particularly difficult Stilo's exquisite little church of the **Cattolica**, standing on top of a hill. This is one of the most perfect Byzantine churches – perhaps the most perfect – in all Europe. It is a real Calabrian treasure: the brickwork, of a warm reddish-brown, and the five delicate cupolas (curiously resembling dustbin-lids!) bring to mind similar churches in the Middle East. The church was probably built in the twelfth century. On the left-hand side as you enter is a faded inscription in Byzantine–Greek: the curator told me that it had recently been translated for the first time by a visiting Greek professor as, 'Make ready this, the hermitage and temple of the Lord. Behold, the Lamb of God that takes away the sins of the world.'

The four columns come from an unidentified temple in Magna Graecia; one has been turned on its head – symbol of the submission of paganism to Christianity. The first column on the right bears the Greek inscription, 'God is the Lord who appeared to us', surmounted by a crudely carved cross. The curator would like to think that there was an actual apparition here in Stilo, all those centuries ago. But nobody knows for sure the significance of this inscription.

Before leaving, have a look at the section of the wall above the visitors' book; the paintwork has peeled away in such a way as to reveal four stages of Calabria's domination by foreign powers – there are the remains of Byzantine, Norman, Angevin and Spanish frescoes. It is a miracle that this church has not been shattered by an earthquake.

Locri

Taking the coastal Route 106 south we arrive after 36 km at the town of Locri (population 11,409). From here one may visit both the ruins of the ancient city and the nearby medieval town of Gerace. If you want to stay the night near the ruins, try the Motel Faro, tel. 0964-361015, the only hotel to have been constructed near the excavations.

(Though quite how the owner managed to build on top of an archaeological zone I don't know; best not ask too many questions.)

History

Locri, founded in 673 BC, was the first Greek city to possess a written code of laws. It was conquered by the Romans in 205 BC and completely destroyed by the Saracens in the seventh century.

What to see

Not much of the Greek town remains; and you may be a little disappointed by what there is to see. There are traces of Ionic and Hellenistic **Theatres** and there is a Doric **Temple** (this last situated in a sort of hamlet full of pigs and cockerels). The setting is beautiful. Try to see the ruins at sunset, with the tall sugar-cane rustling in the breeze, the mountains purple in the distance. Whilst I was testing the acoustics in the theatre one evening, the sky reverberated with thunder and in no time it was raining with a vengeance. All manner of heady scents were drawn in the wake of the downpour: dried cistus, thyme, asphodel, wild asparagus and liquorice, the saxifrage that colours the ancient stones with a brilliant enamel of red and yellow. Truly, this is old Calabria.

On the archaeological site stands an **Antiquarium** (open Tuesday–Saturday 9 a.m.–1 p.m., 3.30–7.30 p.m.; Sunday 9 a.m.–1 p.m.). It houses some architectural fragments from Locri and a few old coins and shards of broken pottery. It is well laid out but terribly dull.

Gerace

Situated 9 km from Locri on top of an impregnable crag, Gerace (population 3,500) can be reached by bus from the square in front of Locri station five times daily. It is a rugged and ramshackle town. As Edward Lear wrote: 'Every part of it seems to have been dangerously afflicted by earthquakes, splits, and cracks, and chasms, horrible with abundant crookedness of steeples, and a general appearance of instability in walls and houses.' Traditionally, this is bandit country, and the wildness of the landscape – best appreciated from the vantage point of the Norman **Castle** – leads one to believe it, too.

What to see

Gerace has a lovely Norman **Cathedral**, founded by Robert Guiscard in 1045 and later enlarged by Frederick II in 1222. For your visit, the custodian (or 'watchman' as he prefers to call himself) will expect a hefty tip. Fair enough: this is the largest church in Calabria. The crypt, noticeable as soon as you enter, is supported by twenty-six columns from ancient Locri. The stark Romanesque interior, in the form of a Latin cross plan, is supported on high stilt-blocks resting on antique columns of marble and granite – all of them diversely coloured a red or green, a pink or brown, some of them mottled with chips of white, like a round of Windsor Red cheese. The arches are of different heights. It all looks most eccentric. To the right of the altar is a perfect little Gothic chapel – the *Cappella di Sacramento*, complete with vaulted ceiling.

Down the street and to the right of the Cathedral entrance stands the wonderful **Church of San Francesco d'Assisi**. Consecrated in 1252, the intriguing designs above the portal are distinctly Arabic. But the overall design of the church is Norman, with lancet windows in the outside walls of the nave. Inside is a splendid Baroque altarpiece of 1664, with a marble inlay of extraordinary detail – birds pecking at melons; a bird pecking at a moth; a relief of how Gerace looked in medieval times; nuns playing with a dog. In the same square, the Largo delle Tre Chiese, stands the **Sacro Cuore**, with a curious frilly little dome resembling a party-time blancmange.

Reggio di Calabria

Reggio (population 165,882) is not a pretty city. Already rebuilt after an earthquake in 1783, it was half-demolished by the one of 1908 that destroyed Messina. A grim and undistinguished place, Reggio is consequently made of shoddy tenements and low buildings, most of them constructed from reinforced concrete. Mussolini's favourite poet, Gabriele d'Annunzio, described Reggio's Lungomare as the most beautiful kilometre in Italy. It is a pleasant enough park overlooking the sea and the rugged Sicilian coastline, but nevertheless has little to compare with those magical views over the Bay of Naples.

But there are several reasons for staying a few days in Reggio. The city boasts a wonderful museum which dramatically brings to life the lost cities of Magna Graecia. And it is the ideal point of departure for the so-called Isole Grecanica, primitive mountain-villages where a Greek dialect is still spoken. It is also near the tiny fishing village of Scilla, named after the dread rock of the *Odyssey* – worth a visit even if you can't be bothered with Homer. Reggio is ideal, too, for trips into the pine- and birch-covered Aspromonte mountains. Finally, it is from Reggio that you take the ferry to Sicily. If you are visiting that extraordinary island, and you have time to spare, you could do worse than spend it in Reggio. For a start, the city has some excellent restaurants.

What to see

The Museum

The National Museum (open Tuesday–Saturday 9 a.m.–1.30 p.m., 3.30–7.30 p.m.; Sunday 9 a.m.–12.30 p.m.) houses a superb collection of antiquities from the cities of Magna Graecia, and from nearby Locri in particular, to which city are devoted ten rooms. Among the exhibits you should not miss the set of dramatic tablets illustrating the **life of Persephone** (fifth century BC); the giant **marble foot** (third century BC) in the form of a sarcophagus; the marble **head of Apollo** with sunken eyes. But the real treasures here are the **two bronze statues** of Greek warriors found at a depth of 8 metres off the coast of Calabria in 1972. Nobody knows how the warriors came to rest on the bottom of the Ionian Sea, but the delineation of physical features achieved by whoever sculpted them is awe-inspiring. Originally, both warriors were carrying spears and shields, assets which have never been recovered as they would have been detached from the statues whilst they were on board ship to facilitate transportation. There is today a huge industry in Reggio selling miniature replicas of the famous *Bronzi di Riace*; you can even buy bottles of something calling itself 'Parfum Riax'.

Where to stay
Top range

Excelsior, Via Vittorio Veneto 66; tel. 0965-25801. Four-star, posh and certainly the best hotel in Calabria. But it will set you back a bit.

Continental, Via Florio 10; tel. 0965-24990. Four-star, luxurious but without much style.

Mid range

Hotel Lido, Via 3 Settembre 6; tel. 0965-25001. Three-star, rooms with all mod cons: minibars, televisions, telephones. Comfortable but bland.

Albergo Noel, Via Zebri 13; tel. 0965-330044. My favourite hotel in Reggio. Overlooks the sea; of a pleasing size (only 19 rooms); faded but clean and airy.

Miramare, Via Fata Morgana 1; tel. 0965-91882.

Bottom range

Albergo Abruzzo, Via Capera 5; tel. 0965-23862. Cramped, with lumpy beds; and the grumpy old ladies who run the place are in the strange habit of padlocking you into your room at night. Fine if you don't mind that sort of thing.

Where to eat

Da Peppino, Corso Vittorio Emanuele 27–29; tel. 0965-331224. Here you will eat the best swordfish in Calabria. Large white napkins and tablecloths; no silly frills. I have particularly happy memories of this restaurant as I was once hit on the head there by a flying champagne cork; by way of apology, the management presented me with a whole new bottle of the stuff, on the house. Sadly, two years ago the patron was gunned down outside this restaurant by the *'Ndrangheta*.

Don Pepe, Via Roma 10; tel. 0965-26041. Excellent for fish. Very popular with the locals, so book early. Impressive selection of wines.

The Environs of Reggio

The Isole Grecanica

You may want to spend a day walking in the roughest corner, the Ultima Thule, of Southern Italy. You can be sure that this conglomeration of ancient villages perched way up in the mists of the Aspromonte mountains are well off the beaten track of tourism; they are a last refuge of living Byzantinism. For a bastard Byzantine-Greek is still spoken in these primitive settlements, whose inhabitants are disdainfully referred to by Calabrians in cosmopolitan Reggio as *Turchi*, Turks. Probably, they originally came from Greece as refugees, taking to the mountains for safety.

One village, Bova, its 'houses nestling among huge blocks of stone that make one think', wrote Norman Douglas, 'of some cyclopean citadel of past ages', is said to be a genuine colony of Magna Graecia – the last link with the ancient culture, dating from the time of Locri. Reputedly, Bova was the birthplace of Praxiteles, the Greek sculptor, and in 1911 Douglas was delighted to find that he could communicate in 'fluent Byzantine' with his Bova guide.

The villages up in the Isole Grecanica sprawl unmethodically on top of fantastic rocks, teetering over the edge as though for dear life; earthquakes, mud- and land-slides are indeed a constant danger. Their remoteness from any channels of communication with Reggio means that, for long stretches of your walk, you are unlikely to come across any fellow human beings. For an entire four hours, the only people I saw were two solitary *carabinieri* officers – not surprisingly, as the Aspromonte are a notorious hiding-place for 'Ndrangheta kidnap victims, and for hoodlums on the run. Few people know the lie of the land up here, the twisting mountain paths. On 8 June 1988, the thirty-year-old son of a Lombardian industrialist, kidnapped six months previously by the shores of Lake Como in Northern Italy, was found wandering about the Isole Grecanica in a state of shock, dazed and confused. He had just been released by the 'Ndrangheta. But fear not; there is no danger to you from this fearsome organisation. Watch out for falling rocks, though. You will need an entire day in the Isole Grecanica – paths to villages are often badly-cut, narrow rock steps, so wear a stout pair of shoes.

Roccaforte del Greco   Here is a suggested itinerary. From Piazza Garibaldi in front of Reggio's train station, take the tiny blue *Principato* bus heading for Roccaforte. It leaves at 6.50 a.m. Roccaforte lies some 40 km from Reggio, a steep climb all the way. There are few coffee bars or shops here; this is the back of beyond and people will stare at you as though you had descended on their village like an asteroid from outer space. But you soon get used to it.

From the heights of this village you are afforded a stupendous view of the Amandole River, the largest *fumarole* – an almost vertically descending torrent – in Calabria. On a fine day, you can see it snaking its way into the Ionian Sea. The Amandole is often the ruination of the Isole Grecanica, bursting with tremendous spates and carrying away sheep, cottages, olive and lemon trees. Nature is harsh up here: in summer, the Amandole is dry as bone, dehydrated to expose grey shingle-beds, the gnarled roots of trees. Wild bulls and goats are often to be seen in the parched river bed.

Up in Roccaforte, where the ramshackle Baroque church still respects the rites of Greek Orthodoxy, life is at a standstill. A professor in Reggio told me that 90 per cent of the women here are ignorant of their dates of birth; 82 per cent have never been to a cinema; 84 per cent have never spoken on a telephone. Speak to any of the inhabitants in Italian, and they will probably not understand.

Take the road from Roccaforte to Roghudi (it is signposted). Half an hour down, you come to a deconsecrated thirteenth-century Byzantine church, the **Chiesa dei Tripepi**. It is in the middle of a field; at the battered portals pigs snuffle at their swill in a trough. If you are lucky, a farmer will open the church for you. Inside, there is nothing but a spooky old Madonna in a dusty glass case, dressed up like a doll in wreaths of pink tulle.

Roghudi

A couple of hours later you come to the village of Roghudi, built on the crest of a hill with tumbledown, terracotta-roofed houses fitting into crevices as best they can, hanging on by their eaves. There seems hardly to be any hope for them. In 1972 the village was largely depopulated after a mudslide. Today, ten or so families stubbornly remain, living under the shadow of a further impending disaster. (There is a Calabrian saying that people in Roghudi are constrained to tie even their chickens to the table legs.) The path that climbs upwards towards Bova is beautiful – forests of oak and chestnut, beech and fir trees; highland pasture of Alpine flowers.

Bova

Bova is reached through some of the most beautiful forest in Italy – I had a field day there picking wild cherries. From afar, this aerial town reminds one of an eagle's nest, perched imperiously on a mass of cactus-growing rock. On arrival in Bova, a sign reads *'Kalos Irete'*, Greek for 'Welcome'. There is a ruined Norman **Castle**, well worth climbing up to for the views; and, surprisingly for so small a town, Bova boasts a total of seven churches. In the **Chiesa Matrice**, note the fragment of a marble Madonna and Child mutilated by Turkish pirates.

In Bova's main square there is an extraordinary object on permanent display – a black and red 1911 steam engine. Hence the name of the square: Piazza Ferrovieri d'Italia. As you leave Bova a sign reads *'Metablepite'*, Greek for 'Goodbye'. A strange and very haunting place.

Bova Marina

Descending all the way, we eventually hit the coast at Bova Marina, an insignificant town but with some of the most popular stretches of Calabrian beach. From here you can take the train back to Reggio, your journey into the heartland of Byzantine Calabria complete.

Scilla

Twenty kilometres north of Reggio on the coastal Route 18 takes us to Scilla (population 6,161), a delightful fishing village clustered on a spur behind the famous rock of Scylla which, crowned by a 1225 **Castle**, rises some 73 metres out of the sea. It was between this rock, described by Homer as a monster with a wolf's body and dolphin's tail, and the whirlpool of Charybdis that Odysseus had to pass, homeward bound from Ithaca after the Siege of Troy. 'For on the one side lay Scylla and on the other divine Charybdis sucked down terrifyingly the salt water of the sea.' Today, there are fine views of Sicily across the narrowest point of the Straits of Messina. Scilla has some fine (though somewhat pebbly) beaches.

Bagnara Calabria

Ten kilometres north is Bagnara Calabria, a town perched in a lovely position on steep terraces rising one above the other from sandy

186

bays. It is here that you can observe the Calabrian art of swordfishing; here, the Straits of Messina are at their narrowest, so the fish are easy prey. The wooden fishing boats themselves are peculiar-looking constructions; each is surmounted by a disproportionately tall mast with crow's nest; and from the prow there protrudes a just as disproportionately long sort of proboscis, along which a man runs to harpoon the swordfish. If you ask the fishermen nicely (go down to the harbour at about 7 a.m.), they will allow you to accompany them on the kill. Primitive, bloody and exhilarating.

Gambarie If you do not have time enough to inspect the Greek villages in the Aspromonte, you can always plump for the less arduous (and less time-consuming) option of visiting the tiny Aspromonte town of Gambarie, a popular summer and winter resort in a magnificent position among beech and fir forests. The resort lies 35 km inland from Reggio on Routes 18 and 184. A bus leaves from Reggio's Piazza Garibaldi at 7 a.m.; it takes one and a half hours.

When you get off the bus, follow the signs for *'Garibaldi Cippo'*. Garibaldi's cypress, under the branches of which the hero lay mortally wounded, is reached along a beautiful woodland path, bursting (at the right time of year) with wild mushrooms. After 7 km, it breaks out into meadowland and from that point it is but a short walk to the famous tree – the scene of Garibaldi's capture by government troops on 29 August 1862, when he raised an army of 3,000 volunteers with the call *'Rome or Death!'* in an unsuccessful attempt to incorporate Rome and the Papal States into a united Italy. As it turned out, Rome was not liberated until 1870. Near the tree (encircled by iron railings) stands the **Garibaldi Mausoleum**, a great block of concrete in the Soviet socialist realist mould. Through a little window you can see a bust of Garibaldi, a couple of cannonballs and a tattered, bullet-torn flag. The woods here are everywhere littered with the usual detritus of picnickers; the plastic cups etc. are an unusual way to honour the founder of the modern Italian Republic.

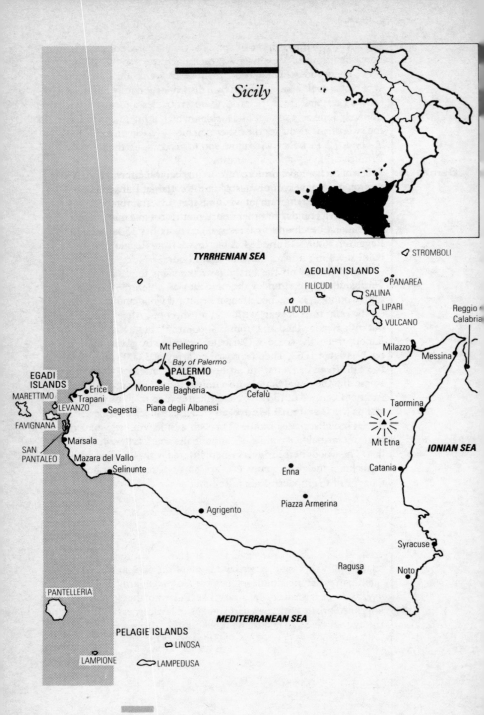

Sicily

TYRRHENIAN SEA

STROMBOLI

AEOLIAN ISLANDS

FILICUDI PANAREA

SALINA

ALICUDI LIPARI

VULCANO

Reggio Calabria

Mt Pellegrino

Bay of Palermo
PALERMO

Milazzo

Messina

EGADI ISLANDS

MARETTIMO

Erice

Monreale Bagheria

Cefalù

Trapani

LEVANZO

Segesta Piana degli Albanesi

Taormina

FAVIGNANA

SAN PANTALEO

Marsala

Mt Etna

IONIAN SEA

Mazara del Vallo

Enna

Catania

Selinunte

Piazza Armerina

Agrigento

Syracuse

Ragusa

Noto

PANTELLERIA

MEDITERRANEAN SEA

PELAGIE ISLANDS LINOSA

LAMPIONE LAMPEDUSA

Sicily

Introduction

Much of Sicily appears more Moroccan than Mediterranean. A joke – though it is not very funny – told in the North of Italy is that Sicily is the only Arab country not at war with Israel. Certainly the Arabs, who invaded in 831, have left their mark on this Mediterranean island; in the capital city of Palermo, an exotic confusion of mosques and pink-domed cupolas, there is an old Mafia stronghold known as the Kalsa. The name derives from the Arab *khalisa*, meaning – ironically – 'pure'.

Palermo is a city troubled for twenty days a year by the *sirocco*, an African wind covering cars and buildings in a film of red sand. In the labyrinth of her daily markets, you see black-clad women winching baskets of fruit to the tops of their tumbledown houses on lengths of rope, for all the world as though they were out of some medieval *kasbah*. But then Africa is only 160 km away. 'It isn't quite like Europe,' wrote D. H. Lawrence of this strange and beautiful island. 'This is where Europe finally ends. Beyond is Africa and Asia.' In Sicily, you feel a million miles from anywhere.

Crime and the Mafia
It was the western part of Sicily that the Arabs invaded, an area which has since become the province of the Mafia. Apparently, this is not coincidental: *omertà*, the Mafia's code of silence – 'which binds so many people in a type of squalid complicity dictated by fear', as Pope John Paul II once said – is Arab in essence. Or so Northern Italians would have one believe; the word 'Mafia', they point out, is itself derived from the Arab *mahias*, meaning bully or braggart.

But then there has always been racialism (and this is not too strong a word) towards the Sicilian; a 1944 *Soldiers' Guide to Sicily*, with a foreword by Dwight Eisenhower, claimed that 'he is well known for his extreme jealousy in so far as his womenfolk are concerned, and in a crisis still resorts to the dagger'. The *Guide* continues: 'Morals are superficially very rigid, being based upon Arab or Spanish codes of etiquette; they are, in actual fact, of a very low standard.' This, need one say, is to exaggerate – in a city like Palermo the streets certainly appear to bristle with menacing omens of lawlessness. But this is not to say that all Sicilians are members of the Mafia; perhaps we have seen too many films and read too much Mario Puzo, author of *The Godfather*.

Looking at Sicily today, it is difficult to see how the island was ever the prize possession of the Arabs – or of the Greeks, Normans, Spanish or Bourbons. Let alone of Benito Mussolini. Blighted by a long and bitter history of colonisation, Sicily is heir to some irresolvable contradictions: the sub-tropical lushness of its cultivated coastal regions, as against a parched and arid hinterland; a population largely devoted to agriculture, often illiterate and desperately poor, as against a prosperous Mafia class that thrives on organised crime; a comparatively law-abiding East as against a lawless West, so lawless that in a city like Palermo even the *carabinieri* drive the wrong way up one-way streets.

History

It is impossible to understand contemporary Sicily without knowing something about her turbulent history. Sicilians have never, in the entire history of their island, been governed by a capable ruling class. Sicily has always been the symbol of a vanquished island, as opposed to the victorious insularity of, say, England. The only time the Sicilians have taken up arms against their oppressors was in 1282, when the population of Palermo ousted the French in the 'Sicilian Vespers', a singularly barbarous revolt in which Sicilian women thought to be pregnant by Frenchmen were ripped open. Typically, the insurrection achieved little; although Palermo was briefly declared an independent republic, the doors were afterwards opened for centuries of corrupt and inefficient rule under the Spanish – a rule to which Sicilians sluggishly acquiesced.

In his classic novel *The Leopard*, Giuseppe di Lampedusa wrote: 'The Sicilians never want to improve for the simple reason that they think themselves perfect; their vanity is stronger than their misery; every invasion by outsiders, whether so by origin or, if Sicilian, by independence of mind, upsets their illusion of achieved perfection, risks disturbing their satisfied waiting for nothing; having been trampled on by a dozen different peoples, they think they have an imperial past which gives them a right to a grand funeral.'

'Trampled' is the right word. During the sixth century BC, Sicily was dominated by a string of Greek tyrants, the most notorious of whom was Phalaris: according to the history books, he had a gastronomic penchant for infant children. At the end of the first Punic War, in 241 BC, Sicily became a Roman province, an imperial granary, 'the nurse at whose breast the Roman people feed', according to Cato's dictum. Damage to the land was considerable.

The Normans were on the whole benevolent rulers: under Roger II there was a unique flowering of Byzantine, Islamic and Western European traditions of art and culture. But William II, who ruled Sicily from 1166 to 1189, was nevertheless typical of Norman despots in his love of Moorish concubines, and of slaves for bodyguards.

The worst period for Sicily, though, was 600 years, commencing in 1282 after the uprising, of Spanish and Bourbon rule. The viceroys were particularly corrupt, trading in nepotism, privateering, piracy and brigandage. Any traveller venturing across the island soon discovered the reality. In 1771 the English writer Patrick Brydone complained of 'deserted fields, barren wilderness, oppressed peasants, and lazy, lying, lecherous monks. The poor inhabitants appear more than half-starved.' The comatose stupor of the ordinary Sicilian in the face of the Mafia is not so different from his helpless acquiescence to suppression under the Spanish.

The British, on the other hand, appeared to have done Sicily some genuine good. Lord William Bentinck, governor of the island from 1806 to 1815, abolished feudalism in 1812 with his 'new liberal constitution'; and Admiral Nelson once fortified the Royal Navy with 40,000 gallons of Marsala, the distant (and perhaps underrated) Sicilian cousin of sherry. Ever since, Marsala has been one of Sicily's more lucrative exports – healthier, at any rate, than its *most* lucrative commodity, which is heroin.

Seen from Reggio di Calabria, it is difficult, at least in bad weather, to believe that Sicily – a large, craggy hump like the back of a semi-submerged Leviathan – could be the centre of a criminal association so vast, so well organised, so secret and so powerful that it can dominate not only half of the island, but half of criminal New York as well. Interpol and the Drug Enforcement Agency now have incontestable proof that at least 60 per cent of European and 33 per cent of world drug-trafficking is Italo-American in origin. The trafficking is mostly centred in Sicily, for the island contains, in concentrated form, all the evils and all the delights that exist in mainland Italy – evils, such as the Mafia, that are nevertheless too diffuse to be adequately noticed. The island is like one of those concave shaving mirrors in which Italy can behold her national faults and virtues distorted and exaggerated. Writing from Palermo in 1787, Goethe seems uncannily to have foreseen this fact: 'To have seen Italy without seeing Sicily', he wrote, 'is not to have seen Italy at all. For Sicily is the key to everything.'

Sicily is incredibly, almost embarrassingly, rich in interest. The Baroque façades of churches in Campania, the Romanesque cathedrals of Apulia, the ruins of ancient Greece in Calabria, the castles, churches and palaces built all over Southern Italy by the invading Normans, Aragonese and Spanish – all of these are to be found in the microcosm island of Sicily.

The natural beauty of Sicily, though, is unique: the final impression one has of the island is of grilling sunshine, of rugged mountains, of vine- and olive-clad slopes, of torrents and of dry ravines, of white roads winding steeply up hills and down valleys, of peasants on mules, and of small, forgotten, medieval towns with narrow streets, perched on hillsides. Of fruit, of fields of lemon and lime trees, there is a cloying abundance. The prodigious fertility of Sicily was once brought home to me by, of all people, a Sicilian taxi-driver. We were perched precariously on top of the dizzy heights of Palermo's Monte Pellegrino (described by Goethe as the most beautiful headland in the world). *'Madonna mia!'* he exclaimed. 'So you don't even grow olives in

England, eh? Let alone oranges. Or lemons, pineapples – prickly pears? Mother of God, but what a miserable place! Wine, then – what about *il vino*?' I replied that we had beer, not much wine. At that point the taxi-driver raised his arms heavenwards. 'So what the devil do you *do* in your country?'

For the independent traveller in Sicily, there is almost too much to do, too much to see. The Aeolian Islands are so beautiful that the inhabitants say you should really have four eyes to see them. Volcanic in origin, these include Stromboli, an ascent of which is an unforgettable, awe-inspiring experience. There is the strange and barren island of Lampedusa, off the coast of Africa, where you are more likely to find a bowl of Tunisian *couscous* than a plate of Sicilian pasta. The provincial towns of Noto and Ragusa in eastern Sicily are an eighteenth-century architect's dream of golden-coloured Baroque palaces and churches, some set behind monumental staircases, others behind lush tropical gardens. The nearby city of Syracuse, the old town a maze of twisting cobbled streets, boasts the finest Greek theatre in the western world, set romantically in a large and verdant park. Palermo, an aristocratic city, is graciously composed of Baroque churches and oratories built by the Spaniards, and formal eighteenth-century gardens laid out by the French. Not to mention the Arab palaces and pavilions.

It is in Palermo, too, that you will see Sicily's famous puppet shows. Traditionally concerned with the deeds of Charlemagne and his paladins, the sword-fights between Saracen and Christian marionettes invariably reach a crescendo of crazed racial odium, their metal armour rattling furiously as they basically beat the hell out of one another. For Sicily is strong in folklore: vans and wagons are often painted in reds, yellows, blues and greens, to symbolise the island's oranges, sun, sea and grass.

Travelling around the coast of Sicily in an anti-clockwise fashion, one could happily spend a fortnight on the island. In Palermo itself, there is certainly more than enough to keep you occupied for a good four days.

With a population of five million, Sicily is the largest of the Mediterranean islands at 25,708 sq km; mostly mountainous, the island forms a continuation of the great Apennine range that stretches across the Mediterranean from the main trunk of Europe to Africa. Etna, the largest volcano in Europe, dominates the east and much of the centre of Sicily. Sicily is almost exactly midway between Gibraltar and Suez, between east and west, Europe and Africa.

The coastal regions are largely devoted to the culture of the vine. In a land where, in the local dialects, there is no future tense for the verb 'to be', and where a markedly cheerful expression has it that *'Finchè c'è morte c'è speranza* [Where there's death there's hope]', wine is a saving grace. Try a bottle of Rapitala, a dry white with a sourish sort of tang.

The label shows two knights in armour, swords about to clash: violent action, gesticulation and bloodshed, characteristics of Sicilian life from its puppet shows to the Mafia's *sanguinoso* 'balancing of accounts'.

Getting there

By air

Palermo and Catania, Sicily's second most populous city, are linked by air services with all major European cities, including London. There are no direct scheduled flights from London, though there are plenty of direct charters. You fly to Rome or Milan, and pick up one of the regular connections to Sicily.

By rail and road

Italian State Railways have a Motorail service to Villa San Giovanni (where ferries operate to the eastern Sicilian city of Messina); and there is also a car-ferry and hydrofoil service from Reggio di Calabria. Other ferries from the mainland operate from Genoa, Livorno and Naples. Crossing time from Reggio to Messina is one hour maximum. The ferry crossing over the Straits of Messina is lovely; and on the train ride from Messina to Palermo you will traverse the spectacular northern coast. Ferries leave from Reggio at 6.55 a.m., 8 a.m., 10.15 a.m., 12.55 p.m., 2.20 p.m., 3.15 p.m., 5.20 p.m., 7.30 p.m., 9.55 p.m. But it is best to confirm.

Getting about

By road

Driving in Sicily presents no particular difficulties. Motorways, which traverse rugged terrain by means of viaducts and tunnels, are a convenient and fast way of travelling; they link Messina to Catania, Catania to Palermo, Palermo to Trapani, and Palermo to Mazara del Vallo. The convenience of being able to reach Palermo from Catania – the cities connecting the northern to the southern end of the island –in less than three hours has transformed communications; it is now possible to see most of Sicily's major sights on day trips.

By rail

Sicily is well served by rail. Trains, though, are often slow; with them, it is almost impossible to cross the island directly in one day. The two main lines, Messina to Palermo, and Messina to Catania and Syracuse, have a frequent service, but almost all the fast trains come from Naples, Rome or Milan on the Italian mainland. However, with careful planning, you should be able to reach most of Sicily's most interesting – though not far-flung – sights by train.

By bus

Buses are faster and more punctual than trains, though they run less frequently, and are more expensive. The fastest way from Palermo to Catania is by direct bus service along the motorway.

Where to stay

With the notable exception of Taormina, there are no long-established resorts in Sicily. Respectable hotels will be found at most towns of any size on the coast of Sicily, and around the main centres of interest in the interior. But the cramped development of hotels along the western coast (most of them built with Cosa Nostra money) is unappealing; in Palermo you would do better to stay in the historical centre rather than along the sea-front. An annual (free) list of *Hotels in Sicily*, giving categories and current charges, is available from the Assessorato del Turismo in Palermo in Piazza Castelnuovo.

Messina

On 28 December 1908 the city of Messina was almost entirely destroyed by an earthquake. The featureless modern architecture of today's city (population 263,000) is designed to resist further earthquakes; buildings are squat (by law, one cannot build higher than 20 metres) and unattractive. Everywhere, there are enormous spaces left by the disaster. Some of them have been turned into sad-looking parks, others merely resemble bomb-sites. For the earthquake was a massive upheaval, causing a 60 cm change in the sea-level of the coast, sending a 6-metre tidal wave crashing along the coast of Calabria. An estimated 84,000 people perished in Messina – two thirds of the population.

On first inspection, then, Messina is an unprepossessing city, dusty and chaotic – not so very different from Reggio di Calabria across the Straits, from where one takes the ferry to this gateway to Sicily. But then Messina has suffered not only from earthquakes. The great 1347 plague of Western Europe broke out within its city walls, and a further outbreak in 1740 took the lives of 40,000 people. In 1854 an outbreak of cholera carried off no fewer than 16,000 victims. Massive Allied bombings during the last war well-nigh razed the city to the ground. So allowances have to be made for the ugliness of present-day Messina. But it is still a convenient stopover, and not without interest.

What to see
The Cathedral

Founded in 1197 by the Norman King Roger II, the Duomo is a superb fake – a reproduction, that is. Following the great 'quake of 1908, it was entirely rebuilt, only to be levelled once more by bombings in June 1943. However, the façade preserves most of its original medieval and Renaissance sculptural decorations – the central **doorway** of 1468 is particularly fine. Note the primitive farming scenes: tiny naked men picking (and even sucking) grapes from vines, or swinging from the branches of trees like monkeys, many of them upside down. The overall effect is distinctly pagan, with the swinging men looking positively high on grape-juice.

The imitation Gothic **campanile** contains an intricate mechanical astrological clock, the largest of its kind in Europe. At midday, the thing goes quite berserk with an explosion of clockwork cherubs. The **interior**, cool with the simplicity of an early Christian basilica, contains little of interest. The Bishop's throne by the main altar is repro.

The Museum The Museo Regionale (open Tuesday–Saturday 9 a.m.–1.30 p.m.; Sunday 9 a.m.–12.30 p.m.) well repays a visit. It is quite some way outside the city centre – from the station, take an 8 or 27 bus. The gardens, romantically planted with a profusion of tropical flowers, are full of fragments from pre-earthquake Messina – Baroque statues of Neptune, rococo fountain decorations. The gardens give one a poignant impression of how splendid a city Messina must once have been.

Inside, the treasures include a beautiful late fifteenth-century **Madonna** by Francesco Laurana; a **polyptich** of the Madonna and Child painted in 1478 by Sicily's greatest artist and one of the great masters of the early Renaissance, Antonello da Messina, and a curious sixteenth-century Flemish work, **Master of the St Lucy Legend**, the canvas surrealistically crowded with symbols from the Passion – a cross, a flaming torch, flails, a pair of pliers, a pike, a sponge, a spade, dice, even a pair of hands, washing themselves in a chalice. There are two masterpieces by Caravaggio: the 1604 **Adoration of the Shepherds** (note the nitty-gritty realism of dirty straw and a wicker basket full of agricultural implements) and the 1609 **Resurrection of Lazarus**.

As you walk towards the station along the Via Primo Settembre, you will pass two Baroque corner fountains which survived the earthquake. Adorned with dolphins and other sea-creatures, they now stand opposite a 'Rent-a-Car' shop.

Turn left down Via Cardine and you come to the **SS. Annunziata dei Catalini**, an exquisite twelfth-century Norman church of the sort that you find in Palermo; the top half (toppled by the 1908 earthquake) has been skilfully restored. The building is now the Messina University Chapel. A temple of Neptune, and afterwards a mosque, are said to have occupied the same site; over the door is a Saracen inscription.

Nearby, sunk in a vacant lot, stand the sad ruins of **Santa Maria Alemanna**. Built in 1220, this church is one of the few Gothic buildings in Sicily. For some reason, restoration work has long since been abandoned; the scaffolding is sprouting weeds, rusty iron prongs protrude from concrete.

The cemeteries To the south of Messina is the picturesque cemetery. A luxuriant garden commanding spectacular views of nearby Calabria, this is where the 80,000 earthquake victims lie buried: 'Morto il 28 Dicembre 1908', read all the tombstones. And there is a fascinating

English cemetery, founded during the Napoleonic Wars. The epitaphs are most poignant: 'In ever loving memory of Frank Tiverton of England, Aged 21 years, Who was taken home by the terrible Messina Earthquake of Dec. 1908. His sun is gone down while it is yet day.' There are victims, too, of the Napoleonic Wars, their tombs adorned with the elaborate heraldry, the fearful symbols, of war: 'Captain Angus Cameron of his Brittannick Majesty's 21st Regt. of Foot. Killed in action, 1809.' It is strange to see so many people from Liverpool, Leeds and Manchester, now lain to rest in this godforsaken plot of Sicilian soil.

Where to stay

Riviera Grand Hotel, Viale della Liberta 516; tel. 090-57101. Four-star, the most elegant of Messina's hotels.

Royal Palace Hotel, Via Tommaso Cannizzaro 224; tel. 090-2921161. Three-star, comfortable; all rooms with televisions and minibars, etc.

Moderno Terminus, Via Primo Settembre 15; tel. 090-710853. As the name suggests, very near the station. Two-star, modest, reasonably priced and clean. Recommended.

Monza, Viale San Martino 63; tel. 090-773755. Two-star, somewhat rudimentary but otherwise fine.

Albergo Roma, Piazza Duomo 3; tel. 090-775566. Almost next door to the Cathedral, this *pensione* is on the top floor of a once elegant *palazzo*. Rooms are enormous, though without bath or shower. The communal lavatories leave a little to be desired; and a distinct whiff of humanity wafts from the kitchens. But no matter; the place is run by a very accommodating (and very elderly) husband and wife. The 'foyer' is chock-a-block with religious artefacts.

Where to eat

Trattoria del Porto, Via Vittorio Emanuele 71; tel. 090-54873. Behind the Duomo. A lot of rough types from the docks eat here, for the food is cheap and very good. If you want atmosphere, this is the restaurant for you.

Osteria del Campanile, Via Loggia dei Mercanti 9; tel. 090-711418. Excellent for local fare. Not particularly cheap, but try the delicious *involtine di pesce spada*.

Donna Giovanna, Via Risorgimento 16; tel. 090-718503. One of the best restaurants in Messina; popular with the locals.

La Trappola, Via dei Verdi 39; tel. 090-718652. Excellent local cuisine.

The Aeolian Islands

The most convenient starting-point in Sicily for the Aeolian (or Lipari) Islands is from the dreary port of Milazzo, 45 km along the coastal Route N113 from Messina. Running time from Milazzo to

Lipari, the best island from which to explore this archipelago of seven volcanic islands, is two hours by ferry, and about half that time by hydrofoil. In summer, there are five trips to Lipari every day, commencing at 7.30 a.m. and ending at 7 p.m. Cars are allowed only on Lipari and Salina, but are hardly necessary; these tiny islands are for walking on.

Named after the Greek god Aeolus, who was fabled to keep the winds imprisoned in his cave at Stromboli, the Aeolians are of a stunning beauty, with vast stretches of beach consisting of volcanic sand, black lava or white pumice; rust-coloured mountains with climbing vegetation; grottoes, islets and lagoons. There is flora in abundance: brushwood, heather, broom, prickly pear, oleander and myrtle. In spring and autumn, migratory birds such as pelicans, red- or ash-coloured herons, cormorants, flamingoes, cranes, wild geese and quails pass over the islands. Near Stromboli, flying fish are sometimes to be seen; many of them are attracted by camp fires specially lit for the purpose along the beach, and fly headlong into the flames. Talk about fast food.

Lipari

The largest of the Aeolians (population 12,000), about 37.6 sq km, shelters a picuresque town of the same name. Its whitewashed houses grow out from the flanks of a promontory on the top of which stands a medieval **Castle**, once the site of an ancient Greek **Acropolis** and now entered through an impressive sixteenth-century Spanish fortification. The Castle is the focus of Lipari's historical centre; around its walls the populations of the Neolithic, Iron, Bronze and Hellenic Ages once settled.

Archaeological finds from this part of the island are housed in the excellent **Museo Archeologico Eoliano** (open Tuesday–Saturday 9 a.m.–2 p.m.; Sunday 9 a.m.–1 p.m.). This occupies two buildings flanking the **Cathedral**, founded in 1084 by King Roger the Norman. The museum contains items from more than 1,300 tombs excavated in the past twenty years, the oldest dating from the fourth century BC.

Adjacent is the **Museo Vulcanologico Eoliano**, which traces the genesis and volcanic activity of the islands. There are plenty of maps, plastic models, graphics and samples of igneous matter, and it is all great fun.

What to do

The best way to explore Lipari is by taking the local bus along its two main routes. Alternatively, you can hire a moped from Foti Roberto, Via Professore E. Carnivale 84; tel. 090-9812587. The bus stops by the Esso station at the intersection of Corso Vittorio Emanuele and Marina Lungo. For one of the most enjoyable excursions, take a bus for the village of **Canetto**.

A ten-minute walk from here brings you to the **Spiagge Bianche**, the White Beaches. These are made up of vast stretches of white pumice-stone, the white pebbles so light it is like throwing bits of popcorn into the wind. You can hire a canoe to explore the secluded coves nearby. The sea is crystal-clear, with bits of shiny black obsidian glistening from the depths.

From these (often topless) beaches, you can take a pleasant hour's walk to **Ponticello**, where the surrounding hills are entirely composed of pumice – a lunar landscape harsh white under the sun. There are spectacular views en route.

Where to stay Since Lipari is the ideal island from which to explore the rest of the Aeolians, you may want to rent an apartment for a few days. To do so, it is best to book through either of these agencies: Costa Agenzia Promozioni, Via F. Mancuso, tel. 090-9812391; or Eolie Immobilliare, Via Garibaldi 19, tel. 090-9512358. The one advantage of renting a flat is that you can cook for yourself; eating out in Lipari is certainly expensive, as all provisions have to be shipped in.

Otherwise, for hotels, try any one of the following:

La Filadelfia, Via F. Mancuso; tel. 090-9812795.Two-star, near the Acropolis. Recently built but tastefully decorated. According to the brochure, the hotel 'rises in the historic hearth [sic] of Lipari'; and 'you will find it comfortable for the hospital of the staff'.

Hotel Oriente, Via G. Marconi 41; tel. 090-9811493. Two-star, modern and perfectly respectable.

Pensione Poseidon, Via Ausonia; tel. 090-9812876. Two-star and, as the name suggests, by the sea. All rooms with telephones and televisions.

Albergo Casa Vittorio, Vico Sparviero 15; tel. 090-9811523. In a secluded part of the island, this pleasant hotel is nestled in a tiny alley among tumbledown eighteenth-century houses. You can book either a room or an apartment. Any food you cook may be eaten on a terrace overlooking Lipari town. For those on a low budget.

Where to eat **E Pulera**, Via Diana; tel. 090-9811158. Restaurant and piano bar. Open only in the evenings, which are enlivened by *musici eoliani*, Aeolian musicians.

Filippino, Piazza Municipio; tel. 090-9811002. Founded in 1910, this is the oldest restaurant on Lipari. Expensive, but recommended for fish and local dishes.

La Ginestra, Via Stradale 10; tel. 090-9822285. Restaurant as well as a pizzeria. Prices not too prohibitive.

Stromboli Monday to Friday a ferry leaves Lipari for Stromboli at 10 a.m., arriving at 1.30 p.m. The seaward aproach to Stromboli is dramatic: a great mass of rock rises majestically to a startling height from the depths of the Tyrrhenian Sea. On the eastern slopes, clusters of whitewashed houses are scattered higgledy-piggledy like so many dice across the slate-grey slopes. Often, the cone will fume great billowing clouds of smoke. One of the most active volcanoes on earth today, Stromboli is particularly violent during the *sirocco*, the harsh wind from Africa.

Only 400 people live on Stromboli, but the main village, made up of the two hamlets of San Batolo and San Vincenzo, has hotels enough. Tourism was late in taking off; it began only in 1949, with the release of Roberto Rossellini's film *Stromboli*, a melodrama starring Ingrid Bergman as a Lithuanian refugee who marries a fisherman and throws a fit every time the volcano erupts. Even today, Stromboli appears the most remote of the islands in the Aeolian archipelago; probably, there are more wild goats than humans, and there are no restaurants to speak of. There are good beaches, however – the black sand a dramatic contrast to the inky-blue sea.

What to do   It is best to climb the 927 metres to the summit of Stromboli with a guide. The ascent can be dangerous (a Spanish boy was killed in 1986 by a boulder of molten lava) and if you do not already have such objects, the guides will insist that you come equipped with walking shoes, a torch, a pullover and a rucksack. You should wear ankle- or knee-length socks; otherwise your shoes will fill up with volcanic dust.

The ascent takes the best part of five hours and you should take with you a goodly supply of dark chocolate; the going is tough and you will need all the energy you can muster. Indeed, my travelling companion nearly fainted before she reached the top.

To spend the night watching the fiery bubbles of lava exploding with tremendous noise is an unforgettable experience. Every half-hour there is a great vomiting into the sky of enormous incandescent blocks of igneous matter, of showers of molten stone breaking out into a thousand splinters like the sparks that fly out from red-hot iron hammered on the anvil. Flashes of molten slag are reflected, eerily, in the sea way down below.

The descent is made by an extinct *sciara* – a stream of molten lava which has now turned to volcanic dust. You slide down it by the light of the moon, knee-deep in black sand. It is great fun; you could almost roll down, the sand is so soft.

For guides, I suggest you contact Nino, Prospero and Antonio (tel. 090-986093, 986175). Hardened mountaineers, they passed their *Club Alpino Italiano* proficiency examinations scaling the heights of Mount Etna. They take parties up Stromboli at 6 p.m. and return them safe and sound by 1 a.m. You will afterwards be amazed by the amount of volcanic dust to be blown from your nostrils.

Where to stay   **La Sciara Residence**, Via Soldato Cincotta; tel. 090-986004. Stromboli's one and only 'luxurious' hotel, though at three stars not *that* luxurious. Perfectly respectable, though.

Locanda Stella, Via F. Filzi 14; tel. 090-986020. As with most *pensioni* on Stromboli, this one deals only in full board. For dinner, you can either eat in the restaurant or have the kitchen staff fix you a packed lunch to take up Stromboli. One-star, but not that cheap.

Miramare, Via Nunziata 3; tel. 090-986047. Similar to the above.

Pensione Roma, Via Roma (a five-minute walk from the port); no telephone. For those on a low budget, this is absolutely fine. Rooms are fairly clean, though plumbing is rudimentary. There are fine views of the Aeolian archipelago from the terrace.

Vulcano

The volcanic island of Vulcano, best reached from Lipari, smells –it must be said – of bad eggs. Since 1888, when the now apparently dormant volcano erupted, hurling into the air fiery projectiles known as 'bread-crust bombs', the sulphurous crater has been busily smouldering away. Experts say there may be another eruption within the next twenty years. Vulcano is connected by a thin isthmus to the smaller island of Vulcanello, a now (definitely) extinct volcano which erupted from out of the sea in 204 BC. Some 500 people live on Vulcano, mostly around the small Porto di Levante, where the boats dock. In recent years this part of the island has been spoilt by indiscriminate (and doubtless Mafia-financed) building.

What to do

It is worth climbing to the crater of Vulcano, for which you do not need a guide. However, you should not attempt this one-hour ascent after 7 p.m. as climbing after nightfall is extremely dangerous. Once you have reached the summit, you can take a footpath down into the crater itself. The whole thing is dotted with pockets of activity, fissures from which the steam hisses. The rim itself steams infernally with sulphur vapours.

One thing you might like to do on Vulcano is submerge yourself in a bubbling mud bath; 'taking the lava', the locals call this therapeutic pastime, good for rheumatism. The trough, surrounded by rocks tinged yellow as if they were stained with nicotine, is situated near the Porto di Levante; there is no fee. The gurgling, muddy water is caused by submarine vents through which the volcanic vapours issue. You will see many an overweight and health-obsessed Italian wallowing in the mud like a rotund hippopotamus. After the bath, you can cleanse away the mud in the nearby sea, where there are more vents than you can probably handle: the water seems positively to *seethe* with bubbles.

Where to stay

Hotel Garden Vulcano; tel. 090-9852069. This is at the end of a dirt track and appears to have no address, but is nevertheless both signposted and highly recommended. It is surrounded by beautiful gardens abloom with tropical flowers and is owned by an old sea-captain who has decorated the bedrooms with treasures gathered on his voyages – African spears, moth-eaten naval uniforms. Three-star, with 30 rooms. 'Mineral therapeutic showers coming directly from the craters.'

Eros, Località Porto Levante; tel. 090-9852007. Two-star, of an intimate size, with only 14 rooms. Modern, clean and comfortable.

Casa Sipione, Via Levante 55; tel. 090-9852034. Delightful ranch-style pension; the owners are hospitable and speak near-perfect English. For those on a low budget. One-star, but perfectly all right.

Where to eat

Trattoria al Cratere, Porto Levante; tel. 090-9852045. On the road to Vulcano and crouched seemingly at the foot of the volcano, this is excellent value, particularly good for fish, and there is a pleasant open-air terrace.

Lanterna Blu, Via Lentia; tel. 090-9852178. Again, excellent for fish. The unusual advertisement runs: 'On your plate you will find a paradise heap of fresh fish, not to mention the truthful Aeolian cooking.'

Other Aeolian Islands

The other Aeolian Islands – Salina, Panarea, Alicudi and Filicudi – are much smaller than their more famous cousins, but are worth visiting if you have the time.

Cefalù

The beautiful little port of Cefalù (population 13,300), 184 km from Milazzo along the coastal road N113, is that very rare Sicilian thing – a popular package tour resort with fairly good beaches. But Cefalù is also a picturesque fishing town, its winding back streets a fascinating hive of Southern Italian activity. Black-clad women hang out their linen, old men in fedoras snooze outside their front doors on chairs. You may want to wind down in Cefalù for a day or two, before you take to the pleasures of raucous Palermo.

What to see
The Cathedral

The Norman Cathedral is one of the most exquisite buildings in Sicily. Situated dramatically at the foot of a barren and precipitous limestone promontory, the church was begun by Roger II in 1131. The austere façade rests upon gigantic blocks of hewn stone, made all the more austere by the two imposing towers enlivened by a double row of arches resting on massy columns. Lofty palm trees soften the architectural drama.

The impressive interior, built to a conventional Latin cross plan, has sixteen columns with Byzantine and Roman capitals supporting stilted Gothic arches. One's attention is immediately caught by the magnetic power and simple beauty of the **mosaics** which occupy the conch of the apse. Purely Byzantine in style, they show a colossal Christ in benediction. In His left hand He holds the Bible, open at the text in Latin, *'Ego sum Lux Mundi* [I am the Light of the World].' The figure is flanked by a hierarchy of apostles and archangels, and by peculiar six-winged angels with only heads, it seems, for bodies. The glimmering tesserae of the mosaics are ordered in extraordinary detail; note, for example, the shading on the cheekbones of Christ, and the single lock of hair that falls across the forehead.

The Museum

No visit to Cefalù would be complete without a call to the Museo Mandralisca (open daily 9.30 a.m.–12 noon, 3.30–6 p.m.). This houses a rich array of archaeological finds, Greek ceramics and Arab pottery. Its most famous work is a portrait by Antonello da Messina, *Ritratto di Ignoto* (Portrait of an Unknown Man), showing an impish-looking fellow with raised eyebrow and enigmatic smile – a perfect image of what Italians call *furbo*, cunning.

The wash-house

On the way to Cefalù's beaches, take a look at the curious Lavatoio. Approached by a wide flight of slimy steps, this is an ancient public wash-place converted in the ninth century into an Arab bath-house. It bears an Arab inscription.

Where to stay

Baia del Capitano, Via Mazzaforno; tel. 0921-20003. Three-star and perhaps the most luxurious of Cefalù's hotels, with swimming pool, sauna, tennis courts. According to its brochure, 'situated in the middle of Saracen olive-yards'.

La Siesta d'Oro, Località Kalura; tel. 0921-21761. Two-star. This modern hotel is 2 km outside Cefalù, but very tranquil – hence, no doubt, its name of Golden Siesta.

Villa Belvedere, Via Mulini; tel. 0921-21593. Two-star, 27 rooms with 52 beds, so not of an unmanageable size. Has an antique charm, with a pleasant palm tree garden. Up in the hills of SS. Salvatore, overlooking Cefalù.

Locanda di Bella, Via Umberto Primo 26; no telephone. For those on a low budget. Situated above a ramshackle food store, this must be one of the cheapest hotels in Sicily, if not Europe. The rooms not a little resemble prison cells, but most of them have balconies on which you can dry your clothes. One of the permanent lodgers is an Egyptian chap who has set up a private business selling papyrus. If you see him, please say hello.

Where to eat

Ristorante Rustico da Nino, Via Lungomare; tel. 0921-22582. Open all year. Specialises in typical Sicilian fare. The interior is indeed rustic; it seems to have been made entirely from planks of wood.

Da Saro al Gabbiano, Via Lungomare; tel. 0921-21495. A very respectable pizzeria and beer-house. Good for snacks.

Osteria Magno, Via Amendopla 8; no telephone. Excellent, unpretentious pasta dishes. For those travelling on a shoestring, there is a *menu turistico*.

Palermo

Think of Palermo and you think of the Mafia. The connection seems as inevitable as Las Vegas and gambling or Bangkok and sex. But there is more, much more to Sicily's capital. After Rome, Palermo is, I think, the most fascinating city in all Italy. And it ought to be said, here and now, that as a tourist in Palermo you would certainly be unlucky to tangle with the Cosa Nostra. The danger, rather, is in what Italians call *scippatori* – street urchins who scoot about in pairs on souped-up Vespas, ever on the lookout for the unsuspecting tourist.

Before you have time even to think, they accelerate away with your wallet or handbag. But today this is a problem in any major Italian city. It is certainly a problem in Naples; and the precautions you should take whilst exploring Palermo are the same in Naples (see pp. 73–4).

The atmosphere of Palermo is one of poetic desolation. The 'historic centre' remains untouched since the Allies bombed it in 1943. Great fire-blackened *palazzi* loom large on the main streets, the broken statuary and crumbling stucco a sad testament to regal days bygone. Children kick footballs against the decayed walls of deconsecrated Baroque churches. It is hard to believe that at the end of the eighteenth century Palermo outrivalled even Milan as a centre both of culture and of commerce.

In the slums, people look as though barnacled to their shell-pocked hovels for the centuries to come. Beggar-women, their children swaddled in rags, cry for alms from the steps of churches; old men, dressed in heavy black corduroy with battered fedoras to match, play at cards on upturned wooden crates; hot-chestnut vendors out-yell one another from street corners, the smell of burnt shell wafting sweetly from their tinsel-bedecked stalls; linen – almost luminous with a Mediterranean sun behind it – flaps a brilliant, starchy white from broken windows and rusty balconies.

Yet Palermo's setting is of a legendary beauty. The city stands at the head of a wide bay on the north coast at the foot of Monte Pellegrino and on the edge of the Conca d'Oro, a lush vale of citrus groves where palaces built for the Norman rulers were, in the words of the twelfth-century Arab traveller Ibn Jubair, 'strung round the hills like pearls around the throat of a woman'. But even here there is desolation, for the Conca d'Oro is disfigured by thousands of shoddy tenement blocks built by the Mafia in the late 1950s during the building boom. A large percentage of Palermo's 666,500 inhabitants now live in such dwellings: not Cosa Nostra members themselves, of course – they live in the vulgar villas out in the suburbs. The snarling Dobermans that guard the garden gates tell you as much.

Notwithstanding Palermo's poverty, the sheer *miseria* of the place, you could happily spend four or five days in the city. Besides, Palermo is a convenient point of departure for the Albanian mountain village of Piana degli Albanesi, and for such interesting eighteenth-century towns as Bagheria. And if you have not already been there, you could make a pleasurable day-trip from Palermo to Cefalù.

Palermo is not the sort of city for those who want a quiet holiday relaxing on beaches; the interest, rather, is in the architecture and in the atmosphere, in its hybrid of Latin, Byzantine and Islamic cultures. Between the ninth and twelfth centuries Palermo was one of the largest and most important cities in the world, and she still possesses some of the great Arab–Norman buildings erected at that time. The city is full of red Islamic domes atop Norman churches, of decayed Arab pleasure palaces adorned with swirling Cufic inscriptions. With the *souk*-like atmosphere of Palermo's public markets, dark and obscure with an eastern promise, you might think yourself in Tangier or Fez. In the cafés, wrote Norman Lewis in his classic book on the Mafia, *The Honoured Society*, 'every Palerman becomes a pasha for an hour'. The drinking of strong black coffee is 'a public display of leisure inherited from turban-wearing ancestors'.

History
Ancient

The history of Palermo is not so different from that of Naples. Between the eighth and sixth centuries BC the city was a Phoenician settlement and, until the Roman conquest of Sicily, one of the most important of Carthaginian strongholds. It was fiercely disputed during the First Punic War. After the Greeks, who named it Panormos ('entirely harbour'), and the Romans, Palermo fell in AD 535 to a succession of Byzantine emperors. Little remains in present-day Palermo from this period of history.

Medieval

Three centuries later, the Arabs invaded. Under Muslim rule, Palermo, capital of an emirate, rivalled Córdoba and Cairo in splendour, and was greater than any Christian town except Constantinople. On the whole, the Arabs were lenient; many churches became mosques, but Christians were in general left alone, forbidden though they were to read the Bible within earshot of Muslims. Otherwise, Palermo became a truly cosmopolitan city; among its inhabitants were Greeks, Lombards, Jews, Slavs, Berbers, Persians, Tartars and Africans, while Arabs came from Spain, Syria and Egypt.

With the ousting of the Arabs by Roger de Hauteville in 1072, Palermo was for 150 years ruled by the Normans. Under King Roger II (1137–54), it became the centre of trade between Europe and Asia. Nevertheless, Norman feudal practices tended to prevail; Sicily was not a free island.

The Spanish dominion

After 1266 the Anjous ruled Palermo, but were expelled with the Sicilian Vespers of 1282 (see p. 190). But Palermo's gradual decline began under its Spanish rulers. Their tyranny, and a famine brought about through harvest failures in 1647, led to a fierce insurrection – the peasants skewered a loaf of bread on a pole and thrust it, symbolically, at an image of Christ on the altar. Aristocrats tried throwing coins to the mob; the Archbishop armed his clergy. Typically, nothing came of the rebellion; the Archbishop absolved the ringleaders, exorcising the 'demons and witches' that had caused them to rebel. The fundamental inertia of Sicilians in the face of their oppressors won through; and the nobles afterwards lacked any practical interest in economics or agriculture, surrendering to the sensual attractions of the Palermo court.

A brief viceroyalty (1781–86) under the Marquis Domenico Caracciolo, a Neapolitan who had lived in Paris and London, brought a degree of economic and political reform to Palermo. Caracciolo had been schooled in the enlightened philosophies of Voltaire and Rousseau and was of the opinion that Palermo was 'inhabited only by oppressors or the oppressed'. Feudalism was weakened and taxation of the peasants made less prohibitive.

The Bourbons

But in 1799, when the Bourbon King Ferdinand IV, on expulsion from Naples, took up residency in the Royal Palace at Palermo, a dark age returned once more. For rule under the Bourbons was quite as despotic as under the Aragonese, even though Palermo was in 1811 granted a temporary constitution by the British. In 1820, the Palermans rebelled; again in 1848, and in April 1860.

Garibaldi

They rebelled, in fact, until rescued by Garibaldi, accompanied by his thousand eager but ill-armed volunteers, on 27 May 1860. But with the absence of a monarchy, the Mafia – the Sicilian despots of today – began to gain an evil footing. Sadly, Garibaldi's 1860 Revolution offered plenty of opportunities for ambitious new men to make good. There is a famous fictional representation of this 'new man'. We find him in Giuseppe di Lampedusa's *The Leopard*; his name is Vincenzino. 'With his low forehead, ornamental quiffs of hair on the temples, lurching walk and perpetual swelling of the right trouser pocket where he kept a knife, it was obvious at once that Vincenzino was a "man of honour", one of those violent cretins capable of any havoc.'

Getting there

From Cefalù Palermo is 76 km away. The city is reached along the coastal Route N113. Ferries go to Palermo from Genoa (22 hours), Cagliari (14 hours), Livorno (18 hours), Tunis (11 hours) and Naples (9½ hours; daily at 8.30 p.m.). The airport, Punta Raisi, is 32 km west of the city centre.

Getting about

To find your way around Palermo, bear in mind that the two main axes of the city are the Via Maqueda and the Corso Vittorio Emanuele. These intersect at Piazza Vigliena, known as the Quattro Canti. East–west Vittorio Emanuele and north–south Via Maqueda divide the historical centre of Palermo into four almost equal quadrants. If you need a detailed map, go along to the Tourist Office, at Piazza Castelnuovo 34, tel. 091-583847, where you can also pick up a copy of *Un Mese a Palermo*, the monthly What's On.

By road

Buses are usually overcrowded and slow, owing to the traffic congestion. However, in the early hours of the morning, before the rush hour, numerous buses ply a regular course up and down the Via Maqueda, the Corso Vittorio Emanuele and Via Roma, the main shopping street.

Taxis are hired from ranks at the station and in all the main squares. In general, Palerman cabbies are honest (unlike their Neapolitan counterparts, that is), but you should nevertheless agree on a fare before you reach your destination. Taxis without meters are best avoided. Driving a car in Palermo is likely to be a nightmare – quite as bad as trying to dodge the traffic in Naples.

PALERMO STREET MAP

PLACES OF INTEREST
1 Tourist Office
2 Palazzo del Municipio
3 Villa Bonanno
4 Palazzo dei Normanni
5 Palazzo Chiaramonte
6 Regional Gallery
7 Puppet Museum
8 Villa Giulia
9 Archaeological Museum
10 Capuchin Catacombs
11 La Zisa
12 Villa Malfitano
13 Politeama Garibaldi
14 Teatro Massimo

CHURCHES
15 San Giuseppe dei Teatini
16 San Cataldo
17 Martorana
18 Gesù
19 Duomo
20 Cappella Palatina
21 San Giovanni degli Eremiti
22 San Francesco d'Assisi
23 San Lorenzo
24 La Magione
25 San Domenico
26 Oratorio del Rosario di San Domenico
27 Santa Zita
28 Oratorio del Rosario di Santa Zita

On foot

If I were you, I should walk everywhere. The historical centre is not that extensive; with careful planning, you should be able, on foot, to visit its most important sites in the space of a leisurely two days.

From the Quattro Canti to San Giovanni degli Eremiti

The Quattro Canti

'The Four Corners' is a small octagonal piazza, its four façades embellished with statues of the seasons, and of four kings of Sicily. The Canti date from the early seventeenth century and are usually impossible to admire because of the dirt and traffic. Adjacent is the **Piazza Pretoria**, almost entirely occupied by an enormous sixteenth-century marble fountain, the basin of which is adorned with statues (many of them vandalised) of naked women. Palermans nickname this part of town Piazza Vergona, 'Square of Shame', owing to the saucy looks which the statues appear to be casting at one another. Flanking the piazza is the sixteenth-century **Palazzo del Municipio**.

S. Giuseppe dei Teatini

Across Via Maqueda from Piazza Pretoria stands one of the most magnificent of Palermo's Baroque churches. The façade is plain but the interior is a rococo riot, with marble angels in gold loincloths upholding the ceiling. And don't miss the two marble angels supporting the stoups by the main entrance – tumbling down from the skies in a whirl of cloud, they look as though they might at any moment hurtle against the floor. This is high-class Baroque, as though a posh box of chocolates had suddenly exploded.

Piazza Bellini

A few steps down Via Maqueda, and we come to an enchanting square, with, to the right, the early twelfth-century **San Cataldo**, a Norman church topped by rose-red Arab cupolas. In 1787 this church served as a post office. Next to it is the **Martorana** Church, originally erected during the first half of the twelfth century by Georgios Antiochenos, grand admiral of Roger II. It was here that the Sicilian Parliament met after the Sicilian Vespers and decided to offer the crown to Peter of Aragon. The exterior is dull, with the Baroque west front adjoining a decayed and indifferent Norman campanile. But the interior, though damaged by many a Baroque excrescence, is stunning, its dome adorned with dazzling twelfth-century mosaics. Probably the work of Greek craftsmen, these show Christ with four angels; in Arabic lettering, a verse from a Byzantine hymn adorns the cupola's rim. The mosaics continue around the drum and side vaults, a universe of gold. In bygone days, the nuns here were celebrated for their preserved pumpkin, blancmange and *frutti* of almond paste. No doubt it was the Saracens who first bit a sweet tooth into Sicily.

The Gesù

Via Ponticello, across Via Maqueda from Piazza Bellini, snakes its way through a bomb-scarred but lively neighbourhood to the first church in Sicily to be erected by the Jesuits (1564–1633). It is popular with the poor on account of the fairground garishness of its Baroque decorations; the depiction of the Last Judgement in particular is almost fluorescent. If you stand in the courtyard of this church, you can see the pock-marks left in the stonework by the American bombings of the Second World War.

Quartiere dell'Albergheria

We are now on the outskirts of one of the poorest quarters in Palermo, much of it devastated in 1943. It is worth investigating: of an evening, it resembles a scene from wartime Casablanca. Tunisian butchers whisk away flies from the severed heads of cows; rusty army-green vans are piled high with watermelon; hot-chestnut vendors and kebab-friers shout their wares; in squalid cantinas marble-topped tables are awash with wine. All this colourful action takes place in **Piazza Ballaro**, which is overshadowed by the dome (bright majolica tiles of green and gold) of the seventeenth-century **Chiesa del Carmine**.

Piazza Bologni

If you return to the Quattro Canti you can begin to walk westwards down the **Corso Vittorio Emanuele**. Passing many delightful shops selling secondhand books, puppets and clothes, you soon come to the Piazza Bologni on the left-hand side, with its tumbledown Baroque palaces and ridiculous statue of Charles V. The king has been made – accidentally, one should think – to appear emaciated and spindly, and seems to be saying, 'Look, I *know* how I look, but please don't laugh.'

The Cathedral

In a couple of minutes you confront the exotic exuberance of Palermo's Duomo. Founded in the late twelfth century by Palermo's English Archbishop Walter of the Mill (who is reported to have attained office 'less by election than by violent intrusion'), this great sandstone mass of a building is a hybrid of diverse architectural styles. In general appearance, the Cathedral is that strange mixture of Byzantine and Norman so peculiar to Sicily, but the huge dome is eighteenth century and looks jarringly out of place. Nevertheless, the sharp lights and shades of this edifice, the saw-toothed triangles around the roof, the golden colour of the stone – all these impress one with the force of an apparition.

The **main doorway** is on the southern side, a beautiful Gothic porch with a column emblazoned with words from the Koran. The nineteenth-century interior, grim with grey plasterwork, is less impressive: the floor is of plain, cold marble. Interesting, though, are the six **royal tombs** in the first two chapels of the south aisle. Two of them have marble canopies inlaid with glittering mosaics; Roger II's tomb, though, is none too thrilling. The **treasury** is worth investigating, if only for the peculiar crown of Constance of Aragon – found in her tomb in the eighteenth century, it almost exactly resembles a bejewelled and really rather lovely bathing-cap.

It was from the pulpit of this Cathedral that, in the winter of 1982, the Archbishop of Palermo, Monsignor Pappalardo, delivered a sermon that has since gone down in the history of Sicily as the 'anti-Mafia Mass'. The occasion was the brutal murder of General Dalla Chiesa, prefect in charge of Mafia investigations in Palermo for precisely 100 days. Dalla Chiesa's wife was also machine-gunned to

death, the first time the Honoured Society had ever killed a woman.
'Whilst Rome does nothing,' preached Pappalardo, 'Palermo burns.
God help us, God help poor Palermo.' He quoted from St John
the Apostle, directing the lines against the Mafia: 'He that is of
God heareth God's words: ye therefore hear them not, because ye
are not of God.' This sermon was one of the Church's very rare con-
demnations of organised crime in Sicily. Pappalardo ended with the
words, *Ecco il grande silenzio della morte* [Here is the great silence that
is death].'

Palazzo dei   Walking further down the Corso Vittorio Emanuele, you pass on
Normanni   your right the headquarters of the Palermo *carabinieri*, opposite the
lush **Villa Bonanno** public park. Then you come to a vast collection
of buildings of many periods and different styles, known as the Normans' Palace. In the ninth century the Arabs built a military post
here, later enlarged by the Normans and decorated in the Arab and
Byzantine styles. The Spaniards added the principal façade. Today it
is used by the Sicilian government.

The Palace is open Monday–Saturday 9 a.m.–1 p.m., 3–5 p.m.
Guided tours are available during these times. First on the list of
things to see is the fantastic **Sala di Re Ruggero**, King Roger's Room
– a miniature chamber adorned with gold and green mosaics of hunting scenes, birds and trees, convoluted foliage and botanical motifs.
The mosaics are bold and simple, more Norman than Arabic.

The high point, though, is the **Cappella Palatina**, built by Roger
II (1132–40). The bronze doors open on to a dazzling jewel box of Saracen art (only occasionally illuminated for the benefit of tourists – you
have to badger the sluggish curator). The wooden roof, carved into
stars, stalactites and honeycomb niches, shows miniature scenes of
Arabic life: men playing at chess and drinking, a lion in combat with a
giant serpent, camels, palm trees and white peacocks. Gazing up at it,
you are spirited away to muse on sultans, minarets and the Arabian
Nights. (It is a good tip to have a pair of binoculars with you to appreciate the detail.) The walls are adorned with glittering mosaics representing subjects from the Old Testament. Beside the pulpit stands a
beautifully carved giant candlestick, probably presented by the Archbishop of Palermo in 1151. This magical chapel, so radiant with oriental splendour, is Sicily at her most ineffably beautiful.

S. Giovanni   Walk south down the nearby Corso Re Ruggero and take the first
degli Eremiti   major turning on your left. Cross the busy road here (one of the most
hair-raising spots in all Palermo for the helter-skelter of its traffic) and
turn into the Via dei Benedettini. At number 3 stands what is perhaps
the most charming spot in Palermo – the garden and cloister of the
Church of St John of the Hermits. This is one of the earliest existing
Norman churches and still presents an almost entirely oriental aspect.
Built in 1132, the nave is divided into three parts, each crowned by a
Saracen red dome. The **gardens** are a confusion of flowering shrubs –

date palms and figs, grapefruit, banana trees and mandarins, cacti and prickly pears. The church is in a markedly squalid part of Palermo, a rich jewel in a dunghill.

From San Francesco to the Villa Giulia and the Chiesa della Magione

S. Francesco d'Assisi

Walking down the Corso Vittorio Emanuele east towards the sea (the opposite direction from the Cathedral), take the Via Paternostro off to the right until you come to the thirteenth-century San Francesco d'Assisi, one of the most important churches in Palermo. The façade, graced with a rose window, is embellished with a striking zigzag ornamentation, a refreshing respite from Palerman Baroque. The heavily restored Gothic interior houses, in the fourth chapel to the left of the entrance, an exquisite 1468 **Renaissance triumphal arch**, the earliest sculpted Renaissance work in Sicily, an island which was pretty much a stranger to the Renaissance.

If you have had your fill of Palerman churches, I suggest you drop in at the **Antica Focacceria S. Francesco** (tel. 091-320264), just across the road from the Assisi house of worship. Founded in 1834, this elegant snack bar (quite unknown to tourists) is fitted out with wrought-iron marble-topped tables and park-benches for seats. The speciality here is the very Palerman one of *milze e polmone e tracchia*, the spleen, lungs and trachea of cow. From an old cast-iron stove the organs are served up in hot baps with a sprinkling of grated cheese. Even if you aren't wild about innards (and I for one can't stomach them), it is certainly worth coming here to savour the unusual atmosphere, and to drink a long cool beer.

Oratory of San Lorenzo

A few doors down from San Francesco, at Via Immacolatella 5, is an oratory embellished by the master of stucco decoration, Giacomo Serpotta (1656–1732). You might have trouble gaining entrance; the custodian, who certainly won't open the doors without a handsome payment in return, may tell you that the oratory is 'sotto restauro', even if it isn't. If you come after midday, she may also inform you that there is not a 'good enough light' with which to appreciate the interior.

Perhaps the custodian's reluctance to permit entrance is to do with the fact that in 1969 Caravaggio's *Nativity*, his last known work, was stolen at dead of night from the confines of this oratory. At the time of writing it has not been recovered. As a consequence of this theft (though it is a bit late in the day) six padlocks have to be unlocked before you can enter the building. But no matter: the interior is a joyous and thoroughly impish explosion of three-dimensionally carved cherubim, the stuccoed creatures seemingly *flying* away from the walls. Note the beautifully wrought male figures high on the wall and the scenes from the martyrdom of St Laurence, all in a perfect dolls'-house miniature.

Piazza Marina

Down the Vittorio Emanuele you soon come to a square arranged around beautiful public gardens in the middle of which rises a fantastic banyan, sending out roots like giant boa-constrictors. The tree was once a traditional trysting place for Mafiosi living in the nearby Kalsa slum quarter. The square is dominated, massively, by a grim medieval edifice, the **Palazzo Chiaramonte**, which from 1605 to 1782 was the seat of the Spanish Inquisition. Numerous dissenters were burnt in its forecourt. Etched into the prison walls are some fascinating graffiti; particularly poignant is the inscription reading, quite simply, 'Pane, pazienza e tempo [Bread, patience and time].' They speak books, those words.

Regional Gallery.

From this infamous edifice, it is but a short step to Via Alloro, where stands the part-Gothic, part-Renaissance Palazzo Abatelli. The palace houses my favourite museum in Southern Italy (open Wednesday, Friday, Saturday 9 a.m.–1.30 p.m.; Tuesday, Thursday 9 a.m.–1.30 p.m., 3–4.30 p.m.; Sunday 9 a.m.–12.30 p.m.). Among the numerous treasures are a twelfth-century **Arab door frame**, with incredibly intricate latticework of wood, and a large and terrifying fresco, **The Triumph of Death**, by an unknown artist. It shows Death, the great leveller, on a spectral horse, piercing with arrows the complacent and well-fed – bishops, lawyers, princes and grandees. Probably the artist (a Fleming of the fifteenth century) had witnessed an epidemic of plague, a frequent occurrence in Sicily. There is an exquisite thirteenth-century **Arab vase** with large wings for handles; next door, a fine fifteenth-century alabaster bust of **Eleanor of Aragon**. Upstairs, one of the great treasures of Sicilian art: the **Annunciation** by Antonello da Messina. With her left hand, the Virgin holds the folds of her blue garment and wears a smile so enigmatic that it mesmerises.

Puppet Museum

Nearby to the north is the delightful Museo Internazionale delle Marionette at Via Butera 1 (open Tuesday–Friday 10 a.m.–1 p.m., 5–7 p.m.). This houses over 2,000 puppets – French marionettes, glove puppets from Brazil and China, shadow figures from Indonesia, Malaysia and Cambodia, and knights in armour from Sicily. It is the largest collection of its kind in the world.

Villa Giulia

Retrace your steps westwards down the Via Alloro and turn left into Via Torremuzza. Walk along this until you hit the broad Via Lincoln. Cross this road and you come to the Villa Giulia, a spacious park with bandstand and many an itinerant ice-cream seller. The park houses the **Botanic Gardens** (open June–September 9 a.m.–2 p.m.; October–May 9 a.m.–12 noon, 2–4 p.m.; closed Sunday). Numerous plants are kept in a late eighteenth-century neo-Classical building, which deserves a visit from botanists and amateurs alike. You can marvel at the strange-sounding names: *Cyperus papyrus*, *Ficus magnolioides*, *Araucaria cookii*, *Coffea arabica*, *Citrus deliciosa*. Goethe, himself an enthusiastic botanist, came here in 1786. 'Among this multitude,' he wrote, 'might I not discover the Primal Plant? There certainly must be one. Otherwise, how could I recognise that this or that form *was* a plant if all were not built upon the same basic model?'

La Magione

A turn to the north off the Via Lincoln takes you into the Via Magione, on which stands, alone in the middle of a bomb site, a Norman church of the same name. In 1193 it was transferred to the Teutonic Knights by the Emperor Henry VI as their mansion. Palm trees mark the spot; there are beautiful gardens.

From the Church of San Domenico to the Grand Hotel des Palmes

San Domenico

About halfway up the Via Roma, north of Via Vittorio Emanuele, you will find the Baroque Church of San Domenico, which looms large in the lively piazza of the same name. Rebuilt in 1640, this church is the traditional pantheon for the most respectable of Palermans. The not very interesting interior contains the tombs of lawyers, surgeons, painters, historians and army colonels. None of them led particularly unusual lives – it's just that they had enough money with which to afford elaborate tombs.

Oratory of San Domenico

Behind this church, in Via Bambinai, opposite a tobacco shop, stands the Oratorio del Rosario di San Domenico, now used only for the occasional mass or wedding. To gain admission, ring the doorbell at number 16; presently, the elderly custodian will emerge, jangling a bunch of keys like a janitor and mumbling, *'Ma non mi da qualcosa?* [Aren't you going to give me anything?]'. Once you have surrendered a few thousand lire, the doors will open.

The oratory contains a great **altarpiece** by Van Dyck, representing the Virgin of the Rosary, with San Domenico and Santa Rosalia, patron of Palermo, kneeling in intercession for the end of the plague; one of the children is holding its nose as protection against the stench of rotting corpses. The aisles are decorated with twelve allegorical statues by Serpotta – Humility, Patience etc. Most curious is the statue of Fortitude – a coquettish young woman, hand on hip, bedecked in a rustling silk ball gown. She was modelled on a courtesan of Louis XIV.

Santa Zita

The street becomes Via Squarcialupo ('Wolf ripped to pieces Street'). On it stands the Church of Santa Zita, rebuilt 1586–1603. Because of its proximity to the port of Palermo, and to what used to be a set of army barracks, this church was badly bombed during the last war; look at the way great chunks of marble have been blown out of the entrance steps. It is still surrounded by a vast and desolate bomb site: nothing has been done to clear it up because, in Palermo, money destined for public works usually ends up in the (well-lined) pockets of the Mafia.

Inside this church, take a look at the extraordinary **Chapel of the Rosary**, to the right of the choir. Constructed in 1696, this is a colourful riot of marble inlay – Baroque *putti* playing cellos or upholding vast cornucopiae, eagles, sea-shells and exotic plants. The chapel survived the bombing by being piled, floor to ceiling, with sandbags.

Oratory of Santa Zita

On the left of the church is the Oratorio del Rosario di Santa Zita. Ring for the custodian at Via Valverde 7; it is worth waking him up. The oratory, approached up a flight of steps through beautiful gardens, contains what is perhaps Serpotta's masterpiece – a stucco work of the **Battle of Lepanto** (where Cervantes, author of *Don Quixote*, lost an arm). It is all incredibly fine, the oars of each ship depicted in web-thin plaster.

Archaeological Museum

The nearby Museo Nazionale Archeologico (open Tuesday–Saturday 9 a.m.–2 p.m.; Sunday 9 a.m.–1 p.m.) has a most interesting collection. It is laid out in the seventeenth-century courtyards of a vanished monastery – they boast a fountain of Triton, blowing sea-water through an upheld conch-shell; papyrus plants, palm and banana trees. Most famous here are the celebrated **Metopes of Selinunte**, the sixth-century BC figures skilfully blended into a reconstructed Doric frieze. In Room 13 on the ground floor are Hercules, in combat with an Amazon; Actaeon, torn to bits by dogs (the vicious-looking hound on the right has razor-sharp teeth), and Athene overcoming a great hulk of a Titan named Encelado.

Upstairs, in the **Bronze Department**, is the Greek third-century BC Ram of Syracuse, and the bronze, found in Pompeii, of Hercules subduing an Arcadian stag. For some reason the animal looks as though it might be smoking a cheroot; presumably, the cigar is part of a water-spout.

Grand Hotel des Palmes

Regain Via Roma and continue north until you come to number 396. This is a splendid turn-of-the-century establishment where, in November 1881, Wagner wrote parts of his opera *Parsifal*. The owners will gladly show you the sumptuously decorated salon where he composed at the piano; the ritzy bar contains Wagner's plush-red piano stool, kept under glass. The Palmes was also where the French surrealist Raymond Roussel, author of such travel classics as *Locus Solus*, committed suicide. His corpse was found in Room 224 on 13 July 1933. And Salvatore Luciano, the Mafia's infamous wartime boss, used to hold court in the elegant dining room. Indeed a waiter once insisted on giving me the table where 'Lucky' Salvatore used to sit. As Signor Luciano had been largely responsible for turning the Mafia into what it is today, a body of para-political drug-peddlars, I protested that it could not reasonably be expected much of an honour to sit at his place. 'But no!' retorted the waiter, apparently quite offended. 'Salvatore was a real *Signore*. And he dressed as elegantly as a banker, too.' An interesting way of looking at Lucky, but there you are. This hotel is an excellent place to come for a preprandial cocktail. You may even want to book into the place.

Other sights

Catacombs

If you are an admirer of the Hammer House of Horror you should visit Palermo's Capuchin Catacombs on Via dei Cipressi, west of the city centre (open Monday–Saturday 9 a.m.–12 noon, 3.30–5 p.m.). To reach them, take bus number 27 from Piazza Castelnuovo. The most lively burial place in town, this dungeon-like, eighteenth-to-nine-teenth-century necropolis contains the corpses of 8,000 Palermans. All have been mummified – either soaked in arsenic or quick-lime or left to dry out in the sun.

The mummies, most of them in a pretty bad way, have been segregated into different corridors according to their past professions: lawyers, surgeons, university professors. There are also sections for *bambini* and *vergine*. The priests, you may notice, are the best preserved of the lot – not surprisingly, as in times of calamity they are regarded by Palermans with a superstitious dread. However, when I last visited, one nineteenth-century bishop had been made to look as though he was reading a recent copy of the *Corriere della Sera* newspaper – a spirited, if ghoulish, joke.

If you are wondering why most of the corpses have lost their glass eyes, it is because they were taken by American soldiers as souvenirs during the last war!

La Zisa

Not far from the catacombs stands the Zisa. (Take bus number 24 and get off at the Piazza Gugliemo il Buono.) This Islamic pleasure palace takes its name from the Arab *aziz*, meaning splendid. A perfect example of Arab–Fatamid architecture, it is in the middle of a rubble-strewn slum, and I advise that you hang on to your wallet or handbag when visiting.

The Zisa was built by Williams I and II in the second half of the twelfth century. The interior contains a beautiful frieze of mosaic decoration with peacocks and hunters and a stone honeycomb ceiling. However, you may not be able to gain entrance; in all likelihood, the Zisa will be 'under restoration'. But the palace is nevertheless worth seeing from the outside.

Villa Malfitano

Outside the Zisa you may notice a rusty iron gate with the words '*Educatorio Whitaker*'. Nothing remains of this English Marsala merchant's school, but his villa, the wonderful Malfitano (Via Dante 167), is still standing. To visit, telephone the Whitaker Foundation on 091-560522.

Surrounded by 17 acres of giant yuccas and bamboos, the nineteenth-century Malfitano is now inhabited by a grey-haired gentleman who was once Joseph Whitaker's valet. Since his master's death, this *cavaliere* (an Italian term of respect, akin to our knight) has single-handedly assumed charge of the villa – pottering about among the Louis XVI furniture, dusting the mahogany chairs emblazoned with the initials 'JW'. As he courteously guides you through the old ball-, billiard- and smoking-rooms, he will tell you of how he once danced attendance on a German Kaiser, and on the Prince of Lampedusa, author of *The Leopard*. And he will show you sepia photographs of Edward VII and George V, both of whom once visited this villa. It is all quite an experience, and I thoroughly recommend that you visit.

The environs of Palermo

Monreale

No visit to Palermo would be complete without a visit to the small hill town of Monreale (population 24,900), which commands fine views of the Conca d'Oro and the Bay of Palermo. To get there, take bus number 8 or 9 from Via M. Stabile; they leave every 20 minutes.

This is so idyllic a spot that Palermans have the saying, '*Chi va a Palermo e non vede Monreale, asino va e asino torna* [Visit Palermo without seeing Monreale – as an ass you go, and as an ass you return].' The town owes its fame to the **Norman Cathedral** founded in 1174 by William II as the seat of an archbishopric.

The church is one of the wonders of the medieval world. On a sharp winter morning, its vast and austere interior, glittering with the gold tesserae of a thousand mosaics, is suffused with a clean light – truly uplifting after the dark Baroqueries of Palermo's seventeenth-century churches with their puffy cherubim and chiselled skulls. Profiled and clear in this luminous light, the Cathedral – a gracious union of Byzantine splendour and Arab purity of volume – gives an overwhelming impression of majesty, intimating things beyond the comprehension of man. It literally needs to be seen to be believed. (A touch of bathos, though, may be provided by the roly-poly sacristan who lies in wait behind the bronze doors, ready to cover the plunging necklines of unthinking tourists.)

Adjoining the Cathedral is the Benedictine monastery, also built by William II. Little remains of the original building except the remarkably beautiful **cloisters**, the pointed arches of which are adorned with glittering mosaics and supported by 216 columns. In spring, there is an overwhelming scent here of orange blossom.

Bagheria

An interesting excursion may be made, too, to the small country town of Bagheria (population 38,700). To visit, take the blue AST bus from Piazza Lolli; it leaves every 30 minutes.

Here you will find the *circoli* so typical of provincial western Sicily – gentlemen's clubs where the members (dressed as though for church in their hand-me-down finery of black suits and hats) drink wine, play at billiards, read newspapers and smoke evil-smelling cigars.

Best of all about Bagheria is the eighteenth-century **Villa Palagonia** (open daily 9 a.m.–1 p.m., 4–7 p.m.), the folly of a prince so eccentric, many of his contemporaries deemed him mad. One can see why. The garden walls are surmounted by sixty-two stone monsters – hunchbacks, dwarfs, dragons, harpies, an orchestra of monkeys, the head of a horse with a human body, a woman with three breasts, a ram's head growing out of the side of her own. Goethe was disgusted with this delirious display of anti-Classical design, these 'deformed and revolting shapes botched by inferior stone-cutters'. See what you make of it – I find it all great fun.

Piana degli Albanesi

One of the strangest excursions to be made from Palermo is to the chilly mountain village of Piana degli Albanesi (population 6,300), 24 km south-west of the city. To get there, take a bus from the Via Balsamo, next to Palermo's central station. (The bus company is called 'Prestia Comande'.) Buses run every two hours from 6.30 a.m. to 9.50 p.m.

This fifteenth-century colony of some 7,000 Albanians has seven Greek Orthodox churches. For both Epiphany and Easter the women wear the traditional costumes of their Balkan ancestors. It is not a particularly beautiful town, but the drive up through the hills of the Conca d'Oro justifies the excursion.

Monte Pellegrino

Finally, you can make a short excursion to the **Sanctuary of Santa Rosalia**, a dank, cold cave on the top of Monte Pellegrino. Take a bus number 12 from Piazza Ignazio Florio.

The cavern, down the walls of which trickles a water which is held to be miraculous, was consecrated in 1625. It contains a reclining statue of the hermit–saint, patroness of Palermo, covered in beaten silver. Goethe thought it wonderful: 'A beautiful woman who seemed to be reclining in a kind of ecstasy . . . I could not take my eye off this picture, which seemed to me to possess a quite extraordinary charm.' You will notice how the cave is hung with all manner of votive offerings from the cured – horseshoes, silver amulets, a lifeboat ring, a crash-helmet, a large rubber tyre and countless limbs from plastic dolls.

Theatre and opera

Once upon a time, operas took place at Palermo's **Teatro Massimo**, a powerful neo-Classical theatre constructed between 1875 and 1897; it is the largest opera-house in Europe. For the past ten years, though, this has been 'under restoration'; at the time of writing, it shows no sign of re-opening.

The exiled opera and symphony perform at the nearby **Politeama Garibaldi**, a huge circular theatre with a triumphal arch entrance crowned by a bronze chariot and four horses. The season runs from 7 January to 16 June; the box-office number is 091-584334.

The Sicilian **puppet show** should not be missed. The most popular theatre is the **Cuticchio Giocomo** in Vicolo Nicolo Raguso 6; tel. 091-329194. Performances depend on the number of people who come along, but there are usually two or three a week, commencing at 9 p.m. The shows are quite violent: up to the mid-1950s puppet theatres employed overseers to thwack any more excitable members of the audience with a long bamboo cane. One show I saw, *Roger the Norman Conquers Sicily*, was an absolute riot – every time Roger killed an Arab, vigorous applause went up, accompanied by a maniacal stamping of feet.

Shopping

There is little to be found in Palermo that you will not find in other Italian cities. However, I recommend a visit to Palermo's lively **Vucciria**, a busy fish, fruit and vegetable market situated halfway down the Via Roma, beneath the Shanghai restaurant. Wandering around the stalls, you really do feel as though you had been transported on a magic carpet to some Middle Eastern *souk*. In the labyrinth of its cobbled streets hang all manner of grisly meats – the innards, eyes and ears of pigs, cows and sheep. And *'Bello! Bello!'* bellow the fishmongers over their multi-coloured fare – squid, sword- and tunny fish, mullet, lobster and bream.

Palermo has a flea market, *mercato delle pulce*, of sorts – the tiny **Papireto** in Piazza Peranni, not far from the Cappella Palatina. Here you will find smashed plates, bits of crockery, old Sicilian puppets, ancient Remington typewriters, car mirrors, rusty electric shavers. Fun; but there probably isn't an awful lot that you will want to buy.

Nightclubs

Palermo is not well served on this front; but here are some recommendations.

Villa Boscogrande, Via T. Natale 91; tel. 091-241179. A ritzy hotspot much frequented by the young. Situated near Palermo in the seaside resort of Mondello, the club is in a gorgeous *palazzo* where Visconti filmed parts of *The Leopard*. To join the bright young things, take bus 3 or 14 from Via della Libertà near the Teatro Politeama.

Play Time, Via dell'Artigliere 25; tel. 091-250463. Cute name, and there's a very cute piano bar, too.

Villa Igiea Grill, Via Belmonte 43; tel. 091-543744. Part of the elegant hotel of the same name; glamorous piano bar.

Where to stay
Top range

Grand Hotel des Palmes, Via Roma 396; tel. 091-583933. Four-star, see p. 213 for description. The modern rooms do not live up to the stylish Art Nouveau of the dining room or foyer. (And I was surprised to find a plump cockroach in my room one night.) But it is worth it, if you have the money.

Villa Igiea, Via Belmonte 43; tel. 091-543744. A castellated villa built at the turn of the century for wealthy travellers. Five-star, with enormous rooms – much more elegant than the majority of those in the rival des Palmes. A very elegant and civilised place in which to stay.

Politeama Palace Hotel, Piazza Ruggero Settimo 15; tel. 091-322777. Four-star, modern and a trifle bland.

President Hotel, Via Francesco Crispi 230; tel. 091-580733. Modern, clean, very luxurious.

Mid range

Centrale, Corso Vittorio Emanuele 387; tel. 091-588409. Three-star, with a sort of faded thirties charm. Conveniently situated near the Quattro Canti.

Sole, Corso Vittorio Emanuele 291; tel. 091-587344. Pleasant old-fashioned hotel.

Bristol, Via Maqueda 437; tel. 091-589247. Two-star, old-world style. Not far from the beautiful Martorana Church.

Le Terrazze, Via Roma 188; tel. 091-586365. Two-star. In a noisy part of Palermo, but very reasonably priced.

Confort, Via Roma 188; tel. 091-324362. Two-star. Not quite so comfortable, actually; but otherwise fine.

Wagner, Via Ammiraglio Gravina 88; tel. 091-585311. Two-star. Particularly recommended by the Tourist Office, which considers this hotel a real bargain.

Bottom range   **Albergo Rosalia Conca d'Oro**, Via Santa Rosalia 7; tel. 091-6164543. One-star, if that. A few turnings off the Via Roma as you walk down from the station, this is a fairly ramshackle establishment. I was surprised to find a German backpacker asleep in my bed there one night – an administrative error, I was assured. But if you don't mind the chaos, and the (it must be said) dirt, this is fine. And cheap.

Albergo Orientale, Via Maqueda 26; tel. 091-6165727. One-star. Beautifully situated on one side of a magnificent Renaissance *palazzo*. Kindly proprietor.

Albergo Odeon, Via E. Amari 140; tel. 091-6165727. One-star. Excellent location near the train station.

Where to eat   Palermo is one of the gastronomic centres of Europe; there is an almost embarrassing variety of restaurants to choose from. I make only a few personal choices. All restaurants along the Corso Vittorio Emanuele should be avoided: they stink of Mafia money.

Shanghai, Vicolo dei Mazzani 34; tel. 091-589702. For me, this is the greatest restaurant in Southern Italy. Situated in a decayed eighteenth-century house overlooking Palermo's lively marketplace, its fish are hoisted up from the stalls below in wicker baskets. The restaurant is run by a portly chap named Benedetto Basile, who is something, I am told, of a poet; he gave his restaurant an oriental name as the market stalls below are covered, on a busy day, in sail-like tarpaulins which apparently lend the place an atmosphere of Shanghai.

The swordfish is excellent. This restaurant is very, very cheap, and of a slightly ramshackle aspect – of the sort that might be termed extremely crummy. But take courage in your hands . . .

Pizzeria Bellini, Piazza Bellini; tel. 091-230413. This restaurant, popular with the locals, is romantically situated opposite the Martorana Church with its Saracen rose-red domes. The pizzas are excellent, and so is all the food. It is not at all expensive. The restaurant has an interesting autograph book; among the signatures is that of Marlon Brando, with the ecstatic recommendation, 'It's fabulous!'

Al Fico d'India, Via E. Amari 64; tel. 091-324214. This place has eccentric decorations – puppets hanging from the ceiling, old wagon wheels, indifferent oil paintings. It resembles the interior of an artist's attic. Come early, as the restaurant gets crowded: it has the best antipasta in town, and is reasonably priced.

Charleston, Piazza Ungheria 30; tel. 091-321366. A high-class joint, and expensive. The *maître*, Hassan, is very courteous and will recommend that you try the *involtini di pesce spada*, stuffed swordfish rolls.

Regine, Via Trapani 4; tel. 091-586566. One of the finest restaurants in town, in terms both of the ritzy furnishings and the food. It is run by the Barone brothers, who are the inventors of the delicious *filetto al Robespierre*. Very expensive.

Al Buco, Via P. Granatelli 33; tel. 091-323661. One of the most popular of Palermo's *trattorie*, with excellent service. The manager, Signor Lo Nigro, will recommend his excellent *bucatini al Buco*. Reasonably priced.

Papoff, Via La Lumia 28; tel. 091-325355. This is *the* restaurant in Palermo for Sicilian specialities: *'u maccu'*, broad beans seasoned with fennel, are scrumptious. Reasonably priced.

Useful addresses

● **United States Consulate**, Via Vaccarini 1; tel. 091-291532.

● **British Consulate**, closed in 1980.

● **English Church** (Holy Cross), Via Maria Stabile 118; near the Hotel des Palmes.

● **Post Office**, Via Roma, by the Museo Archeologico. Open Monday–Saturday 8.15 a.m.–7.40 p.m.

● **English bookshop**, S. F. Flaccovio, Via Ruggero Settimo 35.

● **Car hire.** Try the **Maggiore** office at either the Punta Raisi airport (tel. 091-591688) or at Via Agrigento (tel. 091-6259286).

Trapani

Trapani (population 70,500), 96 km west of Palermo along the coastal Route N186, is a fly-blown Mafia port, infamous for the laundering of proceeds from heroin. The modern town is, not surprisingly, a dump, but the old one is not without a moderate interest. Trapani is anyway the ideal place from which to make excursions to the exquisite medieval mountain village of Erice, to the far-flung Egadi Islands, haven for fishermen and scuba-divers, and to the wonderful Greek temple at Segesta. The principal sights of Trapani itself can all be seen within a leisurely two hours. In the course of your sightseeing, you will notice that Trapani has an extraordinary number of banks – more banks, in fact, than Milan. The reason for this is that the Mafia all have their own banks. Do not try to change your money in Trapani.

What to see

You should try at least to see the following.

The exhibits of the **Museo Nazionale Pepoli** (open 9 a.m.–2 p.m., Sunday 9 a.m.–1 p.m., closed Monday) are contained within a former Carmelite convent. They include Arab funerary inscriptions, some elaborate objects in coral from the seventeenth century, and sixteenth-century jewellery from, of all places, Nuremberg.

The Renaissance **Church of Santa Maria** (open only on Sunday and Monday) is situated on the Corso Italia, near the old Jewish quarter. It contains a beautiful marble *baldacchino* of 1521 which shelters a terracotta Madonna by Della Robbia.

Sant'Agostino has a fourteenth-century façade with a Gothic portal and rose window. It is in the charming Piazzetta Satturno; the statue of Saturn is late sixteenth-century.

A fine seventeenth-century building, **the Municipio**, marks the beginning of the Corso Vittorio Emanuele. The pink marble, and the clock-dials with the eagle in between, are eccentric.

Completed in 1635, the **Duomo** has a lovely dome of gold and green tiling; the portico is from 1740.

Appropriate that a Mafia town should have a church called **Chiesa del Purgatorio**; it is concealed down a side street, Via Giglio, to the left of the Cathedral. The church is of an unusual aspect, with a tessellated dome of green and gold with blue marble baubles about the cupola's rim. Inside are the wooden 'Misteri' – twenty groups of wooden figures carved in the eighteenth century, which are carried in procession around the town on Good Friday.

Where to stay

The Tourist Office lists only eight hotels for Trapani. At all costs, you should avoid the **Hotel del Sole**, a one-star Cosa Nostra brothel near the station. But try any of the others.

Nuovo Russo, Via Tintori 6; tel. 0923-22166. Three-star, near the port. Small, but by far the most elegant hotel in Trapani; old-world and moderately faded.

Vittoria, Via Francesco Crispi 4; tel. 0923-27244. Two-star, modern and apparently reputable. Thirty-three rooms.

Moderno, Via Tenente Genovese 20; tel. 0923-21247. One-star and for those on a low budget. But not bad at all.

Where to eat

Trattoria Salina, Piazza Umberto Primo; no telephone. Across the road from the station. Gloomy but with ramshackle style; good for fish and African *couscous*.

Pizzeria Calvino, Via N. Nasi 79; no telephone. In the heart of the old city, this is the best place for pizzas.

Erice

Inland from Trapani, 14 km along a twisty road, is the watchtower, the supreme vantage point, of Sicily. This small, grey, fortified medieval town (population 24,500) is huddled on the top of an isolated mountain over 750 metres above sleazy Trapani. Even in summer, it can get extremely cold in Erice; often, the entire town is enveloped in mist. At such times, you would not think yourself in Sicily. Erice has the aspect, rather, of a northern European fortress-town, its grey stone walls damp with condensation. Wonderful views are to be had from all points of the compass. On a clear day, you can see beyond Trapani to the Egadi Islands and even to Cape Bon in Tunisia.

History

The origins of Erice are ancient. A legend persists that it was founded by Eryx, son of Venus. Later, a cult to Venus flourished and a temple was erected for her honour. Sailors coming to Erice in Roman times would be welcomed to the town by Venerean priestesses, *Ierodule*, who, according to the sacral laws, were obliged to provide sailors with amorous favours in return for handsome rewards. Erice has long been famed for the beauty of its women. The Arab chronicler Ibn Jubair described them as the loveliest in the whole island. But times have changed, no doubt.

What to see

Opposite the defunct funicular, which used to haul people up from Trapani, stands the **Chiesa Matrice**, a small fourteenth-century church with a detached bell-tower built by the Aragonese as a lookout tower. It is the largest and most interesting of Erice's churches.

From here, ascend through the town to the ivy-clad **Castle**. Perched on top of a rugged rock, this Norman edifice occupies the site of the famous Temple of Venus, and contains fragments of the shrine in the stonework. The views from here are superb: in spring, the whole district at your feet is clothed with the most luxuriant verdure.

Depending on the time of year, you might find that Erice is teeming with studious-looking types clutching briefcases and buff-coloured files. Erice houses the famous *Centro Internazionale di Cultura Scientifica 'Ettore Majorana'*, named after a Sicilian nuclear physicist who disappeared under mysterious circumstances (see p. 180).

Where to stay   You may want to stay overnight in Erice.

Hotel Elimo, Via Vittorio Emanuele 75; tel. 0923-869377. Opened in September 1987, this three-star hotel is plumb in the middle of the historical centre, and converted from a seventeenth-century *palazzo*. Quite pricey.

Ermione, Via Pineta Comunale; tel. 0923-869138. A first-class hotel with 70 rooms.

Pensione Edelweiss, Cortile Piazza Vincenzo; tel. 0923-869158. The cheapest place to stay – simple rooms; the doubles all have private baths.

Where to eat   Erice is well served on the restaurant front. All of the following are excellent.

Al Ciclope, Viale Nasi; tel. 0923-869183.

Re Alceste, Viale Pepoli; tel. 0923-869084.

Ulisse, Via Chiaramonte 7; tel. 0923-869333.

La Vetta, Via Fontana 5; tel. 0923-869404.

The Egadi Islands   These islands (and several others so small as to resemble rocks) are off the western coast of Sicily and have not yet been discovered by tourists in a big way. There are very few hotels; on those islands where there are *no* hotels, you will have to put up for the night in a fisherman's house. Though without the paradisiacal beauty of the Aeolian Islands, the Egadi are interesting for their natural springs and grottoes, and for the neanderthal paintings etched into the walls of certain caves. Some of the islands have a rugged beauty, parched and baked under a grilling sun. Occasionally, dolphins are to be seen leaping in and out of the waves.

Getting there   Ferries and hydrofoils leave Trapani for the Egadi. The best island from which to commence your explorations is Levanzo; in the summer, six *aliscafi* (hydrofoils) leave for this island every day. Travelling time is only 20 minutes; tickets are bought from Siremar Biglietteria, Via Ammiraglio Staiti; tel. 0923-40515. As you sail out of Trapani harbour, you will see extensive salt-works – the salt is stored in huge, tent-shaped heaps or saltpans, and the odd windmill survives.

Levanzo   There is only one hotel on Levanzo (population 150), and you are well advised to check into it as soon as you arrive, as rooms may otherwise fill up. The **Pensione Paradiso**, Via Calvario (tel. 0923-924080), may be described as a rudimentary or low-key establishment, but dinner (excellent *couscous*) on the terrace is a delight.

There is no night-life on Levanzo – only the hooting of owls. Of animal life there is nothing – except a solitary mule, that is. Insects, though, are well represented by thousands of grasshoppers. Beaches are rocky, barren and inaccessible, though the crystal water is well worth testing should you manage to reach it.

The above-mentioned mule belongs to Signor Castiglione, a well-known island wit and raconteur. For a small fee, you may ride the beast overland to the extraordinary **Cava del Genovese**, a grotto with primitive cave designs; discovered in 1949, the paleolithic paintings are the only ones of their kind in Italy. The caves are some 5 km away from Levanzo port; the scenery as you approach them (with or without mule) is dramatic – sheer drops into the sea, virtually no trees. A visit is highly recommended.

Marettimo   The most beautiful of the Egadi Islands (population 400), Marettimo boasts bays, reefs, multi-coloured grottoes and a small village of whitewashed Arabic houses by the port. Samuel Butler claimed that it was the island of Ithaca in *The Odyssey*.

There are numerous wild boar, rabbit, eagles and quail on Marettimo – but no hotels. Of necessity, you will have to stay with a family of fishermen. I recommend that you ask for an old seadog who goes by the name of Signor Bevilacqua ('Mr Drinkwater') – everyone on the island knows him and, besides, he is easily recognised by a fine set of chipped teeth. If you're lucky, he'll have a spare room, single or double, in his daughter's house.

Signor Bevilacqua is also your man if you are interested in a circumnavigatory tour of the island. For about 30,000 lire he'll take you in his tiny boat (motorised, just about) to see some spectacular grottoes and rock formations to which he himself has given individual names. There are the giant 'camel's head', the *'grotta del tuono'* (so called because the ceiling of this grotto, resembling a giant cathedral dome, reverberates with a noise like thunder when the sea is turbulent), and the *'fica della Madonna'*, which is best left untranslated.

As you might expect, there are few restaurants on Marettimo; however, you might want to try the excellent **Trattoria il Veliero** down by the sea-front (tel. 0923-923195). Run by relatives of Signor Bevilacqua (who else?), it will serve you a slice of *ricciola* fish, in a piquant wine or onion sauce. This goes down very nicely with a bottle of chilled *Regaleali*, a Sicilian white.

Other islands   **Favignana** is famous for its tunny-fish industry; the killings take place from 10 April to the end of July and are worth watching if you like your sports bloody. The islets known as **Le Formiche** ('The Ants') are reputed to be the rocks hurled by Polyphemus at Ulysses, and are indeed very small.

They include the beautiful islet of **Palinura** (population 150), named after the captain of Aeneas's ship who fell into the sea somewhere off the coast of Southern Italy, or so they say.

Segesta

The Greek temple at Segesta, 96 km inland from Trapani on the N186, is one of the best-preserved Doric temples in Sicily. Its simple outlines are made all the more majestic by the desolation of the surrounding landscape of lofty mountains and parched scrubland. For many, the temple is one of the most eloquent of all classical sites in Sicily, and this despite the fact that the temple, dating from the fifth century BC, is unfinished. For a start, there is no roof; less obviously, the columns are unfluted, and the steps of the basement half-built, showing the portions added to facilitate the transport of stones. There is about this temple a lonely, rough-hewn grandeur; Segesta is an ideal place to come and read a book, or to eat a picnic. There is a minimum of tourist clutter.

Marsala

Marsala (population 83,000), 40 km from Trapani along the coastal Route N115, takes its name from the Arab *Mars-al-Allah*, Harbour of God. The town was important under the Saracen occupation of Sicily as an avenue of communication with Africa.

Today, it is famous for its (shockingly un-Muslim) production of Marsala, manufactured from Sicilian wines and spirits. Much was done for the production of Marsala by English merchant families. In 1773, John Woodhouse shipped sixty oak barrels of this fortified dessert wine to England. Two other British families, Ingham and Whitaker, followed suit, but were later taken over by the Italian Florio (now part of Cinzano).

Marsala is today a pleasant enough town, not least because of the heady smell of fortified wine which everywhere pervades the air. And the billboards advertising Marsala wines for the benefit of tourists from England, where the drink is thought to be associated with patrician sophistication, are certainly unusual: '. . . A fire place, the golden labrador on tartan rug, so much intimy . . . a smile, a world and then . . . REGINA, naturally! *Queen* of Marsala means . . . *Regina!*'

What to see

Although you will probably not want to stay overnight in Marsala, the town well repays an afternoon's investigation. Before you start, you might like to inspect the cellars of the giant **Stabilmento Florio**, a Marsala distillery down by the port, marked by two large trees and a lofty brick smokestack. You will be invited to taste the wine; I got drunk there on my birthday, and it was most enjoyable. A small museum contains a letter from Lord Nelson to John Woodhouse with an order for Marsala for his fleet. In order to visit, book an appointment at the Pro Loco (city tourist information office), Via Garibaldi 45 (tel. 0923-958097).

The Museo Arazzi (open 9 a.m.–1.30 p.m., 4–6 p.m.), situated behind the Cathedral in the tiny Via Abele Damiani, houses a wondrous collection of **tapestries** depicting scenes from the life of the

Emperor Vespasian. Eight in all, they were donated to Marsala Cathedral in 1589 by Antonio Lombardo, Archbishop of Messina and Ambassador to Spain. The tapestries, made in Belgium and originally in Philip II's palace in Madrid, are of such extraordinary detail that the weavers (all of them followers of Raphael, as can be seen from the design) could only thread 4 sq cm of cloth a day: not surprisingly, the tapestries took twenty years to complete. The Emperor Vespasian is, by the way, easily recognisable from his bronze shin-plates.

The **Archaeological Museum** (open 9 a.m.–2 p.m., 4–7 p.m.), housed in a whitewashed Marsala warehouse resembling a dilapidated French Foreign Legion outpost fort, is interesting for its enormous **Punic ship**, discovered in 1971 off the coast of Marsala. The only ship from this period which has so far been discovered, it is thought to have been sunk on its maiden voyage during the First Punic War. The iron nails which riveted the prow together have miraculously survived uncorroded. The museum contains objects found in the ship's hold – coils of rope, wine bottle corks, olive stones, a stove.

Nearby, on the sea-front, is the site of **Lilybaeum** (open 9 a.m.–12 noon, 2.30–dusk), where the remains of a third-century BC Roman villa can be seen. A beautiful mosaic shows various hunting scenes.

From here it is a short walk to **San Giovanni**, an unprepossessing-looking church in the middle of a wasteland named after St John, the patron saint of the Marsala sword-fishermen. Beneath the foundations is the **Grotta della Sibylla** (open only in summer), a dank and slimy cave where the Sibyl is said to have performed her oracles through the medium of water. Some curious murals survive.

Mozia

If you have time, a visit from Marsala to Mozia, on San Pantaleo, one of three islands in a shallow lagoon, should not be missed. The embarkation point, in the rural district of Spagnola, is 8 km from Marsala on the main N115 road. It is best to telephone from Marsala and ask to be met by the boatman; his number is 0923-959598. The lagoon – *Stagnone* to the locals – is full of bass and goldfish, cuttlefish, sole, mullet and scorpion fish; but there are only ten fishermen on the island.

Mozia is a mysterious place, and takes its name from a mysterious legend. Hercules, who lived in the fertile plains around modern-day Marsala, was one day robbed of his oxen. Searching high and low for the missing beasts, he was approached by a woman named Motya, who revealed to him the cave in which the oxen had been hidden. In memory of this obliging woman, Hercules founded a town on the island, naming it Motya. Stuff and nonsense, of course; probably the Phoenicians, who had set up numerous wool-weaving works around Marsala, named the town Motya because in the Semitic language the word means spinning-wheel.

What to see

The town was founded in the mid-eighth century BC by the

Phoenicians, and excavations have brought to light a Punic **sacrificial burial ground** where child-sacrifices were immolated. These excavations were largely the work of the English Marsala merchant Joseph Whitaker, who owned the island and was a friend of Henry Schliemann, the archaeologist who discovered Troy.

The Whitaker villa, which stands near the docks of Mozia, houses a **Museum** (opening hours depend on the whim of the custodian), showing Phoenician ceramics, Corinthian vases, and Attic black-and-red figure vases. There is much Phoenician jewellery, including scarab-rings imported from Egypt. For those with a taste for the eccentric, it is highly recommended.

Selinunte

Continuing further down the coast, 80 km from Marsala along roads N115 and N115d, you will come to the most remarkable Greek city in Sicily. It took its name, poetically, from the local abundance of wild celery, *selinon* in Greek. The ruins are impressive because they stand abandoned, far from any modern developments. And ruins they really are: fallen capitals, uprooted columns, smashed entablatures. Nearby is the sleepy little hamlet of Marinella, with excellent beaches.

Selinunte was one of the great colonies of Sicily, a bustling commercial metropolis and important trading centre with Carthage. In the fifth century BC the seven great temples were built, but the city was destroyed by Hannibal in 409 BC. It seems unlikely that his 10,000 men could have toppled the temples; the massive chaos of piled-up blocks was doubtless caused by an earthquake, undoing in ten minutes what it had taken over a century to build. The site was rediscovered in the sixteenth century by the Spanish, but systematic excavations were commenced only in 1822 by the English. Selinunte was built on three hills separated by two rivers. The eastern hill, on which now stand the most impressive ruins, was occupied by three huge temples, the second by the acropolis, with more temples (and now a museum) inside its defences. The **acropolis** is open daily from 9 a.m. until dusk.

Agrigento

Agrigento (population 50,000), 80 km east of Selinunte along the coast, was the only Greek colony in Sicily to rival the power, wealth and artistic achievement of Syracuse. Today, the city is known for its 'Valley of the Temples', the most important archaeological site on the island, dotted about with no fewer than twenty temples, of which the Concord is one of the best-preserved Doric temples in the world.

Modern Agrigento, on the other hand, is a concrete jungle of shoddy tenements. During the 1950s, the city was one of the worst examples of Mafia building speculation; the reason being that the exclusively

Christian Democrat administration (the so-called 'Party of God') was open to pretty well any form of connivance, so long as the Cosa Nostra bribes were good enough. On 19 July 1966 a large part of the housing collapsed when the building work caused a landslide; 7,543 people were made homeless.

If possible, you should stay overnight in Agrigento, as the temples are best seen in the early morning, before the crowds. Besides, the port of Agrigento is the point of departure for the strange Sicilian island of Lampedusa, closer to Africa than to Italy. If you are adventurous, you may want to sail out there.

Ancient Agrigento

In order to reach the temples, take bus 8, 9 or 10 from Agrigento station, and ask to be let off at San Leone. From this stop it is but a short walk to the tiny thirteenth-century Church of San Nicola. It has a Gothic doorway and a Doric cornice, the material for which probably came from a Roman building. Inside there is a magnificent Roman sarcophagus, with a delicate relief showing Phaedra transfixed by the arrows of Eros. The church is built on the site of a Greek sanctuary; from its main portal are fine views of the temples down in the vale below, each of them placed strategically on the crest of a hill.

The Museum

Adjoining the church is the Museo Nazionale Archeologico (open Tuesday–Sunday 9.30 a.m.–1.30 p.m., 3–5 p.m.). It is a good idea to explore this excellent museum before descending into the Valley of the Temples; the exhibits give one a palpable sense of how wealthy a city Agrigento must have been in ancient times. There are some outstanding Attic black-figured **vases**, including amphorae; there are remarkable **lion-head spouts** from the Temples of Heracles and the Temple of Demeter. And there is the extraordinary **Gigante**, an enormous human figure designed to uphold part of a temple; its primitive outlines remind one of some monolithic Henry Moore sculpture.

Walk down from the museum along the Via dei Templi; in ten minutes you will arrive at the 'Snack Bar dei Templi', an over-priced café. On entering the archaeological park, the first ruin on your right is the **Temple of Heracles** – this is the oldest of the Agrigento temples, built in about 520 BC. Only eight columns still stand.

Proceed uphill until you come, on your right, to the Paleochristian Necropolis – dank, musty and in summer blissfully cool; this is a miniature city of the dead, riddled with twisting labyrinthine corridors and blind alleys.

Temple of Concord

The next stop is the Temple of Concord, the best preserved of all Greek temples after the Theseion in Athens. If you are lucky, you may see a wedding here, for it is traditional in Agrigento for newly-weds to have their photograph taken outside the temple. Not so pagan a custom, actually: the Concord was converted in the sixth century into a church by S. Gregorio delle Rupe, thus saving it from destruction by Christians who considered it pagan. For twelve hundred years this temple served the Christian faith, right up until 1748.

The temple has six columns on each façade, and thirteen on each side, making a total of thirty-four; the stone has been burnt by the sun into a rich, tawny golden-brown. Nearby is a giant fig-tree – the only shade from the sun for seemingly miles around.

Temple of Juno

The next temple, crowning an eminence in the distance, was dedicated to Juno, or Hera. En route, you will pass many a Byzantine tomb-recess built into the old city walls of Agrigento; these provide excellent shade from the sun. The temple was built in 460–40 BC. Its structure was composed originally of thirty-four columns; today, twenty-five whole and nine broken ones survive. On the south-east side, the columns have been badly worn by the *sirocco* wind.

In 406 BC the temple was vandalised by the Carthaginans; it still bears traces of the destruction, the yellow stone scorched a rose-red by the flames of fire. On the eastern side a sacrificial altar still exists.

Temple of Jupiter

We now retrace our steps to the 'Snack Bar'. Cross the road, and the first site is the Temple of Jupiter. This is an extraordinary pile. The ruins, which remind one of those in Selinunte for the way in which they have tumbled, were once part of the largest Greek temple ever constructed – intended by the tyrant Theron to celebrate the victory at Himera of the Agrigentines over the Carthaginians.

Inside the perimeter of the ruins, which cover an area of 112 by 56 metres, is a sandstone copy of one of the *Gigante* (or Telamones) used as supports for the huge structure. Lawrence Durrell likened this figure to an Easter Island statue lashed to the ground, like Gulliver by the Lilliputians. Amid the ruins, note the U-shaped notches and grooves in the stones, used to facilitate hauling during construction. The temple was further demolished in the eighteenth century when its stones were plundered to build the jetty at Agrigento's nearby Porto Empedocle.

House of Pirandello

From the temples you can make an enjoyable excursion to the house in which Luigi Pirandello, Sicily's greatest playwright, was born. Sicilians have an enormous respect for Pirandello (bus-drivers will talk to you about him); Agrigentines, though, are uneasy about the writer's characterisation of their city, where (in his own words) 'taciturn apathy, suspicious mistrust, and jealousy have remained indelible in the souls and customs of the people.' Prophetic words, when one remembers how they were written before the rise of the modern Mafia.

Take bus number 11 in front of the 'Snack Bar' and get off at Villaseta. From here a short walk takes you to the hamlet of Caos (appropriately named, considering Pirandello's great psychological theme was the split personality), where stands the house. There are no official opening times; the doors open when the custodian is around, which is pretty well always, since the black-clad lady seems well-nigh barnacled to the place.

There are some fascinating exhibits – photographs of Pirandello

receiving his graduation certificate at Bonn University, where he
studied philology; of Pirandello standing by the Agrigento temples,
after he had won the Nobel Prize for Literature in 1934; and a signed
photograph of Bernard Shaw sent to Pirandello by the great (and
vain) man himself. The house is beautifully situated on a spur of land
which juts dramatically out into the sea; in a lonely field stands a lofty
pine tree, under which the ashes of the playwright, author of *Six Characters in Search of an Author*, are buried.

Modern Agrigento

There is really little worth seeing. The Salita Santa Spirito, a tiny
road off the Via Atenea, a busy thoroughfare and shopping street,
ascends steeply to the abbey church of **Santa Spirito**. This is now a
complex of chapel, chapter house and refectory founded for
Cistercian nuns at the end of the thirteenth century. The Baroqued
church has stucco works by Serpotta, and a fifteenth-century Byzantine wooden ceiling. In my experience, the nuns here are sometimes
reluctant to open the doors to their church unless they can sell you
some of their marzipan sweetmeats: *kus-kus*, they call them. The
courtyard leading to the refectory has some stunning Arab–Norman
arches.

The **Duomo**, on the north side of the town, was begun in the fourteenth century, and has an unfinished Gothic campanile. The north
aisle was dislodged in the 1966 landslide, but has been restored.

Where to stay

Villa Athena, Via dei Templi 33; tel. 0922-23833. Four-star. A
handsome eighteenth-century villa overlooking the Valley of the
Temples, with beautiful gardens. The restaurant is very popular with
local Agrigentines, particularly for Sunday lunch – the highest compliment you can pay the food.

Hotel Pirandello, Via Giovanni XXIII; tel. 0922-595666. Three-star. My favourite hotel in Agrigento, with large, spacious rooms of a
curiously 1930s aspect.

Della Valle, Via dei Templi; tel. 0922-26966. Three-star. Some of
the rooms have panoramic views of the temples.

Bella Napoli, Piazza Lena 6; tel. 0922-20435. Two-star. For those
on a low budget. In a quiet part of town, with perfectly respectable
rooms, though very hot!

Where to eat

Trattoria Black Horse, Via Celauro 8; tel. 0922-23223. Excellent
family-run restaurant. I have no idea why the walls are covered in
photographs of horses; it certainly isn't anything to do with the food.
The *antipasto fantasia* is superb. Very reasonably priced.

Trattoria Pizzeria Vulcano, Contrada S. Anna, on the N115
road, at the railway crossing; tel. 0922-57592. A little way out of town,
but worth it if you have a car. Has an open terrace overlooking the
temples. Excellent Sicilian specialities; moderate prices.

Leon D'Oro, Viale Emporium 102; tel. 0922-414400. Close to both
the temples and the sea. You should try the superb *rigatoni Leon D'Oro*
and the grilled fish. Moderate prices.

La Corte degli Sfizi, Cortile Contarini 3; tel. 0922-595520. The chef here, Nino Russo, allows you to cook your own meals. Order, say, veal, and the meat will come with a red-hot marble grill. A bit of a gimmick, but fun all the same.

Lampedusa

Along with Linosa and Lampione, Lampedusa (population 4,500) makes up the Pelagie Islands, which lie on the African continental platform, about 200 km south-west of the mainland of Sicily, and 110 km from Tunisia.

How to get there

A ferry leaves every day for Lampedusa from Porto Empedocle, near Agrigento, at midnight; it returns at 8.15 a.m. Sailing time is approximately nine and a half hours. A ticket for two costs 120,000 lire – expensive, but the price includes a berth with shower and lavatory. Bookings should be made in the offices of the Siremar shipping company, down by the port.

You may find that you have time to spare before sailing. If so, it is an idea to dine in the excellent **Ristorante Paris**, Via IV Novembre 4; tel. 0922-67456. Hard by the port, it is a simple, no-nonsense trattoria with large white tablecloths. The wine is cheap, the fish scrumptious, and the service formal.

With a flora and fauna similar to that of the Libyan and Tunisian coasts, Lampedusa is fondly referred to as a 'gift from Africa to Europe'. The feel of the place is certainly Arab; on the island are still to be found whitewashed dwellings with cupola-like domes called *dammusi*. There is very little vegetation; it never rains. Wild goat and rabbit are more populous than human beings. Probably, there are not a few Mafiosi here; Lampedusa is a favourite hideout for hoods on the run. The smell of Lampedusa is a potion of red clay and goat dung.

The beaches are delightful. The waters around Lampedusa are the only stretches of the Mediterranean where you can still see the parrot fish, with its colours of bright green and yellow. Turtles lay eggs on the beaches. It is a paradisiacal island; and the peace and quiet was disturbed only in 1986 when a Libyan motor launch fired two rockets at the island in retaliation for the US bombing of Tripoli. The projectiles plopped harmlessly into the sea, short of the beach. Why shell Lampedusa? The reason is that the United States Coast Guard has a radar base on the island. The boys are an awful long way from home (Lampedusa is 4,000 miles from the east coast of the USA) but they are there, presumably, to watch the threatening movements of the monster fleet of the Evil Empire. Parts of the island are therefore out of bounds, but no matter – there is enough of Lampedusa to delight without the barbed wire.

Before we set sail, an interesting historical fact: Lampedusa surrendered during the Second World War to a British pilot who landed his plane on the island when it had run out of fuel.

As you disembark on your arrival in the morning, beware of the sharks – the crooked money-changers, I mean, who ask if you are looking for a hotel. They will fleece you rotten. In particular, look out for a fat man in his mid-thirties, with pock-marked complexion, longish curly blond hair and a heavy gold chain about his neck.

There are not many hotels on Lampedusa: I suggest you check into the Medusa (see below). It is a bit of a haul from the port, but everyone has heard of it. You can buy a map and hire a bicycle from the reception; it will be a bone-shaker, but cycling is nevertheless the best way to explore the island.

What to see

Map in hand, our first stop is the **Santuario di Porto**, a tiny church in a leafy garden all abloom with bougainvillea and sub-tropical foliage. A notice on the doors will caution you to enter dressed decently – swimming-trunks, for example, are a bad idea. The church contains a Madonna which is brought out in procession, annually, on 22 September. The festivities, which last for 15 days, are in remembrance of King Ferdinand II of Bourbon, who in 1843 purchased Lampedusa, allowing Sicilians to settle there. The church is surrounded by strange cave-like grottoes – ancient hideouts for pirates, slaves, castaways and Saracens. Or so they say.

Remounting your bicycle, pedal in the direction of the **Isola dei Coniglii**, Rabbit Island. En route, you will pass several *dammusi*, Arabic dwellings with a curtain for door. Families will willingly let you inside; note how incredibly thick the whitewashed walls are – they keep out the heat during the summer months. The landscape here is astonishing – barren stretches of clay-coloured rock, with here and there the odd cactus or thistle. You could almost be in the Nevada desert.

You will soon come to the island, on the thorny scrubland of which live thousands of rabbits. The waters leading out to it are breathtakingly beautiful, and so limpid you can see the bottom for miles out. If you come here at night, between mid-July and mid-August, you can watch turtles laying eggs in the sand. But you should not make a sound; you must respect a reptile's right to silence.

Where to stay

Medusa; tel. 0922-970126. Clean and spacious rooms, though saltwater unfortunately comes through the taps. I should stock up on bottles of mineral water. Reasonably priced.

There are few restaurants on Lampedusa; the best:

Where to eat

Gemelli, Via Cala Piglia 2; tel. 0922-970699. An expensive restaurant run by Lampedusans born in Tunisia; the decorations are a bit yuppy-hippy, with kaftans and oriental brass pots hanging from the walls. And the service is a trifle laid-back-cool. Nevertheless, this must be *the* place in Italy for *couscous*. The fish variety of this African dish you may order straight away; but if you prefer lamb, put an advance order in over the telephone.

Syracuse

The successor of Syracusae, which rivalled Athens as the most magnificent city in the world, Syracuse (population 119,500) is 150 km east of Agrigento along the southern coast of Sicily.

History

According to the experts, the name derives from Syraka, a neighbouring marsh whose name in turn derived from a Carthaginian word meaning western place; the Carthaginians founded the city. Greek Syracuse reached the height of its power in the fifth to fourth centuries BC, when its population of 500,000 ruled all of Sicily. The fortunes of the city rapidly declined, however, after its conquest by the Romans, who laid siege in 214 BC. Even Archimedes, a resident of Syracuse, was unable with his ingenious inventions (mirrors and magnifying glasses to blind the enemy) to repulse the invaders, who gained the city after two years. He was run through whilst reading at his desk – musing, no doubt, over his recent *'Eureka'* experiment. Syracuse was sacked once again by the Saracens in AD 878.

The ruins of this breezy seaside city survive in the archaeological site of Neapolis, situated in a verdant park. Syracuse, like the cities of Taranto or Bari in Apulia, is divided into an old and a new town – the new town is boring; the old is fascinating. Named Ortygia, the old is built on an island linked to the modern city on the mainland by two bridges, and separates Syracuse's two harbours – the large to the south and the small to the north. A maze of winding streets with tumbledown dwellings, Ortygia owes something to the *souks* of the Middle East. Piazza del Duomo, centre of the old town, is one of the finest Baroque sights in the whole of the Italian South: Sacheverell Sitwell claimed it was the best on earth.

In the eighteenth century, though, the sad dereliction of Syracuse led travellers to make some pompous pronouncements about the tragic decline of empires. When Patrick Brydone arrived in 1770 he found that 'this proud city that once vied with Rome itself is now reduced to a heap of rubbish'. Well, all that has changed. Compared to cities in the west of Sicily, Palermo in particular, Syracuse has an air of gracious civility, the broad, seaweed-scented streets divided by formal gardens of palm trees and rhododendrons. The Mafia has not much of a holding on Syracuse; and, somehow, it shows. For the city is suffused with light – it is open and spacious, not, like Palermo, closed and suspicious. Syracuse is an up-and-coming, bustling city, and the ideal place from which to visit the eighteenth-century towns of Ragusa and Noto. You could happily spend two or three days here.

The Ancient City

The **Archaeological Park of Neapolis** (open 9 a.m.–6 p.m.) is spoilt by wheeler dealers selling map of Sicily tea towels, and by touts for pony trap rides. Ignore them and head for the Greek Theatre. En route, you will pass **Hieron's Altar**, the base of a huge sacrificial altar from the third century BC. Perhaps the largest altar ever erected by man, it saw up to 450 bulls sacrificed on the stones – and that was every day, so we are talking about a lot of bulls.

The Greek theatre

Hewn entirely out of rock, this is the largest Greek theatre in Europe – 138 metres in diameter. Constructed in the fifth century BC, it was here that the Greek tragedian Aeschylus first performed his play *The Persians*, probably during the early hours of springtime. The *cavea*, auditorium, had forty-six tiers of seats, all of them still visible; and it is estimated that another fifteen extended as far as the summit of the excavation. The theatre could have seated some 15,000 people. Around the gangway, at the top of the theatre where the rows of seats now end, you can see etched into the stone the names of various notables who attended spectacles here: Hieron and Philistis, his wife and Queen. There is even an inscription to Zeus Olympus, though I should think he was too busy, up in the clouds, to attend. The view from the theatre, particularly at sunset, is spectacular – the town, the harbour, the Ionian Sea.

The Ear of Dionysus

From the theatre, you descend into the exquisite Paradise Quarry, an overgrown garden of jungle liana and sub-tropical fauna. Here you will find a very peculiar grotto, the Orrechio di Dionisi; it was the painter Caravaggio who, struck by the resemblance of the cave's entrance to a human ear, gave it this name. Fancifully, he conceived the idea that Dionysus, the tyrant of Syracuse, had constructed the cave in this shape to serve as a prison; by listening at a hole above ground, he could hear, thanks to the echo, the hushed secrets exchanged by the prisoners. Coming to the cave in this modern day and age, we would probably be more inclined to name it after Doctor Spock of *Star Trek*.

The mystery is that this massive cave was man-made – you can see the chiselled excavation marks and the indentations of pick-axes, in the walls. What purpose it served, no one knows. Possibly, it functioned as a sort of primitive sounding-box for the nearby Greek theatre – a testing-ground for acoustic properties. Whatever the verdict, the cave impresses one with the force of something very strange. Bats and pigeons whirl about the ceiling; shout, and your voice is magnified ten-fold, carried way up there to the bird nests.

The Roman amphitheatre

Nearby is the huge Roman amphitheatre. Constructed in the second century BC, it was used exclusively for gladiatorial purposes. There is a massive trench-like recess in the middle of the arena, which, filled with water, may have been used for mock-sea battles of the sort that Nero had made popular. Or it may have been stuffed with crocodiles or hippopotamuses, to be netted, speared and hacked to death by gladiators.

The catacombs

Walking from Neapolis down the broad and busy Viale Teocrito, turn left into the narrow Via San Giovanni. At the end of it stands the

tiny San Giovanni delle Catacombe; the catacombs, creepy but blissfully cool, were tunnelled out of the rock from AD 315 to 360. The
church itself is a romantic ruin. It occupies the western portion of an
old basilica, once the Cathedral of Syracuse; inside is the fourth-cen-
tury crypt of San Marciano, said to be the first Christian church in
Sicily.

Archaeo-
logical
Museum

Further down the Viale Teocrito, you soon come to the excellent
National Archaeological Museum (open Tuesday–Sunday 9.30 a.m.–
2.30 p.m., 3.30–5 p.m.). Of a space-age modernity (children will have a
whale of a time with the push-button and hands-on working displays),
this museum houses some of the most interesting archaeological
material in Italy. In the Prehistoric Section one can find such delights
as the teeth of sharks and bones of hippopotamuses, the tusks and
skulls of elephants. There is much Bronze Age material from the
Neanderthal settlements around Syracuse, including a very bizarre
representation of the sexual act. There is an enormous amount, too, of
fragmentary material from ancient Syracusae.

Ortygia
The
Cathedral

The Duomo, in a beautiful piazza, is one of the strangest churches
in Southern Italy. Sicily is full of churches that incorporate elements
of Greek or Roman temples, but nowhere is the original more evident
than in Syracuse Cathedral. It is a seventh-century conversion of a
Doric temple dedicated to Athene – walk down the street running
down its north wall (the appropriately named Via Minerva), and you
can see the twelve columns of the original temple, plastered over and
looking distinctly lop-sided.

The **interior** is now impressively bare – compared, at least, with
the description that Cicero left us of the original Greek temple, which
had doors of gold and ivory, and walls painted with battle scenes and
heroic portraits. On your right as you enter, note the antique marble
water font with Greek inscriptions, resting on seven bronze lions. The
second chapel on the right contains an ornate 1599 statue of Saint
Lucy, patron of Syracuse. In effigy, she looks remarkably composed,
notwithstanding the dagger sticking out of her throat.

Fountain of
Arethusa

From the piazza you can walk down the Via Pincherele to the
ancient Fontana Aretusa, a charming (though dirty) duck pond.
Around the edges grow papyrus plants, originally imported by the
Arabs. The pond was not always dirty; originally a source of fresh
water, it was thought to be a resurgence of a river that disappeared
underground at Olympia. In June 1798, Lord Nelson drew fresh water
from the spring, to refresh his men aboard the fourteen ships anchored
in the harbour.

Museum of
Art

Nearby is the medieval Palazzo Bellomo, which houses the Museo
Nazionale d'Arte Medioevale e Moderna (open Tuesday–Saturday
9 a.m.–2 p.m., Sunday 9 a.m.–1 p.m.). The building itself is worth seeing; there is a vaulted Gothic ceiling above the ticket-office. Here you
will see a wonderful (though badly-damaged) 'Annunziata' of 1474 by

Antonello da Messina, and many Sicilian ceramics from the Middle Ages. Caravaggio's magnificent 'Burial of Saint Lucy' has been on 'temporary display' here since time immemorial – its rightful place is above the altar in Syracuse's Chiesa di Santa Lucia, but the priests do not have alarm systems.

The Castle

Adjacent is the Castello Maniace, built in the twelfth century by Frederick II. Since this is now an army barracks, entrance is problematic – an army officer there told me that, in order to gain entrance, I would have to obtain a permit from the Lord Mayor of Syracuse. At the time, this seemed too much like hard work but the castle is well worth seeing from the outside.

Where to stay

Villa Politi, Via M. Politi 2; tel. 0931-32100. Four-star, dilapidated grand hotel with great charm. Excellent swimming pool.

Grand Hotel, Viale Mazzini 3; tel. 0931-66729. Two-star. My favourite hotel in Syracuse – large, elegant rooms of a 1930s aspect, many of them with balconies overlooking the port.

Riviera, Via Eucleida 9; tel. 0931-68240. A little way out of town (near the monument to those who fell in Mussolini's African campaign), but pleasant enough. A trifle shabby.

Como, Piazza Stazione; tel. 0931-61464. Small, modern, clean; convenient if you have an early morning train to catch.

Gran Bretagna, Via Savoia 21; tel. 0931-68765. Excellent value. Many of the rooms retain their original nineteenth-century frescoes and pleasant family atmosphere. One lavatory, however, cannot reasonably be expected to serve everyone.

Where to eat

Trattoria Archimede, Via Gemmellaro 8; tel. 0931-69701. The best swordfish in town. I have great admiration for the waiters here as they let me stay drinking, one lunch time, until 4 p.m. The place is decorated with taste. Not cheap.

Ristorante Darsena, Riva Garibaldi 4; tel. 0931-61595. Excellent for fish; overlooks the port. Waiters a bit surly, though. Reasonably priced.

Trattoria La Foglia, Via Capodieci 41. This place is so hip and cool, it doesn't even need a telephone number. You can get vegetarian pasta dishes here and the house white wine is the most potent brew this side of Christendom. Decorations are weird, to put it mildly: but it's fun to observe the bright young things of Syracuse at play. Reasonably (though not *so* reasonably) priced.

Ristorante Gran Bretagna, Via Savoia 21; tel. 0931-68765, Beneath the hotel of the same name, an excellent place for cheap pizzas.

Environs of Syracuse

Noto

This eighteenth-century country town (population 25,000), 33 km inland from Syracuse, represents the perfection of restrained Baroque. In the buildings there is not a single instance of disproportion, all are constructed according to the architectural geometries, the stringent harmonies, of the Enlightenment. The old town was destroyed by the earthquake of 1693 and abandoned; the new one was entirely designed by a local architect named Rosario Gagliardi – a genius whose talents have not received their due. It is the exterior of buildings that attracts the eye; apart from the church of the **Crocifisso**, which contains a beautiful Madonna by Francesco Laurana (1471), the interiors are dull and can be avoided. The façades are manufactured out of a wonderful golden limestone, 'ranging from an almost crocus-yellow through fawnish sand to rose,' writes Vincent Cronin in his Sicilian classic, *The Golden Honeycomb*, 'yet keeping always within the limits of honey-colour.' One wonders what Noto would look like were its buildings constructed out of grey stone – not half so attractive, probably.

The carved animals and grotesque figures supporting the balconies of the **Palazzo Villadorata** in the Via Nicolaci are particularly famous. The balconies themselves billow out in extraordinary half-circles of bulging metal, like the wind in a ship's sails, or like a scallop shell. They are the perfection of the eighteenth-century Sicilian balcony. They are far too good to hang one's washing on.

Ragusa and Ibla

Architecturally, Noto's twin town is Ragusa (population 65,000), 60 km west on the N115. It too has churches designed by Rosario Gagliardi. Ragusa is, accurately, two hill-top towns: the old town, named Ibla, is connected to the modern one by a narrow isthmus in the form of an immensely long flight of steps – 242, to be precise. It rests on a hump-like crag at the bottom of a gorge. Ibla is unspoilt to the point of being dead; it suffers from depopulation, and many of its ramshackle houses are nailed up with slats of wood, as though hit by some terrible plague. With its air of poetic desolation, of picturesque squalor, Ibla could not be more different from the bustling go-ahead Ragusa on the other side of the gorge, which is the main town of the south eastern corner of Sicily, wealthy from oil discovered in the 1950s. On the outskirts of modern Ragusa, you will see derricks, rigs and nodders, the mechanical trappings of petroleum extraction.

What to see

So called because it claims to occupy the site of the ancient Sicel town of Hybla Heraea, Ibla is the more interesting of Ragusa's two towns. The **Church of San Giorgio** is a picture of grace on a grand scale. Designed by Gagliardi, the sandstone edifice is advantageously displayed high up on a platform above a sloping, palm-tree lined piazza; fifty-four steps take you to the main portal. The church is the high point, the finest expression, of Sicilian Baroque. The interior, however, is a feeble reflection of the façade – which is nearly always the case with churches in south eastern Sicily.

Nearby is the pretty **Giardino Ibleo**, with a palm avenue flanked by the ruins of several small churches. It is the ideal place to come and read a paper, or take a picnic. The gardens are often used for public functions. In June 1988 I attended an Italian Communist Party rally here; afterwards, there was wine and food in abundance but it took three hours to be served, and the Christian Democrat Mayor of Ragusa left in disgust.

Where to stay

If for some reason you find yourself stranded in Ragusa, you might want to stay the night in the **Hotel Mediterraneo**, Via Roma 189; tel. 932-21944. It is a modern, two-star 1950s hotel with good rooms. Needless to say, it is in modern Ragusa; in Ibla there are neither hotels nor restaurants.

Catania

A great sprawling city, Catania (population 380,328), 60 km north of Syracuse, is the most populous in Sicily after Palermo. Economically, it is the most important city on the island; indeed, Catania now has Sicily's main international airport. It is without the charms of Palermo; the centre is almost entirely eighteenth century, and buildings are more likely to appeal to the student of provincial Baroque than to the amateur traveller.

Catania is an ideal base for trips to nearby Mount Etna; and for an excursion to Piazza Armerina, where there are some superb Roman mosaics. So the advice is: do not be put off by the bustle and dirt. The city is not a favourite with tourists, but it has a fascination of its own. And above all, Catania has the feel of a real city, quite without the gracious suavities of, say, Syracuse.

History

Catania has an interesting history. As with all Sicilian cities, it is a history of terror and of destruction. Founded originally by the Greeks, who established themselves in 792 BC on the southern slope of Mount Etna, the city was destroyed and rebuilt by the Romans, who gave it the name *Catana* (meaning 'Greater', according to Plutarch). Despite a serious volcanic eruption from Mount Etna in 121 BC, Catania had its moments of glory during the Roman period. A huge amphitheatre was built, the remains of which can still be seen, and the poet Ausonius placed Catania among the twenty most important cities on the Mediterranean – superior, even, to Messina.

Under the Norman occupation, 15,000 Catanese were killed in an earthquake. In 1194, the entire city was razed to the ground by

Barbarossa (Red Beard), son of King Henry IV; it was rebuilt, but destroyed once again by King Frederick II, in 1232. Following the death of this Swabian monarch, the Aragonese elected Catania as the capital of Sicily. On 15 January 1296, Frederick III of Aragon was crowned King of Sicily in Catania Cathedral.

Etna and earthquakes

There followed centuries of relative calm, until disaster struck: Catania, like Noto, was entirely destroyed by the earthquake of 1693, in which a bare third of the city's population of 24,000 survived. Catania was rebuilt, on a regular plan of straight lines, more or less overnight. And this is the city which stands today as modern Catania, all of it designed by the architect Vaccarini. But if Noto is a town of honey-coloured buildings, Catania is a city of buildings black and grey – for the majority were constructed out of volcanic stone from Etna, the great mound of which looms ominously large over the city.

Literally, Catania is crouched at the foot of the volcano: it could become a modern-day Pompeii – there is no saying. The last eruption, in April 1983, caused chaos. It lasted for seven weeks, and a flow of lava actually reached the city but luckily stopped short of the harbour. About twenty-five houses were destroyed. In the magazine *Oggi* there was a description by local hunters of how birds, made delirious by the eruption, flew madly around and, tired, alighted on the lava where they were burnt. Rabbits and foxes, terrified, took to their lairs and were baked alive. I often wonder about the fate of the hundreds of sheep that one sees grazing on the fertile slopes of Etna; should there be another eruption, they would become a kind of instant kebab.

What to see
The Cathedral

We start with one of the most beautiful squares in Italy, the Piazza del Duomo. At its centre is the curious **Fontana dell'Elefante**, Elephant Fountain. Made of black volcanic rock, the (smiling?) elephant is surmounted by an Egyptian obelisk of granite. Since Vaccarini designed the fountain in 1736, this elephant has become the symbol of Catania.

The Cathedral was built in 1092 and, after the 1693 earthquake, almost totally rebuilt by Vaccarini. Little of the medieval edifice remains, but if you walk down to number 159 Via Vittorio Emanuele you will see parts of the original apses made out of a particularly porous sort of lava stone. You can't miss them: they are opposite the 'Taormina Ice Cream Parlour'. Six of the granite columns that now adorn the Baroque façade of the Cathedral were stolen from a Roman theatre – vandalism in the name of Christianity.

The Cathedral, be warned, has the most absurd opening-hours: 7–11.30 a.m., and 5.30–7.30 p.m. If you miss these times, I should bribe the custodian and demand that you be allowed inside. Around the high altar are the sarcophagi of sundry Aragonese sovereigns; the **Chapel of Sant'Agata** (patron saint of Catania, who was thrown to the lions by the Romans in AD 252) to the right in the apse contains the Saint's crown, said to have been presented by Richard the Lionheart.

Every February, the silver sarcophagus containing the corpse (or the remains of it) is conveyed through Catania by men decked out in hoods and white robes.

Bellini's birthplace

Along the sloping Via Vittorio Emanuele eastwards towards Mount Etna you will eventually pass the remains of a Roman theatre at number 266. In the adjoining Piazza Bellini stands Bellini's birthplace. The house, with its Baroque façade, was made a national monument in 1923: today, it houses a delightful museum containing original scores of the composer's work (open 9 a.m.–1.30 p.m.).

San Nicolo

From here, the Via Gesuiti, with its curious herring-bone pavement, leads to San Nicolo, an unfinished (though domed) church of frightening aspect. Indeed, the eight massy stone pillars flanking the façade give the edifice the appearance of a grim factory, or of some fantastical Babylonian temple from the Hollywood set of a Cecil B. De Mille epic – abandoned and spooky. Things look as though they have everywhere been amputated, truncated, lopped off; in fact, the church was begun after the earthquake of 1693 and then abandoned. As it stands, this is still the largest church in Sicily.

From the dome (rarely open, for some reason), there is a superb view of Catania; and an interesting feature about the interior is the meridian line on the floor telling the date from the position of a shaft of light shining through the roof in the middle of the day. The church stands in the middle of a graceful eighteenth-century square, which fans out around the unfinished building in a beautiful half-moon.

Next to the church is a former convent, one of the largest in Europe. In the eighteenth century it was converted into a library. Now abandoned, it is nevertheless worth exploring; the iron balconies are beautiful. Walk along the nearby Via San Giuliano until you hit Via Etna; halfway down, in Piazza Stesicoro, you will find the remains of a *Roman amphitheatre*; made entirely out of black lava, the theatre dates from the second century AD. Possibly, this was where Sant' Agata was sent to her death, the arena being one of the largest after the Colosseum in Rome. In 1693, the municipality used the theatre as a dump for the ruins of the earthquake.

Public gardens

If you have time, you should go for a promenade in the Gardino Bellini, Catania's wonderful public gardens. They are full of palms and Brazilian *Araucaria*; of considerable botanic interest is the large *Ficus* tree. Part of the park is designated the *Labirinto*, after its numerous winding paths, all of them leading to large bird cages. In 1882 a lovely bandstand was erected here called the 'Chinese', owing to its pagodalike design. From the heights of this luscious garden you are afforded superb views of Mount Etna.

Where to stay

Villa Dina, Via Caronda 129; tel. 095-447103. Three-star. Converted from an eighteenth-century *palazzo*, the hotel is plumb in the middle of the 'historical centre'. Elegant, highly recommended, reasonably priced.

Hotel Savona, Via Vittorio Emanuele 210; tel. 095-326982. Rooms large and spacious; hotel centrally located. One-star, but it should have two.

Moderno, Via Alessi 9; tel. 095-326250. Two-star, a converted eighteenth-century palace. Not so cheap, though.

Pensione Corona, Via Crociferi 81; tel. 095-327708. For those on a shoestring: the rooms are enormous, dank and often smelly, but the pension is situated in Catania's most beautiful street, the length of it lined with eighteenth-century churches and convents. Many of the *palazzi* have gardens of banana trees. The elderly owner, however, is mad: she thought I was the reincarnation of a *Luftwaffe* pilot who had commandeered the hotel during the last war.

Where to eat

Turi La Paglia, Via Pardo 23; tel. 095-346358. Near the Duomo, this is a delightfully run-down trattoria specialising in sea-food. Best value, and best atmosphere, in town. Highly recommended, if you don't mind a dose of sleaze. Try the swordfish.

Metro, Via Crociferi 76, tel. 095-322098. A very trendy place, this: not so much a snack-bar as a 'Ristorante-Pub-Birreria-Tea Room'. Definitely for the young; you can dance.

Gastronomy C. Conte, Via Etnea 158; no telephone. Excellent food for a plain *tavola calda*. Popular with the locals, so come early.

Costa Azzurra, Via De Cristofaro 4; tel. 095-497889. The most famous of Catania's restaurants. Excellent Sicilian specialities: *the* place to come if you feel like splurging.

The Environs of Catania

Mount Etna

Mount Etna is the biggest thing in Sicily. Look at a map of the island – the volcano spreads out as a massive expanse of brown, like a great skin disease. Throughout the centuries, this volcano has instilled in poets and artists a wonder bordering on fear. Homer, Pindar, Ovid and Dante have offered placatory verse to the monster; even the intrepid Goethe had his doubts about making an ascent. 'Most foreign visitors', he wrote, 'are too apt to consider the ascent a trifling affair. But we, who are near neighbours of the mountain, are content if we reach the summit twice or thrice in a lifetime, for we never attempt it except under ideal conditions.' Legend has it that Empedocles hurled himself into the crater in the hope of persuading everyone, by disappearing, that he was a god. A pair of golden sandals were afterwards vomited up, proof if ever of divinity.

Boots or stout walking shoes, however, are the thing for you; climbing Etna is arduous work. Flip-flops, for example, will probably melt. And take an extra pullover, too: the volcano can get very, very cold. But the wind, on Mount Etna, is the main problem (one is advised not to wear a kilt or skirt). When I was last on the summit, my pages of notes for this book were blown away in a single gust of wind – all of them flying off, irretrievably, in the direction of the Ionian Sea.

For the last few centuries the rim of the crater has stood at about 3,000 metres, double the height of any Sicilian mountain. To travel around the base would take you on a journey of 212 km. You will be struck by the fertility of the slopes; up to a height of 500 metres there are citrus groves, and above them vines and olives flourish to about 2,000 metres. The gnarled and twisted lava blackness of the solidified igneous matter around the actual summit is not a pretty sight, but fascinating none the less. Such cinematic Biblical epics as *Barabbas* and *The Ten Commandments* were partly shot on the heights of Etna.

Getting there

In order to visit Etna from Catania, take the blue AST bus from in front of the station. It leaves at 8 a.m. and the distance is about 40 km. You will be deposited at Etna's 'Rifiugo Sapienza', a huddled mass of tourist kiosks. Touts will no doubt try and sell you bottles of 'Vino Fuoco di Etna'; do not succumb to their blandishments – the liquor is dreadful. It is not a good idea to climb Etna on your own; for a start, it will take you an age and a day, and furthermore going solo can be dangerous. As a notice puts it: 'We do inform all excursioneers that, in spite of all precautions taken by the organism responsible of the security of persons and objects, the excursions upon Etna always allow for some degrees of dangers.' You have been warned.

The thing to do, then, is to pay an expensive fee of 30,000 lire and have a guide take you up the volcano in a four-wheel-drive jeep. Once you get to the top, you may feel you have been taken for a ride; unless you are very lucky, there will be no lava activity. For miles around there stretches out a seeming infinity of solidified black lava. You may wonder, with a force-ten gale blowing in your face, what you are doing here. You may begin to think, too, that the most exciting thing that can happen to you on Etna is to get yourself killed. (Although one shouldn't joke; in 1979 an unlucky group of tourists were swallowed up near the summit, and in 1985 two Frenchmen were killed.) Nevertheless, the views on a clear day are marvellous: you can see all the way to Calabria.

Piazza Armerina

The quickest way to get from Catania to Piazza Armerina, for the stunning Roman mosaics, is to take the A19 motorway to Enna (a dreary town), and from there the N117. All in all, it is about 80 km, but it is worth travelling the distance.

The town of Armerina itself (population 22,500) is hardly worth a visit, although it does boast an impressive fifteenth-century **Cathedral** on the crest of a hill opposite a bar selling, of all things, 'Currywürst'.

Mosaics

The mosaics, about 3 km away from the town centre, are the pavement decorations of an Imperial Roman villa (open 9 a.m.–dusk). Nestled in a valley bordered by forests of hazel and oak, the villa, built at the end of the third century AD as a hunting-lodge, probably belonged to Maximian, Emperor from 286 to 305. At any rate, it must have belonged to a wealthy man keen on showing off his wealth; in richness and extent, it is comparable only to Hadrian's Villa at Tivoli near Rome, and to Diocletian's Palace at Split in Yugoslavia. The mosaics are the largest and best preserved of their kind in the world, and cover the floors of some fifty rooms. When Lawrence Durrell visited, he griped that the mosaics give a 'rather ordinary aesthetic experience'. He must have been in a bad mood: the mosaics are the greatest – and certainly the most easily enjoyable – treasures to have survived in Sicily from Roman times. They were excavated only in 1950; the slave quarters have yet to be unearthed.

Probably the work of African artists, they treat mythological, descriptive and decorative subjects; mostly, they are of hunting scenes, of animals about to be killed for the banqueting table. There are boars trussed up in nets, deer pursued by horsemen, a leopard advancing on a sheep, a lion at an antelope's throat or pouncing on a deer's back, blood spouting from the poor creature's nostrils. The mosaic entitled 'The Large Hunt' shows the capture of wild animals in Africa and Asia, and their transport back to Europe for circus or gladiatorial purposes – elephants, camels, tigers. There are delightful fishing scenes, too, with winged cherubs riding the backs of dolphins. Most extraordinary (though crudely executed) is the mosaic of young girls playing with discus, and generally working out in a gymnastic sort of way. They are wearing bikinis; if you thought this article of clothing was invented by Coco Chanel in the 1950s, you may have made a mistake.

Taormina

The most popular resort in Sicily, with over 100 hotels, this small town (population 10,000), 50 km north of Catania, is virtually given over to tourism. In August, the place is quite frankly a nightmare. Much damaged by the Allied bombs of 1943, Taormina has been further, and irreparably, damaged by the mushrooming of ugly new hotels and boring nightclubs and discos. Were he alive today, Taormina's most illustrious citizen D. H. Lawrence would not be amused.

Nevertheless, at any time of the year other than August, Taormina – one of the most famous beauty spots in the world – is a delight. Its mountain-top position is unrivalled, its Greek theatre the most spectacularly situated in the world, and its climate mild. In spring, the medieval part of the town is an explosion of bougainvillea: purple, purple everywhere. And there are good beaches, easily reached by funicular. In short, you may want to relax here for a couple of days. The artistic and architectural sights and sites are not many; Taormina is strictly a town for mooching around in.

What to see

Goethe thought the **Greek theatre** (open 9 a.m.–dusk) commanded one of the most spectacular views in the world. We should not take Goethe's words at face value, since he had not travelled the whole world. But here they are: 'Citadels stand perched on cliffs to the right; down below lies the town. Straight ahead one sees the long ridge of Etna, to the left the coastline as far as Catania or even Syracuse, and the whole panorama is capped by the huge, fuming, fiery mountain, the look of which, tempered by distance and atmosphere, is, however, more friendly than forbidding.' This view has not changed; it is indeed an incredibly beautiful view, best appreciated in the morning, when the sun rises from the sea, to tinge the snowy peak of Etna with pink.

Though Greek in origin, the design of the theatre dates from a restoration carried out in Roman times, when the stage was entirely reconstructed. It is hewn from the rock in a semi-circular form; and is bounded at the upper end on two sides by Roman masonry. Needless to say, the Romans used it for gladiatorial purposes; today, I am glad to say, it is the arena for an annual festival of film and drama.

At the end of the road from the theatre stands the fourteenth-century **Palazzo Corvaia**, today the headquarters of the Taormina Tourist Office. The charming courtyard is decorated with reliefs of Adam and Eve. Opposite is **Santa Caterina**, a pretty Baroque church. Stairs lead down to a funerary chamber, where rest the mummified bodies of five monsignores from the early seventeenth century. You may have difficulty in seeing the corpses; according to the custodian, people insist on mistaking the catacombs for a lavatory, hence the heavy chain about the entrance. Obviously, Taormina had a better class of tourist, once upon a time.

Carry on down the Corso Vittorio Emanuele until you come (on your left) to the **Duomo**. This still preserves its thirteenth-century crenellations, which give it the appearance of a miniature fortress. The beautiful portals are from the fifteenth and sixteenth centuries. The adjoining terrace commands spectacular views. To the north the mountainous Sicilian coast mysteriously converges with the dark hills of Calabria across the Ionian Sea. And to the south, Mount Etna smokes with an almost insolent cool.

Entertainment

If you are in Taormina during the summer months, you will not want to miss the international festival of theatre, film and music. Performances are in the Greek theatre. Tickets are available in the Palazzo Corvaia.

The most popular nightclub is **Le Perroquet**, Piazza San Domenico; tel. 0942-24808. Caters for all sorts, and excellent if you are gay.

Where to stay
Top range

San Domenico Palace, Piazza San Domenico 5; tel. 0942-23701. Five-star, Taormina's grandest hotel. Originally a monastery, the interior is eccentric, filled with antique furnishings and portraits predominantly black or brown. A trifle gloomy, then – but glorious terraced gardens. Extremely expensive.

Bel Soggiorno, Via Pirandello 60; tel. 0942-23342. Three-star. Rooms command superb views of the sea, and expensive with it.

Palazzo Vecchio, Salita Ciampoli 9; tel. 0942-23033. Two-star. Plumb in the middle of the historical centre. Rooms large, and white-washed to keep out the heat. Elegant; reasonably priced.

Pensione Svizzera, Via Luigi Pirandello 26; tel. 0942-23790. My favourite hotel in Taormina. Only one-star, but many of the spacious and airy rooms look directly out on to the sea. It is also conveniently located next to the funicular which takes you down to the beaches. The owner is a charmer; and he seems to speak at least six languages. Excellent value.

Pensione Columbia, Via Iallia Bassia 11; tel. 0942-23423. Strictly for paupers, but a good choice for the off-season. The fresh-smelling bathrooms are unusual for a pension at so cheap a price.

Vicolo Stretto, Vicolo Stretto 6; tel. 0942-23849. The name of this restaurant translates as 'Narrow Little Alleyway'. This is not to exaggerate: the place is situated in an alley so cramped, two people can barely pass one another.

Grotta Azzura, Via Bagnoli Croci 2; tel. 0942-24161. In the heart of town, but a trifle touristy. The food, however, is first-class.

Antonio, Via Crocifisso; tel. 0942-24570. A little outside Taormina town, but this is where you will find the best *cucina casalinga*, home cooking, in Taormina. Sicilian dishes a speciality.

U Bossu, Via Bagnoli Croci 50; tel. 0942-2311. Reasonable food at reasonable prices.

Useful Reading

Works of Literature

John Horne Burns, *The Gallery.* Set in Naples, this is one of the finest novels written by an American about the Second World War; published in 1947, it sold half a million copies more or less overnight. But Burns, an alcoholic, was unable to cope with the success, and died in Florence at the age of thirty-seven.

Luciano de Crescenzo, *Thus Spoke Bellavista.* An entertaining though lightweight novel about Naples, its extraordinary streets and people, the exuberant chaos of the place.

Giuseppe di Lampedusa, *The Leopard.* A classic of contemporary European literature; set in turn-of-the-century Sicily, it describes the decline of an aristocracy and the rise of what was to become the Mafia.

Carlo Levi, *Christ Stopped at Eboli.* Levi, a doctor and an active anti-Fascist from Turin, was exiled by Mussolini as a political prisoner to a remote village in Basilicata. He wrote about the peasants he knew and loved. The book has become a classic of Italian literature.

Leonardo Sciascia, *The Day of the Owl.* Published in 1961, this was the first novel written about the Mafia in the history of Italian literature. A brilliant, hard-boiled, fast-moving thriller by a writer who has not yet received the recognition he deserves in the English-speaking world. Other recommended books by Sciascia: *Sicilian Uncles*, a collection of four excellent novellas; and *The Council of Egypt*, an historical novel set in eighteenth-century Palermo.

Elio Vittorini, *Conversation in Sicily.* A grim though eloquent novel, written during Fascism, about a Sicilian son's relationship with his mother. It is a remarkable piece of writing: 'One puts down this novel,' wrote the poet Stephen Spender, 'feeling that one has had an experience as valid as life and as art.'

Background Information

Pino Arlacchi, *Mafia Business.* By far the best book on the Mafia. Arlacchi was on the Government Anti-Mafia Commission, so he knows what he's talking about. A horribly fascinating read.

Norman Douglas, *Siren Land* and *Old Calabria.* Two books about Southern Italy by one of the greatest travel writers of our time. The humour is waspish, caustic and at times cruel, but Douglas wrote like an angel. Highly recommended.

George Gissing, *By the Ionian Sea.* Published in 1901, one of the earliest books about Southern Italy written by an Englishman. Gissing begins in Naples and ends up in Calabria.

Johann Wolfgang Goethe, *Italian Journey*. Marvellous travel book by this greatest of German poets. The chapters on Naples and Palermo are indispensable.

Edward Lear, *Journals of a Landscape Painter in Southern Calabria and the Kingdom of Naples*. Hilarious account by this tomfool surrealist of his jaunts in the Mezzogiorno.

Norman Lewis, *Naples '44*. A remarkable memoir by one of the best of English travel writers. Concerns Lewis's experience as an Intelligence Officer in the ramshackle city during the last war.

Fiona Pitt-Kethley, *Journeys to the Underworld*. As a calculatedly outrageous book about Southern Italy, this reads as though Casanova had let rip on a Baedeker guide. Pitt-Kethley, wayward poet of all things impolite, has written a sort of freebooter's romp through the Mezzogiorno, a catalogue of conquests amorous and aphrodisiac. Extremely funny and lewd – not for the prudish.

Rulers of Southern Italy

The Normans

1137–54 Roger II
1154–66 William I (the Bad)
1166–89 William II (the Good)
1189–94 Tancred
1194 William III

The Hohenstaufen

1194–97 Henry VI
1197–1250 Frederick II
1250–54 Conrad IV
1254–66 Manfred
1266–68 Conradin

Angevins

1268–85 Charles I
1285–1309 Charles II
1309–43 Robert the Wise
1343–81 Joan I
1381–86 Charles III
1386–1414 Ladislas
1414–35 Joan II
1435–42 René of Lorraine

Under direct rule of Aragon

1442–58 Alfonso V

Neapolitan House of Aragon

1458–94 Ferdinand I
1494–95 Alfonso II (abdicated)
1494–96 Ferdinand II
1496–1501 Frederick of Altamura

1503–1713 In 1503 Naples joined Sicily under direct Spanish rule, each having its own Viceroy
1713–34 Under Austria

House of Bourbon

1734–59 Charles III of Bourbon
1759–99 Ferdinand IV
1799–1806 Ferdinand IV (restored)
1806–8 Joseph Bonaparte
1808–15 Joachim Murat
1815–25 Ferdinand IV (restored again)
1825–30 Francis I
1830–59 Ferdinand II
1859–60 Francis II
1860 From this date on, Southern Italy was ruled as part of united Italy

House of Savoy

1861–78 Vittorio Emanuele II
1878–1900 Humbert I
1900–44 Vittorio Emanuele III
1944–46 Regency
1946 Humbert II (abdicated after five weeks' rule)
1946 Republic

Index

Aeolian Islands 192, 196–201
Aeschylus 232
Agata, Saint 237
agriculture 12, 13
Agrigento 225–9
Agrippa, Marcus Vipsanius 106, 108
AIDS 34, 35
air travel 37
Alberobello 136, 160
Alfonso V, King of Sicily and Naples 77–8, 93
Aliano 7, 29, 163, 167–8
Alicudi 201
Amalfi 128–30
    Cathedral 129
    history of 128
    hotels in 129–30
    restaurants in 130
Amalfi coast 71
Amandole, River 185
Ameno, Lake 123
amphitheatres, Roman 110
    at Catania 238
    at Lecce 152
    at Lucera 139
    at Pompeii 119
    at Pozzuoli 105
    at Syracuse 232
Anacapri 122
Andersen, Hans Christian 121
Andrew, Saint 129
Angevin kings 77, 204
Antiochenos, Georgios 207
Apennine mountains 71
Apulia 69, 135–61
    architecture in 136
    history of 136–7
    industry in 135–6
    travel to 137
    wine from 47
Aquinas, St Thomas 89, 132
Arabs 10, 189, 204, 214
Archimedes 231
Armerina 240
Aspromonte mountains 172, 183, 185
Ausonius, Decimus Magnus 236

Avernus, Lake 106

Bacoli 107–8
Badolate 28
Bagheria 203, 215
Bagnara Calabria 186–7
Bagnoli 72
Baia 107
balconies 32–3
banks 55
Barbary pirates 10
Bari 136–7, 145–50
    Castle 146
    Cathedral 146–7
    festa in 59, 149
    history of 145–6
    hotels in 149–50
    restaurants in 150
    S. Nicola 147–8
    superstition in 29
Barisano of Trani 144
Barletta 143–4
Baroque art and architecture 110, 129, 137, 151, 157, 159, 166, 183
    in Naples 76, 87, 88, 90, 96
    in Sicily 192, 195, 207, 212, 235, 237, 242
Barzini, Luigi 14, 26
Basilicata 13, 69, 163–9
    history of 163–4
    travel to 164
    wine from 47
beaches
    in Apulia 140, 142
    in Basilicata 163, 169
    in Calabria 172, 177, 186
    in Sicily 197, 202, 225, 229, 241
Bellini, Giovanni 97, 149, 238
Benevento 109–10
Bentinck, Lord William 191
Bitonto 150
Bonaparte, Joseph 79, 85
Bonaparte, Napoleon 171
Boniface IX, Pope 154
Botte Donato, Mount 176
Botticelli, Sandro 97
Bourbons 10
    in Naples 78–9
    in Sicily 205
Bova 184–5, 186
Bova Marina 186
bradyseism 105–7
Briggs, Martin 151
Brindisi 150–1
British, in Sicily 191, 205

Browne, Thomas, Sir 87
Brueghel, Pieter 97
Brydone, Patrick 19, 190–1, 231
Bulwer-Lytton, Edward 116
Burning Fields see Campi Flegrei
Burns, John Horne 94–5
Buscetta, Tommaso 17
bus travel 39
Butler, Samuel 222
Byzantine art and architecture
    in Apulia 136, 137, 147, 154, 155, 157
    in Basilicata 165
    in Calabria 174, 178–9, 181
    in Campania 77
    in Sicily 201, 209, 227
Byzantines 77, 136, 173, 184–5, 204

Calabria 7, 69, 71, 171–87
    emigration from 28
    history of 172–3
    travel to 173
    wine from 47
Calvo, Mount 135
Camigliatello Silano 175, 176
Camorra 22, 73–4
Campania 69, 71–133
    industry in 72
    spas in 43
    wine from 47
Campi Flegrei 71, 104–7
camping 43, 172
Canetto 197
Capo Miseno 108
Capri, Island of 37, 72, 121–3
    Anacapri 122–3
    Blue Grotto 121–2
    history of 121
    San Michele 122
    Villa Tiberio 122–3
Caracciolo, Admiral 79
Caracciolo, Domenico 204–5
Caracciolo, Gian 87
Caravaggio 89, 97, 195, 210, 232, 234
car hire 40–1
cars, travel by 39–40
Carthaginians 227, 231
Casarano 154–5
Caserta 110
Casertavecchia 110
casinos 48